A Systems Approach to Decision Making

Policy Analysis in Local Government

A Systems Approach to Decision Making

Kenneth L. Kraemer

Policy Analysis in Local Government

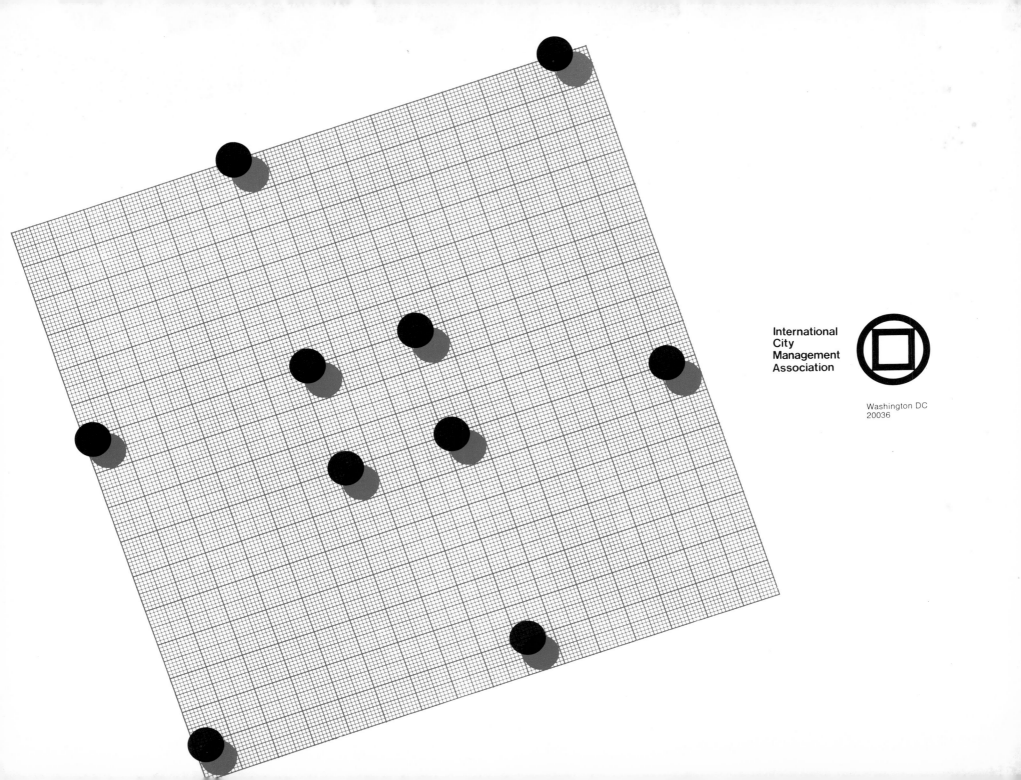

International
City
Management
Association

Washington DC
20036

Municipal Management Series

David S. Arnold, Editor

Managing the Modern City
Principles and Practice of Urban Planning
Municipal Finance Administration
Municipal Personnel Administration
Municipal Police Administration
Municipal Fire Administration
Municipal Public Works Administration
Municipal Public Relations
Management Practices for Smaller Cities
Community Health Services
Case Problems in City Management
Effective Supervisory Practices
Managing Municipal Leisure Services
Developing the Municipal Organization
Policy Analysis in Local Government

Foreword

City managers, county managers, mayors, city councilmen, department heads, and other elected and appointed administrators in local government carry the responsibility for making decisions. These decisions range all the way from the relatively inconsequential to those that involve major aspects of policy. It is the latter kind of decision process, policy making, that is dealt with in this book. Policy making is at the very heart of the governmental process, yet it is a subject that has been dealt with systematically only in recent times.

Policy Analysis in Local Government, which covers the "concepts and principles, tools and techniques, and strengths and weaknesses of policy analysis," is a useful introduction to the still developing area of analyzing information systematically to evolve alternatives for making better policy choices. This book represents the scientific method. It adds a methodology and a way of thinking that will help policy makers to better meet the complex urban problems which they face today.

This book is part of the Municipal Management Series, published by the International City Management Association through a series of training manuals that goes back to the mid-thirties. Each of these books incorporates the latest developments in research and teaching. Each volume in the Municipal Management Series is intended to provide general background as well as specific approaches for practitioners and for those looking forward to careers in local government.

The titles in the Municipal Management Series have been prepared especially for the Institute for Training in Municipal Administration. The institute offers in-service training courses designed specifically for local government officials whose jobs are to plan, direct, and coordinate the work of others. The Institute for Training in Municipal Administration has been sponsored since 1934 by the International City Management Association.

It is a pleasure to acknowledge the fine work of the author of this book, Kenneth L. Kraemer. Professor Kraemer is on the faculty of the Graduate School of Administration, University of California, Irvine. He has experience in the practical applications of policy analysis in cities in California and in other parts of the country and has an unusual educational background, with degrees in architecture, public administration, and urban planning. He is currently director of a research project sponsored by the National Science Foundation to evaluate and synthesize policy-relevant research findings on municipal information systems for use by local government officials.

This book, like others in the Municipal Management Series, has been prepared under the general editorship of David S. Arnold, Director, Publications Services, International City Management Association.

Mark E. Keane
Executive Director

International City
Management Association

April, 1973

Preface

This book is addressed to policy makers in local government and to those preparing for such roles. Its aim is to acquaint them with advances in the art and science of policy making over the last decade and more, as related to public policy. Essentially, the impact of these advances has considerably extended policy makers' potential for exercising reasoned judgment (i.e., for making better decisions). The basic features of these advances are: (1) an increased emphasis on explicit, conscious analysis, and (2) a broader perspective in the conduct of analysis and decision making. These features are referred to respectively as *systematic analysis* and *the systems approach*. Together they are often called *systems analysis*. This term is eschewed in this book, because several other functions and techniques also bear that title.

Policy makers need no longer rely solely on hunch or intuition in approaching problems of urban development and government administration. Intuition is still important, but its dictates can be made explicit and can be examined, aided by quantification, and tested in advance of commitment to action. The process by which

this is done is *analysis,* which involves setting up some kind of model of a system or operation and experimenting on this model to gain understanding, insight, and solutions to problems. In a sense it is not new. Successful policy makers have made up such models and conducted such experiments in their heads. They have considered the interrelatedness of activities in the system or operation which they were studying and they have also considered the larger social, economic, and political aspects of their problems.

The size and complexity of urban government today confounds the efforts of individual policy makers, even the best of them, to continue to operate in this way. Increasingly, reliance must be placed on deliberate, explicit, and conscious analysis. Increasingly, too, such analysis depends on a mix of perspectives seldom found in one individual. The task of choosing among alternative courses of action must still rest with the urban politician or manager. But that choice can be aided by others who engage in the systematic exploration of objectives, of alternative ways of achieving them, and of the consequences of

various alternatives. This activity is *systematic policy analysis.*

The aim of this book is not to train policy analysts. There are courses and textbooks to train analysts in various aspects of the practice of policy analysis. These deal mainly with mathematical and related techniques for solving problems that have been represented symbolically. There are pitfalls in the use of—or failure to use—such tools, but sophisticated quantitative tools are not the major stumbling block in most public policy analysis. One reason is that the simpler and more traditional quantitative tools are adequate for many problems. The important reason, however, is that the greatest difficulties in analyzing the multifaceted problems faced by local government policy makers lie elsewhere.

These difficulties lie in the design and definition of the problems, selection of decision rules, and interpretation of study results rather than in the analyst's use of tools. It is in these areas that the critical errors are most likely to be made and where the policy makers play their greatest role in the process of analysis. Unless policy makers are closely involved in formulating problems, establishing criteria for choice among alternatives, and interpreting the results of analyzed alternatives, it is most probable that the wrong problems may be solved, the relevant alternatives may be overlooked, or erroneous conclusions may be drawn.

This book, then, is intended to acquaint policy makers with the concepts and principles, tools and techniques, and strengths and weaknesses of policy analysis, on the premise that such acquaintance will enable them to participate more effectively in the process of analysis.

However, as there are no exact steps or sets of rules in the abstract which would automatically guarantee a fruitful approach to problems as broad and complex as so many confronting urban governments, the emphasis in this book is on concepts and principles. The book is intended to supply information not found in the usual operations research, mathematics, systems engineering, management science, econometrics, or similar text. It is not addressed to the policy analysts themselves, but is meant to serve as an introduction to the consumers of policy analysis— the local elected officials, board members, chief executives, and department heads, and their staffs.

This work pulls together various concepts, methodologies, experiences, techniques, and issues involved in the application of systematic analysis to urban public policy. It is an integration of material from public and business administration, management science, planning, mathematics, statistics, economics, political science, and sociology. However, it is not a

complete survey and integration of all the aspects of these disciplines (and others not investigated that bear on the development of public policy). Rather, it is a selective account of certain areas that appear to be of immediate and practical utility; some of these are already being utilized, although on a minor scale, and others, though not yet utilized, seem particularly relevant. In a sense, this is a first approximation at outlining some of the major ways in which information can be devised and organized to develop knowledge for use in creating better public policy.

The book is divided into five parts. Part One describes the changing environment of local government decision makers and argues the case for policy analysis. The argument is based essentially on two developments: (1) the emergence of cities as society and the increasing concern that something be done about their plight; and (2) the growing capability for actually changing the urban environment and, through analysis, testing alternative changes in advance of commitment to action. The argument is followed by a brief discussion of the background and emerging status of policy analysis.

The concepts, elements, and process of analysis are discussed in Part Two. The aim is to orient the reader to policy analysis by explaining what it is and what it is not, by identifying the problems to which it may be addressed, and by presenting a strategy for its use. The orientation is followed by a general model of the process of analysis. This section is somewhat abstract, because its aim is to convey a sense of what is involved in all policy analyses, regardless of type of problem, functional area of government, and

other specialized conditions. Part Three illustrates these ideas with selected completed studies. In general, the method employed is to present the cases in considerable detail, using material directly from the original studies or from writings about the studies by those who worked on them. Careful reading of this material should help bring to life the abstract concepts and principles of policy analysis and also should help create a greater understanding of the way analysis works, the results it achieves, and the range of public problems to which it might be addressed.

Part Four presents selected tools and techniques of analysis. These range from the highly quantitative and general, which may be applicable to many different situations (although perhaps in a narrow context), to the essentially nonquantitative, which may be highly specific to a particular situation and rich in terms of the context they describe.

However, the tools of analysis—and, for that matter, the whole process—raise a series of issues in their very application. These issues are the subject of Part Five. One set involves behavioral questions relating to the use and misuse of analysis; the other deals with administrative questions relating to preconditions for the conduct of analysis.

Among the many persons who have been of immense help to me in preparing this book, I wish to thank first the Executive Director and staff of the International City Management Association, who initiated the writing of this book through their Urban Research Program and who provided information and advice at various stages. I should also like to thank the several local government officials—William Cornett, Carl Thornton, and Picot Floyd—who read portions of the manuscript as it developed and who gave of their time to discuss the problems they face in trying to secure improvements in government decision and action. I am also grateful to various reviewers for their helpful criticisms and suggestions. Chief among these are Harry Hatry, William Mitchel, Myron Weiner, and Richard Hanel.

I am indebted to the University of California and the Public Policy Research Organization at Irvine for supporting me during the several summers of research and writing. I especially wish to thank my colleagues at Irvine for their encouragement, stimulation, and constructive comment in the writing and revising of this book, particularly Henry Fagin, Alex Mood, Richard Snyder, Robert Bickner, Norman Duncan, Robert Emrey, Alan Feddersen, and John VanMaanen. I am also grateful to Susi Carrolla and Kathy Burke, who typed the many drafts of the manuscript, and to Helen Van Der Laan, Mary Nelson, and Betty Ann DeDominicis, who assisted them.

My grateful acknowledgments are also due Professor Percival Goodman, of the School of Architecture at Columbia University, and Random House, Inc.–Vintage Books, for their kind permission to quote material and to use various illustrations in my Chapter 7, from the book *Communitas: Means of Livelihood and Ways of Life,* by Percival and Paul Goodman.

I should like to extend my grateful thanks to Herbert Slobin for the design of this book and for its illustrations. Thanks are also extended to the following International City Management Association staff—Emily Evershed for her editorial work and Betty Lawton and David S. Arnold for their production work on this book.

Finally, I wish to thank my wife, Norine, for her patience, understanding, and support, without which I would never have begun, or completed, this book.

Kenneth L. Kraemer
Irvine, California

February, 1973

Contents

Introduction

A city council awakens to the fact that various past municipal policies have tended to discriminate against the poor and against blacks and other minorities in the community but is at a loss as to how to reverse the situation. A public works director, after years of serial reconstruction on the city's streets and utility systems, feels there must be a way of coordinating municipal and private improvements so as to prevent the continual tearing up of the same streets. At the same time, he feels overwhelmed by the complexities involved in trying to change things. A city manager faced with the imminent possibility of a strike by municipal sanitation workers senses that a fundamental change is taking place in governmental employer–employee relations but finds that neither he nor his council are prepared to meet the change in terms of its philosophical, organizational, or financial implications. A planning commission and director, after having encouraged vast public and private expenditures in revitalizing a city's downtown area, come to realize that the municipality's land use, transportation, and taxation policies, in terms of central city and suburbs, have in fact encouraged suburban commercial development to the detriment of the revitalization efforts — and they wonder what to do.

Each of these policy makers and groups senses that things are not as they should be. They would like to make improvements, but they feel that they do not really know what the problem is — that what they now perceive as a problem may be only a symptom or a part of a problem far greater in scope and complexity. They do not know how to find out what they do not know. Given limited time and attention, they are also uncertain as to whether they should tackle this immediate problem or one of numerous others vying for their attention.

These policy makers have some ideas on possible solutions to the problem as they now perceive it, but they would like other ideas and insights. They usually find it difficult to think of alternative solutions radically different from those presently in use, yet they feel that better alternatives could be found. But finding them is in itself a problem.

Although the policy makers may have some ideas about what might be done, they are usually uncertain as to the consequences of taking action, especially in view of their limited understanding of the problem. At the same time, they feel that if they fail to act immediately the problem may get worse. The policy makers are also uncertain as to whether they could secure public support for any particular decision they might make. The council lacks information on how various groups in the community would react to specific proposals. The manager is uncertain as to whether he could get support from his department heads and staff. The public works director is unsure of community, council, manager, and staff reactions. While these policy makers concede the possibility of participation in decision by various groups, they do not know who the relevant groups might be or how participation might be effected. Knowing that many people involved in the decision may be dissatisfied with the outcome, they are fearful of creating their own opposition, both to the reaching of a decision and to its execution.

Faced with this complex set of constraints, policy makers wish to seek advice. But where to go?

They often find that they cannot get the kind of information and advice they need within government. Thus, they turn to universities, research organizations, consultants. Here, too, they frequently find little help. In approaching universities they are faced with a vast gap between concern with the creation and generation of knowledge and concern with the utilization of such knowledge for practical purposes. Often, academics and other experts are not interested in the practical problems faced by these decision makers; or academics may want to prescribe what they think ought to be done, without considering the actualities of what can be done. There is a large gap between the ideals of the academic and the realities of local government decision and action as policy makers know it. The academic tends to speak of large-scale action, expensive research, fundamental and revolutionary change, and a considerable time period for problem study before action begins. Philosophical and ideological barriers also separate the world of the academic and that of the local government policy maker.

When approaching consultants and research organizations, policy makers face difficulties in sorting out the good from the bad, the outmoded from the current, the fashionable from the really useful and helpful. Furthermore, whatever the source of advice, there are language problems. Technical jargon, buzz words, and acronyms abound in the academic, research, and consultant worlds. Finally the policy maker wonders: "If I seek advice, will it really help me?"

Thus, the list of considerations facing policy makers seeking improvement is long indeed. The list of potential considerations—things the policy makers are unaware of—may be even longer. Each presents a difficulty in reaching a decision and then in trying to carry it through. The policy maker may well ask: "Is there an effective way of thinking about these difficulties? Is there a practicable way of handling them? How can I get advice on these points?"

The very technological processes that have contributed to the immense changes facing decision makers in local government today have also greatly expanded the ability to cope with these changes. Unfortunately, in most cases the changes have proliferated far beyond the present capacity of policy makers to handle them. But it is the central argument of this book that:

1. A large portion of what occurs in our communities is determined by the choices—or failures to choose—on the part of men acting either as individuals or as groups.

2. Top policy makers in urban government— politicians, board members, administrators, and staff personnel—can and do considerably influence changes in the character and quality of their citizens' lives.
3. These policy makers often want to utilize any and all available assistance in making various crucial decisions.

The experiential problems of policy makers are beginning to receive explicit attention as a result of developments in the social and behavioral sciences and in decision technology. A whole new field of policy science is emerging which focuses simultaneously on the social context in which and through which decisions are made and actions taken, and on the intellectual process of deciding what to do.

This book, then, as the Preface indicates, is about one aspect of policy science: analysis for policy making. That is, this book is about the intellectual processes by which men (1) perceive things in the environment and focus on some rather than on others for decision and action, (2) invent alternative courses of action designed to solve the problems or deal with the opportunities perceived, and (3) evaluate and choose from among the alternatives for action— or, in some instances, nonaction.

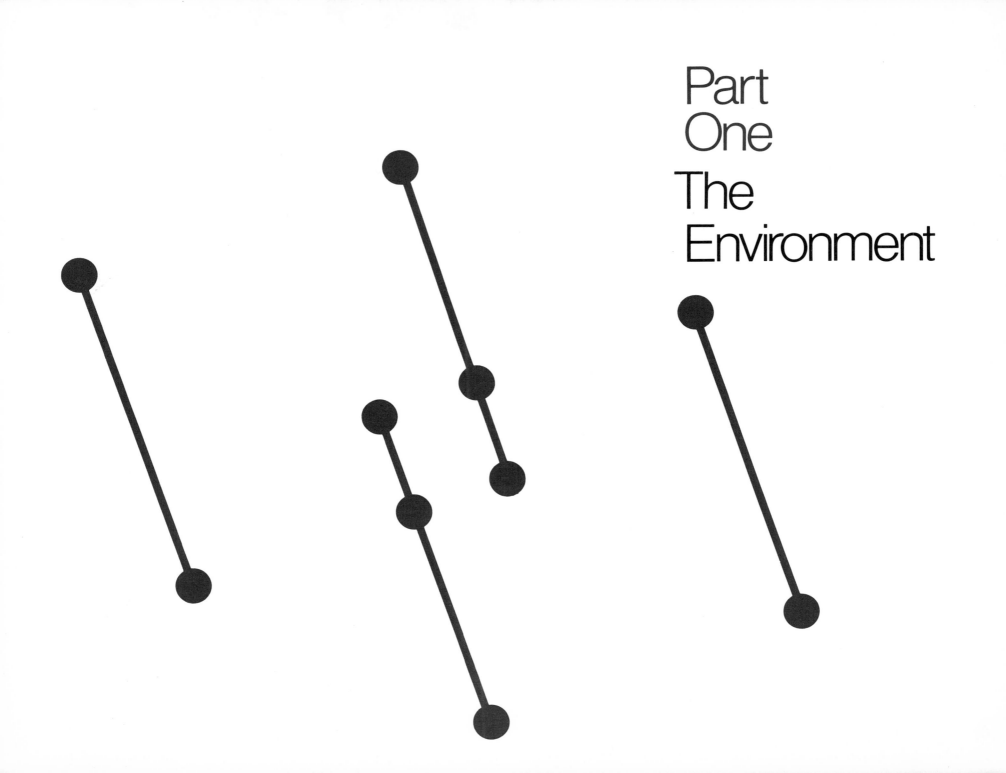

Part
One

The
Environment

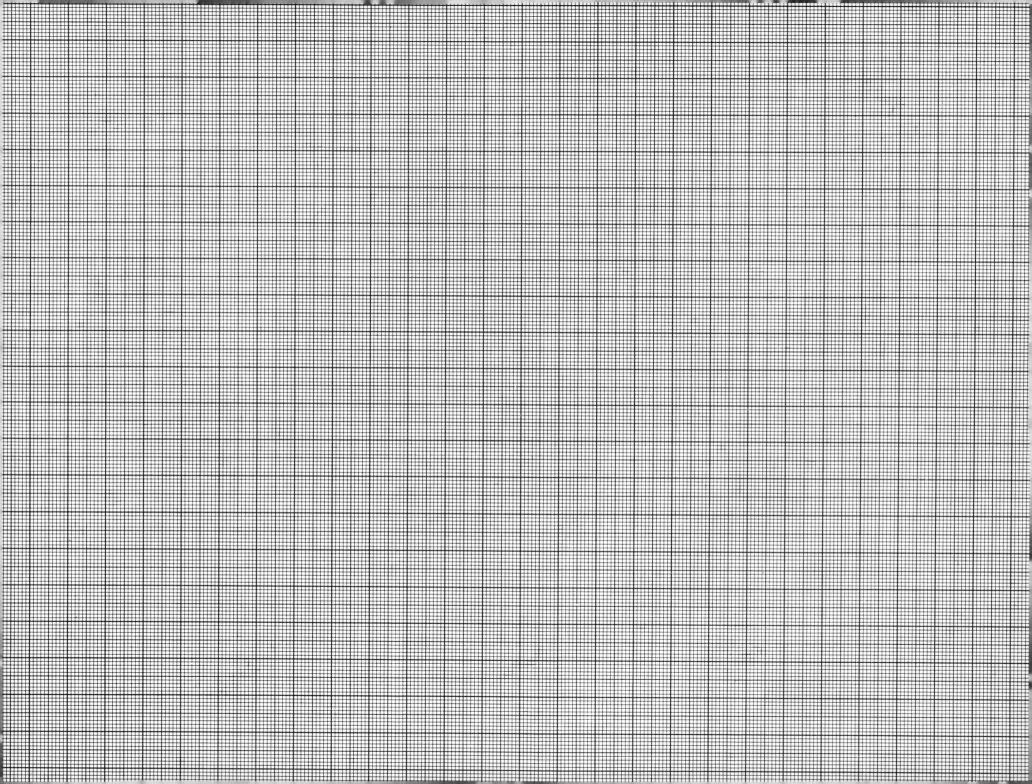

1

The Setting and the Case for Urban Policy Analysis

Before we take up the case for policy analysis, we should consider three features of the current setting: (1) the pervasiveness of change; (2) the potential for the application of science to bring about change and of scientific methodology to help manage change; and (3) the shift in citizens' expectations, which has resulted in a demand that local government policy be oriented to accommodate change. The need for using analysis in making policy rests on this last demand. The case rests on: (1) an increased awareness of the importance of cities in society; (2) the impact of local government decision making in shaping individual and community destinies; and (3) the problems faced by decision makers in developing policy.

THE SETTING

Change is a basic fact of urban life today. It can be managed or it can be chaotic. As a result of advances in science and its associated technologies, man has a greater potential than ever before for handling change. Science can be used to induce massive physical changes directly. In addition, it can provide the methodology for evaluating planned changes in advance of government action. The failure to make such evaluation in the past, as well as the perceived successes of science and its technologies to date, have resulted in changed popular expectations about the role of government policy making. The shift is from a primary concern with mechanics to an equal concern with the substance of what urban government does and the effects that government action has on the daily lives of citizens.

Change: a fact of urban life

Today the city changes daily as a result of a number of factors. Among these are the movements of people, goods, and services in their routine functions. People go to work, to school, to shops, to recreation and leisure activities, and back home again; goods are transported from plants to warehouses to retail outlets, and to households and institutions; services are taken to people on the one hand, and people travel to them on the other.

The city also changes over a long period as a result of decisions to move and to invest by individuals, households, firms, and institutions. The middle class leaves the central city for the suburbs, and so do commerce and industry; lower income groups move into middle class neighborhoods, and blacks move into formerly all-white neighborhoods; migrants from outside the city move into all of these urban areas.

Finally, change occurs in a particular city as a result of changes in the larger area of which it is a part. A central city neighborhood becomes a ghetto; a suburb becomes a city in its own right, with all the advantages and disadvantages of that status; a ghetto becomes a wasteland, whether from urban deterioration or redevelopment or riot; a suburb becomes surrounded by other suburbs; a city is divided by a freeway.

The short-term changes contribute to the everyday problems and the demands for government action. The longer-term changes and the cumulative effect of many small changes can alter the basic character of public action and, thereby, the character of government decision making. For example, urban disorders have worked to alter the function of urban policing from crook-catching to broad social control. As a result of this change, the societal sanctions, permissible police behavior, decision-making structures and processes, and policies deemed appropriate for handling changes have been altered.

Any particular government is characterized by a certain style of its own as it meets the impact of change, whether in its environment or in its own makeup. The government may react to change reluctantly, after the fact, and in a remedial manner. It may seek to anticipate change, to plan for it, to control it—or even to induce it. Or it may opt for some combination of these styles. The style characterizing a particular government is a function of historical precedent, the direction, scope, and magnitude of change experienced by the community, the socioeconomic makeup of the community, the character and quality of its leadership, and many other factors—including change. In any event, a style exists, and it has substantial impact on the quality of life in the community.

Science and urban change
As the ability of urban governments to handle change through policy decisions is sharply increased by advances in science and technology, so also is the necessity. Unattended, scientific technology creates problems. The present distress in urban areas is partly the secondary result of technology's past uses. For example, the automobile produces health and safety hazards, increases urban congestion in central cities, contributes to the costly urban development patterns in the suburbs, and increases public dependence on automotive transportation by preventing suitable alternatives from being developed. In such instances public policy has tended to react to change under pressure and

after the fact. Only in recent years, for example, have safety standards been set for the automotive industry. Effective automobile pollution control policies are still in the development stage. In the future, more attention must be given to the effects of possible technological commitments on the total urban environment, for example, the effects of supersonic transport, nuclear power plants, computers, etc.

The application of science offers the possibility of solving such problems and, to some extent, preventing their future occurrence. It does this by creating (1) new means for physically changing the urban environment,[1] and (2) new methods for evaluating the impacts of actions in anticipation of change. Present-day scientific technologies can generate physical changes on a larger scale and more quickly than ever before. As a result, the time span of physical change can be shortened to the same order as that of social and economic change and government action. That is, whereas in the past large-scale physical change could be carried out only over several decades or more, the time span for similar changes today may be a mere decade, or less. Today, government decision makers can establish a course of action, see it carried out, and witness the results often within a single term of office.

Such capability means that for the first time in man's history it is reasonable to consider the conditions of life in which he would live:

The true significance of . . . this accelerating age of science and technology in which we now live, is that it is beginning to lead us to wonder, once again, about the nature and purpose of man, about what constitutes

the good life and the good society. . . . This is so because the products of science and technology offer us the prospect, at last, of satisfying the material needs of all.[2]

Not only does the application of science permit greater options for physical change; it also provides the methodology for evaluating actual or planned changes. The experimental method, limited to a controlled laboratory setting in the past, can now be extended to the uncontrollable laboratory of the city through the use of "field experiments" and "paper experiments."

The logic of laboratory experimentation can be extended into the field, and into settings not fully experimental, through the use of quasi-experimental research designs. These designs permit an experimental approach to urban improvement in which we try out new programs designed to solve specific urban problems, learn whether or not these programs are effective, and retain, modify, or discard them on the basis of demonstrated effectiveness.

Similarly, modeling and simulation enable us to conduct paper experiments in place of experimentation on the real thing. Such experiments help decision makers to see in advance the consequences of specific actions in all their complexity and interrelatedness, with their respective costs and benefits, and risks and uncertainties. It is possible, therefore, to take science out of the laboratory to use it for public urban purposes. In this way science becomes a potential means to public ends—in both its products and its methodology. This possibility is all the more important because of changing expectations regarding the role of government.

Changing expectations regarding the role of urban government

Historically, urban governments have been viewed as purveyors of collectively required services not provided by the private sector — because they were unprofitable or because they were to be provided on a basis other than ability to pay. Service needs were seen as uniform, and, whether needs could be so standardized or not, uniform services were provided to all groups on the basis of an ideological commitment to equality — defined as equal treatment rather than as equalizing differences among social groups in the community. The business of government was to produce services as efficiently and as cheaply as possible, and this usually meant focusing on minimum levels of service. Thus, the ends of government were clear. Only the means remained to be decided upon, and the choice was among several existing tried and true options. As a result, the attention of political leaders, administrators, laymen, and academics was centered on the mechanics of governing.

The political reality of government decision making and the changing expectations of citizens concerning the role of urban governments was brought home by a series of community leadership studies conducted in the 1950s. While these studies indicated that no single pattern characterizes the manner in which influence is brought to bear on government decisions, they clearly showed that the concern of political leaders, government administrators, and interest groups was with the substance of governmental goals, not simply the mechanics.

The reasons for this shift from expectations of "efficiency" to expectations of "effectiveness" by political, professional, and citizen leadership are difficult to determine. These expectations appear to have grown in part out of the increased reliance on government since the Depression of the 1930s and the generally favorable performance of governments during World War II and the postwar forties and fifties. They also stem from the affluence that has characterized the nation since World War II. Because employment has become widespread, because distribution of the gross national product is such that the average family has a substantial disposable income above that required for food and housing, and because population concentrations are functional as well as dysfunctional, there can be concern for the quality of urban life. In this context, the dichotomy between the haves and the have-nots is more readily apparent and is viewed as unnecessary. The current expectations of improved quality of government services and the availability of economic resources have created a demand for effective urban government action. Current considerations are centered on how to develop institutions which can identify needs for change, develop programs to achieve newly defined goals, and create the mechanics of change where community conditions are viewed as unsatisfactory.

Both the traditional and the new views have been expressed by J. L. Brownlee, a former city manager who sees the city as "a living organism that can be healthy or sick — helping a man find fulfillment in life or crushing him into a misshapen mold . . . ," and, on the other hand, speaks of the

daily management challenges produced by the far-flung organization that is the city government of Fort Worth, Texas. It is a giant business enterprise employing 3,500 people and spending more than $50 million annually as it performs literally hundreds of varied, often unglamorous, but essential tasks.

The responsibilities and workload of the City of Fort Worth, a medium-sized "big" city, are staggering. This municipal organization provides services twenty-four hours a day over a 200-square-mile area where four hundred thousand people live; maintains and utilizes over $215 million in capital assets; responds instantly — day or night — to calls of distress and emergency caused by fire, crime or other disaster; disposes of 440 tons of garbage daily. The city also distributes up to 130 million gallons of treated water through nearly 1,500 miles of water mains each day and performs numerous other tasks from the most mundane to the most vital. The city investigates and handles over twenty-five thousand criminal offenses and ten thousand fire calls annually. It circulates over one-half million books through the public library, cuts twenty thousand blocks of weeds each summer, and offers other services ranging from health care to dead animal pickup, from chughole patching to providing suitable locations for the performing arts.

For all these services, and many more, we pay about 25¢ a day per capita — hardly enough to buy a loaf of bread.[3]

Brownlee's considerable emphasis on the mechanics of government administration is illustrative of the traditional concern of government decision makers, their comfort with the "business" of government, and the magnitude of government operations which tends to force decision makers into a relatively short-term-operations-oriented perspective. However, Brownlee's statement that the end result of these operations in some way affects man's fulfillment reflects the increasing awareness of urban decision makers that governments exist for more than the production of minimal services, and that governments can contribute significantly to the lives of citizens through the character and quality of services they provide.

Change and public policy

The job of urban public policy today must be to anticipate change, to pace it, and to order it. If public policy is to be used creatively, decision makers must shift their attention from efficient production of government services to concern for the quality of life resulting from those services, to creating objectives for the future, and to designing new policies, plans, programs, and actions for achieving those objectives. Urban governments presently tend to make policy decisions out of a known number of means, with a view to achieving a known number of ends. In the future, the making of policy must be oriented as well to what may lie around the corner, and to an unknown number of new means and ends that science and technology or social and economic events will be making possible for the first time.

As a result of this century's scientific and technological revolution, we are beginning to realize that urban areas need not be as they are. We can change them—at will, and massively. We are, therefore, faced with the question, "How and in what directions do we want our cities to change?" This is a question of social values and policy decision. Policy analysis is addressed to these issues, whether in the context of the day-to-day recurring decisions or the longer-term, one-time, decisions of urban governments.

THE CASE FOR POLICY ANALYSIS IN LOCAL GOVERNMENT

The need for policy analysis rests, fundamentally, on the increasing need to achieve a closer re-lation between knowledge and power: that is, between information about the myths and realities of urban problems, and the use of government policy to handle these problems. Unwise policies, hastily (or laboriously) muddled through by rule of thumb or by time-honored methods, can now have unprecedentedly grave consequences. At the same time, the information needed for creating better policies is becoming increasingly available to political decision makers and government administrators as well as to laymen. The result is, on the one hand, greater public demand for better decisions and, on the other hand, greater public dissatisfaction with poor decisions.

The case for using analysis in urban government rests, too, on the importance of cities as such, the impact of governmental decision making in shaping individual and community destinies, and the problems faced by governments as they seek to create a better life for their citizens. If this goal is to be reached, better decisions are needed. Better decisions require, among other things, better information. Policy analysis is aimed specifically at providing information for improved policy decisions.

Importance of cities

In the postindustrial world of the late twentieth century the condition of society is in large part the condition of its cities. Whereas in 1790 only 3 percent of the population of the United States lived in urban centers, in 1965 the figure was 70 percent. Of greater importance than the growth of urban population is the increasing concentration of population in and around the larger cities. By 1960, 69 percent of the population lived in 175 metropolitan areas. The projections for the next three or four decades portend even greater concentration; as Herman G. Berkman has put it:

By the year 2000, we can anticipate forty-one metropolitan areas, each inhabited by a million or more people.

By the year 2000, 350 million people, four out of every five of our population, will live and work in metropolitan areas. Between now and the year 2000, 80% of our population increase will occur in metropolitan areas. We may add an equivalent of fifteen cities of 200,000 each year beginning in 1970. By 1980 we will be adding the equivalent of twenty cities of 200,000 population each.

The single most important characteristic of the United States today is a revolution involving the emergence of the Great Urban Region. By 1960, slightly more than half of all households were living in 213 densely built-up urbanized areas. Of this, almost 60.5% were living in central cities. But the proportion of the urbanized area group living *outside* the central cities of these areas of dense concentration had grown from 30% to 40% in a decade. What this means is that between 1950 and 1960, when the central cities of these heavily urbanized regions absorbed almost ten million, the outlying fringe absorbed almost seventeen million! Over 70% of the increases in urbanized area settlement went into the fringe! While the urbanized settlement in the central cities increased by only 20%, that of the fringes increased by more than 80%. The fringe will hold almost 60% of the entire metropolitan area population by 1975.[4]

Thus, the "urban condition" is a dominant feature of the present and emergent society.

Berkman's statement about the importance of cities is impressive but not new. What is new, and of far greater significance, is the perceived or subjective importance of cities:

American cities, long neglected by scientists, professors, administrators, and politicians on the state and federal levels, and even by their own inhabitants, are now in the limelight. Suddenly, the expert and the man in the street both realize the great importance of our cities and their key role in modern civilization. We now realize that huge cities, with their vast opportunities and with their complicated problems, are not only here to stay, but will continue to expand in size and complexity.[5]

The results of this new awareness are a greater demand for government action to improve urban conditions and a greater dissatisfaction with the failure of particular courses of action.[6]

Urban government decision making and community destiny

Many events that occur in a particular urban area are beyond local government control. Many problems created by such events are not only local but national in impact. Nevertheless, they are local and urban as they affect the individual. Whether problems such as poverty, slums, traffic congestion, land speculation, pollution, segregation, unemployment, and ugliness stem from causes such as mechanistic economic forces, class conflict, the geometry of concentration, the dominance of agricultural values in an urban political context, or technology, these problems manifest themselves in the lives and behavior of urban-dwelling individuals.

This fact suggests two things. First, many urban difficulties must be solved locally and their effects alleviated at a personal, individual level. Second, often the level of government most adequately equipped to deal with the individual and with the characteristics of a problem unique to a particular place is the local level. And, as a result of history, tradition, political philosophy, cultural pluralism, and the legal and political complexities involved in the formation of newer

forms of regional, general-purpose local government, the currently constituted local governments will continue to influence the direction and character of the spreading urban regions which they, in large part, form.[7]

This does not mean that the federal and state governments are of inconsequential importance to urban problems. Many of their actions (or failures to act) precipitate events that create problems in the cities—problems which could be prevented by foresight. Furthermore, many problems can be solved only by concerted national action.[8] Finally, the financial and other resources needed to solve urban problems rest largely with the federal government.

Nevertheless, urban governments do have a significant realm of decision and action open to them. For example, any particular government's influence over the choice of regional locations by major industrial firms is probably negligible. However, once an industry has selected a particular region in which to locate, a local government may have a significant influence on the choice of a specific location—through direct inducement, or, indirectly, through its past history of decisions (e.g., on zoning, tax policy, public services, etc.), or through both.

Within the limits set by nonlocal forces and events, at least three general kinds of policy decisions made by local governments are important in shaping the future of an urban area: (1) those relating to day-to-day operations; (2) those relating to the management of government itself, i.e., to the programming of what it is that government will do; and (3) those relating to planning and community development. The last category—that of development decisions—is

aimed at defining and creating new systems and operations intended to serve objectives in some future time period, usually a distant one. Traditionally, local government development decisions have been focused on the physical growth of an area, i.e., land use, community facilities, transportation, and utility systems. Increasingly, urban governments are becoming concerned also with human and economic development and with organizational development of the government itself (for example, some of the efforts of the last ten years and more in the information systems field are illustrative of attempts to develop new and better administrative systems).

In the past it was generally felt that planning and development decisions were the critical shaping elements of a city's future. No doubt they are important. However, in recent decades we have become critically aware that management and operational decisions are at least equally significant. Management decisions, because they are concerned with programming what government actually will do in the more immediate future, are important adjustments to longer-term decisions. Similarly, operational decisions, in their cumulative effect, often take on the character of longer-term programming and planning decisions. That is, they become broad policy.

Both day-to-day operational decisions and management decisions of urban government shape the community's future in two ways. First, they do so through the cumulative establishment of many individual commitments which, when taken together, have vast consequences. Second, they do so through their modifying effect on longer-term development policies in the very process of carrying out those policies. Thus, local government policy, however established, creates many of the immediate conditions in which most people live out their lives. It is these conditions and the general style[9] that government officials choose to follow in making determinations that create the citizens' valuation and response in a community.

Difficulties of decision making

Urban government decision makers face several problems in attempting to shape community destiny. These concern (1) interrelation of cities and problems, (2) limited resources, (3) uncertainty about a future beyond their control, and (4) difficulty of direct experimentation in the community.

Interrelatedness of cities and problems. The cities in an urban area are bound together by complex social and economic relations and by spatial and temporal proximity—either now or in the forseeable future. The time dimension is most often overlooked, but is important. For example, the city dweller's flight to the suburbs was in part an attempt to escape problems then extant largely in the congested central city. The newly created suburbs were free of these problems for a time. But as growth enmeshed the entire urban area, formerly discrete suburbs became neighbors, both to each other and to the central city. Thus, in the course of time, spatial proximity has been brought about either by urban expansion or by increased accessibility resulting from transportation and communications advances. In turn, the social and economic interdependence of individuals and communities has increased.

Further, the problems of cities are interrelated. The complex social, economic, and physical-ecological interrelations of urban problems are increasingly apparent. Slums, for example, are no longer considered as simply a problem of inadequate or insufficient housing. They are related to tax policy, "a culture of poverty," environmental sanitation, employment and economic activity, ethnic factors, class values, and many other substantive factors. Because of cities' social and economic interdependence and spatial proximity, any factors which constitute a problem in one locality are likely to do so in adjacent areas.

As a result, government decisions and actions directed to urban problems are interrelated in several ways. First, solutions attempted by one locality are likely to affect other communities. For example, urban renewal techniques used for a slum problem in one community often seriously affect other communities by: relocation of former slum residents and businesses to other communities; attraction of new residents and new businesses from other cities; creation of additional demand for public services by slum residents; loss of revenues; and creation of new slums. Second, because of these spillover effects and because some solutions imply resource and other commitments which can be marshaled only by a large-scale cooperative venture, local government actions must be made in concert.

In this context of interrelationship, a major problem for government becomes that of achieving a comprehensive perspective as the basis for decision making on policy questions. Such a perspective takes into account the spatial, temporal, issue, and solution interdependencies facing urban government decision makers. Policy analysis seeks to do just this. It involves striving to view a problem or situation in its entirety with all its ramifications, with all its interior interactions, with all its exterior connections, and with full cognizance of its place in its context.

Limited resources. As noted above, cities are the locus of many problems currently of concern in the society. Urban governments, therefore, should and do bear a major responsibility for solving them. However, the human, financial, and organizational resources of urban governments are seriously limited. To alleviate this condition, federal and some state policies have been increasingly oriented to providing technical and financial assistance to urban governments. These efforts will continue, and probably the magnitude of such assistance will increase. Nevertheless, the amount of resources available relative to that needed for the solution of urban problems will continue to be limited. Urban decision makers, therefore, need some systematic way of assessing problems and resources, setting goals, developing alternative courses of action and considering them in terms of their costs and consequences, and choosing that set of public actions most likely to achieve a desirable ratio of goal achievement to resource expenditure. This is the aim and the opportunity of policy analysis.

Uncertainty about the future. Decision makers must not only seek to understand the complex interrelations of problems and solutions but must also allocate scarce resources now. When inaugurating programs or establishing policies that almost always have consequences for the future, they are faced with the problems of coping imaginatively and realistically with situations they now perceive only dimly. Though aware of their own inadequacies and the probable inadequacies of their advisers, urban public policy makers must nevertheless make decisions and plans which will seriously affect the success or failure of their successors as well as the quality of life of both current and future citizens.

To appraise the future is difficult. Important aspects of it are not only unknown, but unthought of. Those aspects which are relatively accessible to the imagination also may be ignored because each decision maker's view of the future is conditioned by emotional and intellectual biases and by political and social forces. In addition, the future is uncertain in a statistical or probabilistic sense. Some events apparently occur on a purely random basis and, assuming they can be anticipated, can be described only in terms of their likelihood of occurrence, or of their impacts.

Since the policy maker can neither plan for— nor think of—everything, he presumably should try to look at a relevant range of possibilities, remembering the importance of examining possibilities which seem relatively unlikely but which might have very desirable (or very catastrophic) consequences if they occurred. Further, he should see that existing policies, systems, and operations be made as flexible as possible and that new ones be designed to provide future decision makers with the flexibility to muddle through. Unless such a capacity is thoughtfully designed —that is, unless the range of possibilities in future challenges, requirements, and opportunities is adequately foreseen—the decisions made now are likely to prove to have many undesirably inflexible consequences. Policy analysis is specifically oriented to deal with

these problems. It is concerned with prediction so that probable future events can be taken into account now and so that future consequences of present decisions can be explored. It is further concerned with the invention and design of new alternatives which take these predictions into account.

Difficulty of direct experimentation in urban areas. Balanced on the knife-edge of the present, policy makers can obtain information about the past but would also like to obtain information which would aid in predicting the future. Of prime concern is the response to questions of the type: "If I do X now, what will the future consequences be?"

Such questions have traditionally been answered by experimentation in the scientific laboratory. However, the urban area presents a difficult environment for such traditional experimental assessments. The major elements for study often are not susceptible to controlled laboratory experiment, because of the following three factors: (1) they cannot be recreated in the laboratory setting; (2) they require manipulations of human behavior that are socially unacceptable; or (3) they involve large expenditures over extended time periods.

Because much of the urban environment does so resist traditional experimentation, policy makers often need means whereby they can conduct "paper experiments" aimed at an accurate reproduction of selected variables in real world objects and events. This reproduction is attempted through the formulation of a theory or a set of theories about the system or operation being studied. When combined with "facts" about

the actual behavior of the system, the formulation becomes a model. The model can then be "operated" or experimented on by the policy makers for the purpose of predicting the consequences of changing various factors which make up the system.

However, models and experiments with models are not always appropriate, desirable, or necessary. "Field experiments," such as those conducted with pilot programs, may be both more practical and desirable, especially when action must be taken immediately or when acting and observing the result of action are the only ways of determining consequences. Administrators and other local government decision makers frequently adopt new programs designed to provide better services, solve specific problems, or search for more efficient ways of doing things. However, few of these people ever regard such programs, whether trials or full-scale implementations, as potential field experiments subject to scientific evaluation. Yet the logic of such field experiments is similar to the paper experiment and the traditional laboratory experiment. That is, the administrator initiating a new or changed program has at least an implicit theory about the relation of various actions to conditions he is trying to affect. When that theory is made explicit, that is, when it is stated in the form of a hypothesis relating selected actions to expected outcomes, the theory can be tested by observed facts which describe the actual outcomes of the implemented program.

Thus, paper experiments and field experiments may become to the policy maker what the laboratory experiment is to the physicist, chemist, or psychologist. The development of such experiments is a key element in the process of policy analysis. However, this book focuses primarily on paper experiments, on the assumption that

many decision makers are familiar with the concept of field experimentation even if they seldom use this technique. Selected works on

field experimentation for those interested in pursuing the subject are referenced in the notes below.[10]

Notes

[1] Note the phrase is "physically changing the urban environment," not "changing the physical environment."

[2] Walter Orr Roberts, "Science, a Wellspring of Our Discontent," *American Scholar,* XXXVI (Spring 1967), 247.

[3] Jerry L. Brownlee and Errol H. Colley, "A City Manager Looks at the Management Sciences," in *Using Advanced Management Techniques,* ed. by Arthur D. Little, Inc., Series on Critical Issues in Urban Management (Washington, D.C.: Communication Service Corporation, 1968), pp. 3–4.

[4] Herman G. Berkman, "The Scope of Scientific Technique and Information Technology in Metropolitan Area Analysis," *Annals,* Monograph VII (Philadelphia: American Academy of Political and Social Science, May 1967), p. 170.

[5] Brownlee and Colley, in Little, *Advanced Management Techniques,* p. 1.

[6] For example, in the wake of suburban migration many downtown areas have deteriorated. Government action, in the form of urban renewal, has sought to alleviate this condition. In the process, certain businesses have been displaced and others destroyed. Residents have

been relocated, sometimes to better but also higher priced housing, and overcrowding has resulted, thus creating conditions for deterioration elsewhere because relocation policy per se does nothing to improve the general conditions (employment, education, health, etc.) of these people. In some cases, too, the aim of revitalizing the downtown areas by the infusion of new businesses has not been fully achieved.

The net result of all these effects has been dissatisfaction, not only on the part of those who have suffered most, but also on the part of those who seem to have gained the most—the politicians, business leaders, and government administrators who advocated the action in the first place. What lies at the heart of such failure is not necessarily a bad solution (i.e., urban renewal) but a failure to take into account the full ramifications of that solution (e.g., relocation), the uncertainties involved (e.g., Will new businesses locate downtown, and if they do, will people patronize them?), and related government actions which may negate the solution attempted (e.g., tax policy which takes away the economic incentive for being downtown in the first place).

[7] An excellent discussion of these points, related to the use of computers, is contained in William H. Mitchel, "An Approach to the Use of Digital Computers in Municipal Government" (unpublished Ph.D. dissertation, School of Public Administration, University of Southern California, Los Angeles, 1968), pp. 21–38.

[8] For example, short of drastic action limiting the num-

ber of vehicles on city streets and highways, a particular city can do little to alleviate vehicular pollution and noise. Even the state of California has been unable to affect a key source of the problem—the automotive industry. In such instances federal action may be required. Such action may need to go beyond industry regulation. For example, FHA and GI loans have probably had an impact on, and in addition have further contributed to, problems of automotive air pollution.

[9] As mentioned previously, style refers to government's attitude towards change. It also refers to the character of its leadership, organizational response, procedures, and the general feeling of trust engendered in its citizens.

[10] The following references are basic reading. Additional references can be found within these works. Donald T. Campbell, "Reforms as Experiments," *American Psychologist,* XXIV (April 1969), 409–29; Donald T. Campbell and Julian C. Stanely, *Experimental and Quasi-Experimental Designs for Research* (Chicago: Rand McNally & Company, 1969); E. A. Suchman, *Evaluative Research: Principles and Practice in Public Service and Social Action Programs* (New York: Russell Sage Foundation, 1967); George W. Fairweather, *Methods for Experimental Social Innovation* (New York: John Wiley & Sons, Inc., 1967); Donald T. Campbell and H. L. Ross, "The Connecticut Crackdown on Speeding: Time-Series Data in Quasi-Experimental Analysis," *Law and Society Review,* III (1968), 33–53.

The Background of
Policy Analysis

2

Two separate strands of activity characterize the development of policy analysis as it relates to local governments. The first had its beginnings in the federal government's defense and space exploration activities and has evolved into a series of technology transfer efforts in recent years. The second is indigenous to urban governments and represents a continuous effort, dating back to the early 1900s, to improve urban government policy making and action.

THE TRANSFER OF SCIENCE AND TECHNOLOGY

Beginnings in military systems
Recent experiments with the transplant of systems and aerospace techniques in urban government have their roots in World War II. The idea that analysis might be applied to public policy questions was suggested by the success of what came to be called operations analysis (and, later, operations research) in dealing with military operations. The questions addressed were largely tactical: how to use "chaff" as a radar countermeasure; how to determine more effective bombing patterns; how to determine better antisub-

marine search measures. Postwar analyses were also largely defense-oriented, but were concerned with the selection and evaluation of new weapon systems rather than with tactical questions. Analyses were further extended in the 1950s to include questions of national security policy and strategy as the primary concern.[1]

Civil systems transplants
Paralleling these military experiences, and in part emerging from them, analysis also began to be applied, in the 1950s, to problems of space exploration. Here, as in defense, the concerns were initially hardware-oriented but were later extended to space exploration policy.

In all of these efforts, three major groups were involved: (1) the federal government, particularly the Department of Defense and the National Aeronautics and Space Administration (NASA); (2) the aerospace corporations which produced the hardware and developed the new systems; and (3) private research and development organizations such as the Rand Corporation, the System Development Corporation, the Hudson Institute, the Institute for Defense Analysis, and many

others. Not only did the individual and joint efforts of these groups produce new analytic techniques; they also produced new management techniques, such as PPBS (planning-programming-budgeting system), PERT (program evaluation and review technique) and CPM (critical path method). The success of the above efforts suggested the possibility of extending these evolving methods of analysis to the so-called civilian sector,[2] that is, to non-defense and nonspace activities and to other levels and units of government.

One of the first such efforts was initiated in 1963 in the form of a NASA-sponsored conference on whether the national space exploration program could be applied to the daily tasks of people living and working in cities and whether new knowledge and analytic techniques could be used to seek answers to the critical issues currently facing urban areas.[3] Subsequently, NASA funded projects at several university research centers to explore specific neoscientific applications; examples are CAST (Center for Application of Science and Technology), Wayne State University (program budgeting in the Detroit police department); Center for Planning and Development Research, University of California, Berkeley (management science in police and fire operations).

Another transplant effort was initiated by President Johnson in August 1965 by an Executive Order which directed all federal agencies to convert to the budget system of program planning and analysis developed in the Department of Defense. Unlike previous budgeting systems, which were accounting-oriented and concerned with maintenance, personnel, equipment, etc., the new concept, PPBS, emphasized the total monetary cost of achieving stated goals. This concept has been extended to state and local governments under the Five-Five-Five Project directed by the George Washington University.[4] This project is also part of local government indigenous efforts at improvement, as many local governments are independently developing PPBS capabilities.

In 1965 the state of California launched an effort to transfer aerospace industry technology to governmental affairs. Four areas were chosen for study — information handling; waste management; mass transportation; and criminal justice — with Lockheed Missiles and Space Company, Aerojet-General Corporation, North American Aviation, Incorporated, and Space-General Corporation the respective contractors.[5] Subsequently, additional contracts were let: Space-General received a contract to study welfare operations; Lockheed received one to study crime information-handling; and Aerojet-General received a contract to devise a system for coping with pollution in a selected region of California.

Government adoption of systems techniques

In recognition of these various technology transfer programs, and to develop a unified approach, the federal government created, in 1965, a special Subcommittee on the Utilization of Scientific Manpower, of the Senate Labor and Public Welfare Committee. This subcommittee has held periodic hearings on two bills which would make federal funds available for utilizing systems analysis for social and economic problems — particularly in urban areas.[6] In addition, two other federal commissions have recently focused on the application of science and technology to national problems which are essentially urban in their locus. The first, the National Commission on Technology, Automation, and Economic Progress, took a broad look at ways in which technological developments and scientific analysis could be utilized to solve such problems as air and water pollution, water supply, solid waste disposal, urban congestion and blight, deterioration of natural beauty, depletion of natural resources, individual and social disorganization, and unemployment.[7] The second commission (President's Commission on Law Enforcement and Administration of Justice) focused on one specific area for its study — law enforcement and the administration of criminal justice.[8]

The Department of Housing and Urban Development (HUD), the key federal agency responsible for planning and development of urban areas, sponsored nationwide summer study sessions on science and urban development in 1966.[9] Subsequently it created an Office of Urban Research and Technology, concerned with sponsoring research and development programs on a variety of urban problems,[10] and in 1967 it helped create

and sponsor the Urban Institute, a national center for urban research. In 1969, HUD launched Project Breakthrough — a research and development effort aimed at experimenting with mass production of low-cost housing through the use of business and aerospace technology.[11]

Numerous other governmental organizations, private corporations, research foundations, and professional organizations have also begun to use systematic analysis to attack urban problems.[12]

In 1967 both Los Angeles and New York City established entirely new arrangements for conducting systematic analyses. The Los Angeles Technical Services Corporation, consisting then of a half-dozen recruits from the aerospace industry and loosely tied to the city government, was created as a nonprofit organization. Its primary goal was to provide the mayor, the council, the planning department, and the operating departments and agencies of the city with continuing expert advice on technical questions.[13] New York City, by contrast, called upon a large staff from the Rand Corporation to study the problems of eight city agencies which sponsor the work. The areas in which the Rand group is working include: fire protection; housing; criminal justice; health; drug abuse; cost analysis and program budgeting; water pollution; neighborhood analysis; economic development; welfare; and deployment of municipal emergency services.[14]

Further, the American Public Works Association, the trade association of municipal public works officials, has conducted specific studies of snow removal, solid waste disposal, and storm and sanitary sewer problems, and has established mechanisms for liaison between city officials demanding new hardware and the research people capable of developing it.[15] Finally, under HUD sponsorship, the International City Management Association (in conjunction with the Technical Analysis Division of the National Bureau of Standards and the Fels Institute of the University of Pennsylvania) has been engaged in applying systems analysis to operational problems in three participating cities.[16] The problems chosen for study were: fire station location; measurement of the effectiveness of various means of preventing neighborhood deterioration; and determination of community facilities needs, functions, and locations. These last efforts are as much a part of the tradition of local government self-improvement as they are technology transfers.

THE TRADITION OF ANALYSIS IN URBAN GOVERNMENT

The second stream of policy analysis activities consists of those traditionally undertaken by local governments themselves or, for these units, by consultants, universities, and research centers. Although less glamorous and less well funded than the technology transfers, they are equally significant and will undoubtedly continue into the future—though perhaps in modified form. Three major areas have contributed to indigenous urban policy analysis in the past: (1) political science, business and public administration, and industrial engineering; (2) urban planning; and (3) urban economics. At times these contributions have been uniquely identifiable with one of these disciplines or professions, but more often they have been an admixture of all three.

The earliest analysis activities in urban governments were those centered on economy and efficiency; these stemmed from the scientific management movement of the 1920s. Work study, organization and methods study, process charting, Gantt charting, accounting and expenditure control, and time and motion studies characterized these early analyses on the part of urban government.[17]

Between the mid-thirties and the sixties, analysis was extended beyond operational and control problems to management problems. Thus, analysis activities were oriented towards government organization and reorganization studies, budgeting improvement (under the management-oriented concepts of program and performance budgeting),[18] and government performance evaluation.[19] These analyses were related to the overall improvement of a department's or a government's operations and, in some cases, to the designing of better ways to achieve government objectives.

While the above analysis activities were chiefly concerned with internal affairs or urban governments, other activities were developing in response to specific problems in the urban environment—problems such as land use, transportation, and housing. Although there had been a tradition of data collection for planning purposes and some analytic work, systematic analysis in this area really began in the fifties through the impetus of theoretic efforts to understand the interrelations of land use, transportation, and market forces in large-scale transportation studies such as those made in Detroit, Chicago, and Penn-Jersey.[20]

Systematic analysis advanced rapidly toward the middle sixties with the added support of Community Renewal Programs (CRP) such as those in Pittsburgh, Stockton, and San Francisco.[21] Generally, these analytic efforts were concerned with developing policies for better utilization of an existing system or operation. The transportation studies dealt with choosing from among existing alternative systems and networks, taking future factors and consequences into account. The Community Renewal Programs were concerned with choosing from among alternative mixes of existing public programs for urban renewal, also taking future consequences into consideration. Generally, these studies did not involve the development of new policies, systems, or operations. Rather, they were concerned with the programming of existing public actions to achieve some previously determined (or assumed) policy.

Parallel with the transportation and urban renewal studies, economic analysis was extended to urban government decision making in the form of cost-revenue analyses (e.g., annexation cases) and cost-benefit studies of specific programs in such areas as health, housing, education, and urban renewal. Economic analysis was extended later to the entire structure and functioning of an urban area's economy—through economic base and input/output analyses, regional accounting, and other applications of urban and regional economics.[22]

The first attempts to deal with long-range planning and development problems were a product of the mid-sixties. Some grew out of previous traditions, while others developed in entirely new areas. Urban transportation studies, such as

BART (Bay Area Rapid Transit)[23] and NECTP (Northeast Corridor Transportation Project), focused on the design and development of new transportation policies, systems, and operations for ten years and more into the future. In education, the SCSD (Schools Construction Systems Development) Project[24] was concerned with the design and development of new elementary school facilities—to meet current instructional needs as well as those which might be expected to develop over a period of ten years and more.

THE FUTURE OF POLICY ANALYSIS IN LOCAL GOVERNMENT

The two broad strands of activity—technology transfers and indigenous efforts—which characterized the development of policy analysis are beginning to converge in the common arena of the city. Increasing attention is being given to the use of analysis in trying to understand and develop solutions to urban problems. Not only are the subject matter and context of transplant and indigenous policy analysis activity likely to be common; so also are the methodology, language and technique, and arrangements for the conduct of inquiry. That is, both strands are characterized increasingly by: the methodology of scientific inquiry; the systems approach or perspective; the language and techniques of mathematics, statistics, and computer programming; and the use of interdisciplinary teams in analysis.

Whatever the tradition, policy analysis currently is more art than science, more potential than reality. Further, its application to the problems of local governments has been minor compared with its application in other areas and when one considers the potential policy problems requiring such analysis. Support for massive efforts to seek solutions to the problems of urban areas is emerging within urban governments and the traditional disciplines and professions concerned with the city, the federal government, and private industry. These groups are uncoordinated and unfunded as yet, but their eventual coalition and funding is a certainty.[25]

Whatever the scope of emergent efforts, one of the key participants will be private industry, particularly the aerospace and research and development firms that have worked primarily in the defense and space areas. The roles of the more traditional groups concerned about urban government problems are less clear, but they will probably include: (1) conduct of specific analysis independently or in conjunction with private industry; (2) advice to governments on the conduct of analyses by other groups and evaluation of such studies; and (3) consolidation as analytic groups within government agencies for the in-house performance of analysis.

One of the key features of the future efforts will be the concept of technology transfer. The transplant of science and technology to urban areas will be costly, risky, and, in some cases, unsuccessful—but it has the potential of ultimately producing significant improvements in government and in the city.

Finally, local government officials will be vitally involved in these efforts, will be required to make decisions of unprecedented scope and magnitude, and will require policy analyses to aid them in their decision making. Some of these analyses will be provided for them, whereas others will require their own initiative. In either case these local government officials will be intensely involved and will need to develop an understanding of their roles in the sponsoring, production, evaluation, and implementation of policy analysis studies.

Notes

[1] E. S. Quade, "Introduction," in *Systems Analysis and Policy Planning*, ed. by E. S. Quade and W. I. Boucher (New York: American Elsevier Publishing Co., 1968), pp. 2–3.

[2] See, for example, the following work: University of Denver Research Institute, *Defense Systems Resources in the Civil Sector: An Evolving Approach, an Uncertain Market* (Washington, D.C.: Government Printing Office, 1967).

[3] U.S. National Aeronautics and Space Administration, *Space, Science, and Urban Life* (Washington, D.C.: Government Printing Office, 1963).

[4] Council of State Governments, *State Reports on Five-Five-Five* (Chicago: Council of State Governments, 1968); State-Local Finances Project, The George Washington University, *An Operative PPB System: A Col-*

laborative Undertaking in the States (Washington, D.C.: The George Washington University, n.d.); Harry P. Hatry and Joseph F. Cotton, *Program Planning for State, County, City* (Washington, D.C.: The George Washington University, 1967).

[5] Lockheed Missiles and Space Company, *Statewide Information System Study*, Vols. I–III (Sunnyvale, Calif.: Lockheed Missiles and Space Company, 1965); Aerojet-General Corporation, *Waste Management Study* (Azusa, Calif.: Aerojet-General Corporation, 1965); North American Aviation, Inc., *Integrated Transportation Study*, Vols. I–V (Los Angeles: North American Aviation, Inc., 1965); Space-General Corporation, *Prevention and Control of Crime and Delinquency* (El Monte, Calif.: Space-General Corporation, 1965).

[6] U.S., Congress, Senate, Committee on Labor and Public Welfare, Subcommittee on the Utilization of Scientific Manpower, *Scientific Manpower Utilization, 1965–66, and Scientific Manpower Utilization, 1967* (Washington, D.C.: Government Printing Office, 1967).

[7] U.S., National Commission on Technology, Automation, and Economic Progress, *Technology and the American Economy*, and *Appendix Volumes I–VI* (Washington, D.C.: Government Printing Office, 1966).

[8] U.S., President's Commission on Law Enforcement and Administration of Justice, *The Challenge of Crime in a Free Society*, and twelve *Task Force Reports* (Washington, D.C.: Government Printing Office, 1967).

[9] See the summary report: U.S., Department of Housing and Urban Development, *Science and the City* (Washington, D.C.: Government Printing Office, 1967).

[10] U.S., Department of Housing and Urban Development, *Urban Technology and Research* (Washington, D.C.: Government Printing Office, 1967).

[11] "Is a Breakthrough Near in Housing?" *Business Week*, September 13, 1969, pp. 80–110.

[12] William C. Pendleton, *Technology and Cities: A Foundation Viewpoint* (New York: Ford Foundation, 1968).

[13] "Think Factory To Help L.A. Solve Problems," *Los Angeles Times*, October 22, 1967, p. 1.

[14] "N.Y. Obtains Rand's Help on Problems," *Los Angeles Times*, September 22, 1967, p. 1; New York City Rand Institute, *First Annual Report* (Santa Monica: Rand Corporation, 1970).

[15] American Public Works Association, *Prospectus for Cooperative Research* (Chicago: American Public Works Association, 1967).

[16] "Systems Approach to Problem-Solving," *Public Management*, February 1969, entire issue.

[17] The literature of this period and the techniques of analysis are discussed in John M. Pfiffner and S. Owen Lane, *A Manual for Administrative Analysis* (Dubuque, Iowa: William C. Brown Company, Publishers, 1947). The scientific management movement in government is documented in Dwight Waldo, *The Administrative State* (New York: Ronald Press Company, 1948).

[18] The budget reform movement from the twenties to the present is reviewed in: Allen Schick, "The Road to PPB: The Stages of Budget Reform," *Public Administration Review*, XXVI (December 1966), 243–69.

[19] The classic work is: Clarence Ridley and Herbert Simon, *Measuring Municipal Activities* (Chicago: International City Managers' Association, 1943).

[20] See, for example: Robert B. Mitchel and Chester Rapkin, *Urban Traffic: A Function of Land Use* (New York: Columbia University Press, 1954); John R. Hamburg and Roger L. Creighton, "Predicting Chicago's Land Use Pattern," *Journal of the American Institute of Planners*, XXV (May 1959), 67–72; Walter G. Hansen, "How Accessibility Shapes Land Use," ibid., 73–76;

Howard W. Bevis, "A Model for Predicting Urban Travel Patterns," ibid., 87–89; William B. Calland, "Forecasting Traffic for Freeway Planning," ibid., 82–86.

For a summary discussion see: Richard M. Zettel and Richard R. Carll, *Summary Review of Major Metropolitan Area Transportation Studies in the United States* (Berkeley: Institute of Transportation and Traffic Engineering, University of California, 1962).

[21] Ira S. Lowry, *A Model of Metropolis*, (Santa Monica: Rand Corporation, 1964); Ira M. Robinson, Harry B. Wolfe, and Robert L. Barringer, "A Simulation Model for Renewal Programming," *Journal of the American Institute of Planners*, XXXI (May 1965) 126–33; Arthur D. Little, Inc., *San Francisco Community Renewal Program; Simulation Model for Renewal Programming*, (San Francisco: Arthur D. Little, Inc., 1964); Arthur D. Little, Inc., *Stockton Community Renewal Program* (San Francisco: Arthur D. Little, Inc., 1966).

[22] For example, on cost-revenue and cost-benefit, see: Walter Isard and Robert Coughlin, *Municipal Costs and Revenues* (Wellesley, Mass.: Chandler-Davis Publishing Company, 1957); Nathaniel Lichfield, *Cost-Benefit Analysis in Urban Redevelopment*, (Berkeley: Real Estate Research Program, Institute of Business and Economic Research, University of California, 1962); James C. T. Mao, "Efficiency in Public Urban Renewal Expenditures through Benefit-Cost Analysis," *Journal of the American Institute of Planners*, XXXII (March 1966), 95–107.

On analysis of the urban economy see: Werner Z. Hirsch, "Interindustry Relations of a Metropolitan Area," *Review of Economics and Statistics*, XVI (November 1959), 360–69; Amanda S. Rao and David J. Allee, *An Application of Interindustry Analysis to San Benito County, California* (Berkeley: Giannini Foundation of Agricultural Economics, University of California, 1964); Roland Artle, *The Structure of the Stockholm Economy: Toward a Framework for Projecting Metropolitan Community Development* (Ithaca, N.Y.: Cornell University Press, 1965); B. R. Berman, B. Chinitz, and E. M. Hoover, *Projection of a Metropolis* (Cambridge, Mass.:

Harvard University Press, 1960); Harold T. Smith, *The Kalamazoo County Economy* (Kalamazoo, Mich.: W. E. Upjohn Institute for Employment Research, 1960); Pittsburgh Regional Plan Association, *Region with a Future: Economic Study of the Pittsburgh Region*, Vol. III (Pittsburgh: University of Pittsburgh Press, 1963), Werner Hockwald, ed., *Design of Regional Accounts* (Baltimore: The Johns Hopkins Press, 1961).

[23] For further reading on this, please see John W. Dykman, "Transportation in Cities," *Scientific American*, September 1965, pp. 162–77.

[24] Educational Facilities Laboratories, *SCSD: The Project and the Schools* (New York: Educational Facilities Laboratories, 1967).

[25] The major impetus behind this effort and, at the same time, the major stumbling block, was the war in Vietnam. On the one hand, realizing that "peace might break out," government and industry were scrambling to find new ways of keeping the economy going. And recognition that civil spending can be just as great a stimulant for the economy and just as profitable (and less risky) for industry has focused attention on urban areas as the prime beneficiary of the "new socio-industrial complex." On the other hand, the vast war expenditures left little money available for civilian expenditure—and the transition from military to civil spending should be a slow one. See: Los Angeles Times, *West*, Special Science Issue, "Can California Survive with Peace?" July 9, 1967.

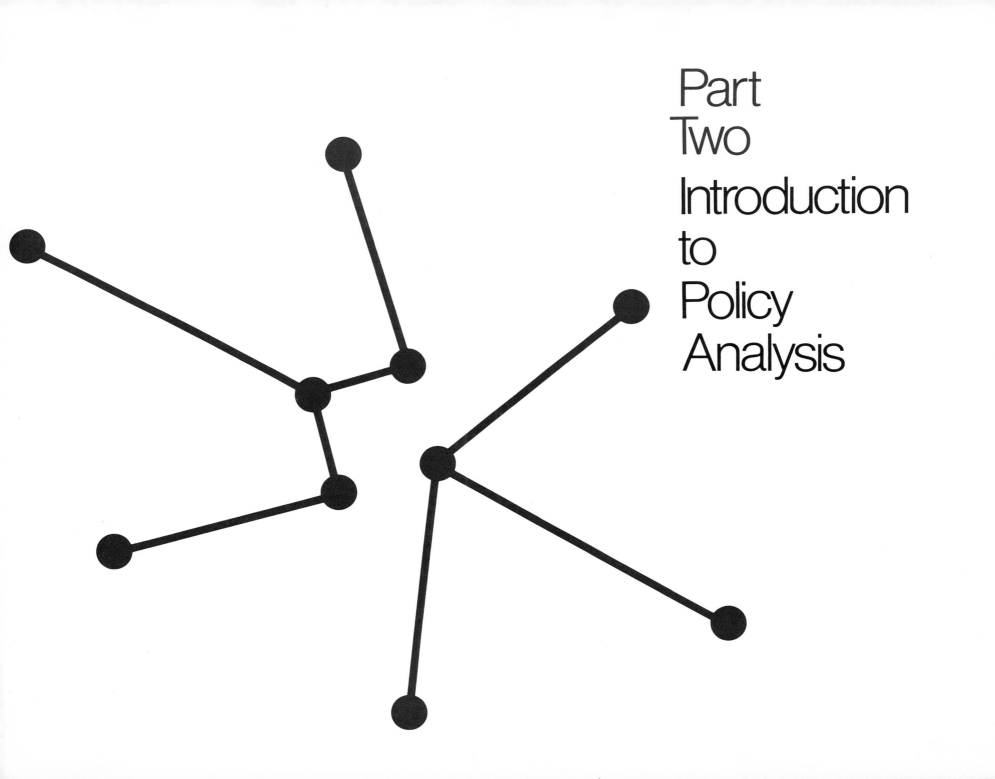

Part
Two

Introduction
to
Policy
Analysis

3

Orientation to Policy Analysis

Policy analysis is a complex, dynamic process. An attempt must be made to define it, describe its key characteristics, indicate the kinds of decision problems for which it may be helpful, and suggest an overall strategy for using analysis in urban public policy making. An attempt must be made also to indicate the relationship between policy analysis as the term is used here and several types of analysis which are kindred.

POLICY ANALYSIS DEFINED

Policy analysis is oriented towards the utilization of scientific method in moving towards the solution of problems of public importance. It is an approach to helping decision makers choose a course of action and carry out that course. It does this by investigating decision problems, searching out objectives and alternatives, and comparing objectives and alternatives in the light of their consequences—using a constructed framework (a model) to bring the decision makers' judgment and intuition to bear on the problems. The aim is to develop guidelines, so that the public and private actions necessary to

solve problems can and will be initiated, and will ultimately result in improvements in the lives of citizens.[1]

THE ESSENTIAL FEATURES OF POLICY ANALYSIS

There are four essential characteristics of policy analysis as it is emerging today. They are: (1) a comprehensive or systems approach; (2) scientific tradition and method; (3) the use of mixed teams; and (4) an action orientation.

The systems approach
In his recent work *The Systems Approach*, C. West Churchman lists four differing definitions of the systems approach as seen by various advocates.

The debaters are these: (1) The advocates of *efficiency*; they claim that the best approach to a system is to identify the trouble spots, and especially the places where there is waste, e.g., unnecessarily high costs, and then proceed to remove the inefficiency. (2) The advocates of the use of *science* in approaching a system; they claim that there is an objective way to

look at a system and to build a "model" of the system that describes how it works. The science that is used is sometimes mathematics, sometimes economics, sometimes "behavioral" (e.g., psychology and sociology). (3) The advocates of the use of human feelings, i.e., the *humanists*; they claim that systems are people, and the fundamental approach to systems consists of first looking at the human values: freedom, dignity, privacy. Above all, they say, the systems approach should avoid imposing plans, i.e., intervention of any kind. (4) The *anti-planners*, who believe that any attempt to lay out specific and "rational" plans is either foolish or dangerous or downright evil. The correct "approach" to systems is to live in them, to react in terms of one's experience, and not to try to change them by means of some grandiose scheme or mathematical model. There are all kinds of anti-planners, but the most numerous are those who believe that experience and cleverness are the hallmarks of good management.[2]

Churchman notes that the recent interest in and thrust of the systems approach has been concentrated chiefly on the scientific version. It is this version which is the focus of his book. Churchman's main point, however, is that the scientific approach is and should be modified by these other perspectives. That is, each perspective raises questions and posits ways of thinking about systems that the others may not. It is this confrontation of perspectives that to Churchman constitutes the systems approach. As he says in *The Systems Approach:* ". . . *the* systems approach really consists of a continuing debate between various attitudes of mind with respect to society."[3]

The systems approach, then, is a way of thinking about systems. Systems are made up of sets of components that work together for the overall objective of the whole. The systems approach is a way of thinking about these total systems and their components. It is an effort to consider a system in its entire context, with all of its ramifications, with all of its interior interactions, with all of its exterior connections, and with full cognizance of its place in its context.

The basic idea is one that is generally accepted by decision makers in principle, but is seldom followed in practice. This idea is that any part of a system or operation has some effect on the activity of every other part. Therefore, in order to evaluate any decision or action regarding a system it is necessary to identify *all* the significant interactions and to evaluate their combined impact upon the performance of the system as a whole. This approach is contrary to the natural inclination of decision makers and analysts to cut a complex problem down to size and isolate it from its environment. Their tendency is to eliminate those aspects of a problem which make it difficult to solve, and thereby to reduce the problem to one that can be handled by standard techniques or by judgment based on experience.

The systems approach is an attempt to move in the opposite direction. It involves deliberately expanding and complicating the statement of a problem until all significantly interacting components are contained within it. The approach consists of looking at the entire area under the decision makers' control rather than concentrating only on one special area. It also involves looking outside the area of the decision makers' control to other systems and operations which affect what the decision makers are trying to do. In most instances these outside forces must be taken as givens or constraints about which little can be done. In other instances, however, by expanding one's perspective, by initiating inquiries into these other systems, and by developing cooperative arrangements with decision makers in these other systems, some greater measure of control can be exerted over these outside influences.

Scientific tradition and method

Along with the systems approach, policy analysis may be characterized by the tradition of science and the scientific method of experimentation. Scientific tradition[4] holds that:

1. Results are obtained by processes that another scientist can duplicate to attain the same results.
2. All calculations, assumptions, data, and judgments are made explicit and are thus subject to checking, criticism, and disagreement.
3. The conduct of analysis is objective; propositions and hypotheses do not depend upon personalities, reputations, or vested interests; and, where possible, analysis is quantitative and experimental.

Equally important to the spirit of scientific inquiry is the experimental method. Experimentation is controlled observation. It involves setting up (or finding) a context in which the analyst can manipulate those elements in which he is most interested in order to determine the impacts of these controllable factors and other, uncontrollable, factors on the elements the decision makers are trying to affect. The most familiar illustration is the laboratory experiment, where the analyst can control the context and the elements, i.e., all the essential features of the system or operation being studied. However, the systems with which urban policy analysis is concerned rarely lend themselves to laboratory experimentation. Further, these systems often are difficult to study and manipulate in the real world, whether in controlled field experiments or in natural experiments such as those created by new or changed government programs. Where such experimentation can be conducted and may succeed, decision makers often regard the potential risk to the organization or themselves as prohibitive for such rigorous evaluation.

The restrictions on the use of the experimental method would appear to be an insurmountable handicap to policy analysis. However, as Ackoff and Rivett[5] have noted, one of the first physical sciences, astronomy, has been in much the same position.

The astronomer cannot bring the solar system into the laboratory or manipulate it in its natural environment (yet). Nevertheless he has developed a theory that is well supported by observation and which can be used to predict precisely.

Since the astronomer cannot manipulate the system he studies, he builds a representation of it. This he calls a "mathematical model." It represents the structure of the real system in quantitative terms. Models can be manipulated and analyzed more easily than the real system and hence permit the analyst, in effect, to carry on vicarious experimentation. He can systematically vary some properties of the system, holding others constant and in this way determine how the system as a whole would be affected if the changes actually did occur. In fact, he simulates the real life alteration and experiments in abstract terms.[6]

The policy analyst also constructs and uses a variety of models and carries out experiments in this symbolic way. The models may be very difficult to construct and may turn out to be extremely complicated mathematical expressions or very lengthy and complex verbal descriptions. However, underlying this complexity there is a relatively simple notion and structure to all these models.

Modeling is an attempt to structure the decision problems of systems so that in the process we can gain a better understanding of what these problems are. The structure developed is artificial in the sense that it is imposed by the analyst rather than found in nature. The structure is an attempt to indicate in a simplified fashion what seem to be the important aspects of a problem. At its simplest, then, modeling is an attempt to determine which aspects of a decision problem are important and which are not, and what the relations are between the important aspects.

The determination of which aspects are important is related to what the decision makers are trying to accomplish (i.e., their objectives). Not everything in a particular problem is important—only those things which aid or prevent

achievement of the objectives. The relations that are of interest, then, are those which aid or prevent goal achievement.

But not every important relationship is subject to the decision makers' control. Some aspects of a decision problem cannot be controlled, either because they are outside the scope of the decision makers' influence or because they represent limits on what can be decided and what actions can be carried out. Those aspects which cannot be controlled are, therefore, taken as givens which limit or constrain what the decision makers can do. Those aspects which can be controlled represent actions that can be taken to achieve a desired objective.

As noted earlier, the decision problems of interest are those of systems. That is, we choose to view our cities, our governments, our departments, our operations, etc., as whole units comprised of interacting and interdependent components or parts. The objectives and the controlled and uncontrolled aspects of decision problems, therefore, are those of some real entity which we have chosen for study and which we are viewing as a system.

Thus, in its basic form, the structure of a model is a statement of the controlled and uncontrolled aspects of a system and the relation between these aspects and some measure of the system's objective achievement. Therefore, as noted by Ackoff and Rivett, all models

take the form of an equation in which a measure of the system's overall performance or benefit (P) is equated to some relationship (f) between a set of controlled aspects of the system (C_i) and a set of uncontrolled

aspects (U_j). Thus expressed symbolically, the basic form of all models is:

$$P = f(C_i, U_j).$$

In words, this statement says that performance depends upon significant controlled and uncontrolled aspects of the system.[7]

The purpose of the model structure, in addition to the increased understanding derived simply from constructing it, is to permit the trying out of various alternative courses of action (the controlled aspects) within a single, consistent framework in order to compare the alternatives and help determine what to do. Each possible action or combination of actions will result in a different level of goal achievement. If there is some way of determining in advance what constitutes a satisfactory result, this determination can be built into the model structure so that the alternatives can be ranked and the preferred one indicated as an output of the model. Where such determination cannot be made in advance or cannot be reduced to a simple enough statement for inclusion in the model, the output of the model will be a statement of the outcomes of each action alternative, without any indication of which is better. These outcomes may then be subjected to comparison by further analysis (e.g., cost-benefit). If further analysis is unnecessary or impossible, the outcomes may be presented to the decision makers, who must compare the outcomes and try to rank the alternatives intuitively, based upon their experience.

Mixed teams

As suggested in part by Churchman's categorization of approaches to viewing systems, seldom does any one individual possess the knowledge, skill, or experience required to analyze systems problems. While this may not be the case with relatively simple and routine problems, it is almost always the case with complex problems —thus the third feature of policy analysis: the use of mixed or multidisciplinary teams.

Further, while it is true that problems have no disciplinary or professional characteristics as they exist in nature, the fact is that we have tended to organize research, knowledge, and education along disciplinary and professional lines. Thus we tend to speak of physical, social, political, and economic problems in one classification schema and of health, transportation, welfare, education, housing, public safety, and leisure problems in another. In fact, however, there are only problems. The various disciplinary and professional perspectives merely describe different ways of looking at and studying the same or similar sets of problems. The need for mixed teams, therefore, is related to the fact that these historical divisions do exist and influence the way in which various people approach problems. The greater the variety of ways of viewing and structuring a problem, the greater the likelihood that one approach, or some combination of approaches, will include all the important aspects of the problem and will yield a satisfactory solution.

Action orientation

The final characteristic of policy analysis is a concern with actual improvements as a result of the research conducted. In essence, this means that the analysis is concerned not only with helping to decide what to do but with the doing as well. It means that the recommendations of policy analysis include specific action proposals for effectuating a decision that takes in

what is to be done, when, where, how, and by whom.

There are several reasons why such concern for and involvement in implementation is required. First, policy analysis can only partially test its recommendations in advance by using the past or the extended laboratory. The real test must come in the application of the recommendations in the real world. Second, despite the most thorough advanced planning, something that was not anticipated always comes up in application—for example, difficulties in the task of implementation, or unexpected results of implementation.[8] Finally, complex problems have a way of never being totally "solved," and major objectives are almost never reached before they are changed. Consequently, policy analysis is aimed at building a process that will evolve and continually improve the way in which situations are met, policies and programs developed, and problems solved within the institutional setting under study. Policy analysis is, then, action-oriented.

THE DECISION PROBLEMS OF POLICY ANALYSIS

Policy analysis can be applied to urban government problems ranging from the routine day-to-day operations of the various departments and subunits to critical one-time decisions on overall community development. This spectrum of decision problems may be divided into the following categories: (1) operational; (2) programming or management; and (3) developmental or planning. This division is an arbitrary one and may involve considerable overlapping in specific instances. It represents a continuum

Table 3-1. A comparison of the three types of decision problems involved in the application of policy analysis.

from a lower to a higher level, or from specific to general policy. Such a distinction is necessary and useful both for purposes of exposition and for coping with actual problems. Table 3–1 summarizes some of the distinctions found in these three types of decision problems.

Operational problems

This category of decision problems includes those generally found in day-to-day operations of urban government. The questions of concern relate to efficiency in the immediate future—for example, "How can an existing system (person, machine, facility) be better utilized?" or "How can an existing operation be better performed?" These problems are relatively simple in that they involve only a small number of interdependent factors. Objectives are singular, known (or readily definable), and agreed upon. The criterion for choice of one system or operation over another is fairly obvious and straightforward.

Analysis of these problems is subject to fairly rigorous quantification. Except for the specific context of urban government, much of the analysis is essentially like that used for decision making in business, industry, or defense. In other words, a general characteristic of problems in this category is that they are, or can be, well structured. Thus, decision makers can be helped simply by applying systematic computational

Dimensions for comparison	Types of problems		
	Operational	**Programming (management)**	**Development (planning)**
Objectives	Single objectives; known or readily defined; agreement easy; efficiency-oriented objectives	Multiple objectives; difficult to define; conflicting; consensus difficult to achieve; effectiveness-oriented objectives	Setting objectives is key problem; values-oriented objectives
Criteria	Single criterion can usually be defined and quantified and indicates best solution	Multiple criteria; choice may depend on intuitive evaluation of net benefit from costs and benefits	Evaluation of alternatives largely intuitive but may be aided by expert advice or by qualitative models
Alternatives	Many alternatives available and usually easy to identify	Alternatives limited; new alternatives often not very different from existing ones; inventing alternatives is difficult	Inventing alternatives is key problem
Models	Standard models exist and can be applied to many situations; machine or man–machine models	Same as operational problems plus ad hoc (computer and gaming) models; man–machine or behavioral models	Same as management problems plus verbal models; political and social models
Techniques	Mathematical, statistical, economic	Same as operational problems plus qualitative techniques, e.g., simulation and gaming	Same as management problems plus Delphi, scenarios, paradigms, etc.
Quantification	Quantifiable	Quantitative–qualitative	Largely qualitative; may involve quantification of parts of the problem
Time	Short-term	Mid-range	Long-range
Uncertainty	Uncertainty statistically describable	Ranges of uncertainty describable	May only be able to indicate that uncertainty exists
Solutions[1]	Solutions can be derived analytically; usually a best one	Solutions usually derived by trial and error or approximation; sometimes solution not possible—best obtainable may be aid to logical thinking about a problem	Same as management problems; often only insight, understanding, elucidation sought—not solutions
Examples	Stock control; personnel assignment; distribution routing; replacement; maintenance	Budgeting; organization design; scheduling; financial and operations management; certain planning problems	Policies planning; transportation, building and other systems development; alternative futures

[1] As used here, solution refers to the notion of a single best answer.

routines to a "generic" model that can be made relevant to a wide variety of operations merely by modifying certain features. Several standard models and techniques have been developed for many such problems. When new techniques are developed they are most readily transplanted. Examples of problems in this category are buying policy and inventory control, personnel assignment (to jobs, training, locations, etc.), distribution routing, replacement and maintenance, waiting lines, location of facilities, and search or detection (such as police patrol detection).

Programming (management) problems
This category includes problems involving the integration of various systems and operations to attain some overall objective. The questions of concern are those regarding the effectiveness and appropriateness of a system beyond the immediate future—for example, "How can an existing system be redesigned (or a new one designed) to function better as a whole?" or "How well do alternative systems (including existing ones) achieve some overall objective?" These problems involve many interrelated factors, and the choice of which to include in analyzing a problem is a key issue. Further, because these problems are concerned with the future, uncertainties become important. And the more extended the future time period is, the greater are the number and degrees of uncertainties. These uncertainties may be about planning factors such as service demands or revenues, the strategic context or environment, technological development, or change elements in the real world.

Multiple and conflicting objectives and criteria for choice also characterize management problems. The selection of objectives and criteria is

frequently the central issue—for example, "What do we really want our systems to accomplish?" and "How do we test the alternative systems to see which accomplishes our objectives best?" Time phasing is also important here, for what is appropriate for one time period may not be for another. For example, "Should urban governments go into operation now with some particular computer configuration, or should they wait until better computer systems are developed?" Configuration A may be suitable for 1970 but not especially workable for 1975, whereas the reverse may be the case with configuration B.

Analysis of programming problems is rarely subject to complete quantification and solution by mathematical techniques, although various parts of a problem may be. Often, all one can do is develop an imitation of the system and work towards a solution by trial and error techniques of simulation. The models used will, therefore, most often be ad hoc. That is, they will be models developed to represent a specific system rather than general models which fit a wide variety of contexts. However, they may be utilized again and again in the context of the specific system modeled.

Illustrative problems in this category include budgeting (whether capital, operating, or program), organization design, scheduling and control of projects and operations, operations management, financial management, facility layout, and some planning problems.

Development (planning) problems
This category of problems includes those which involve determining objectives for future systems, inventing alternatives, and planning the composition of alternative systems. The questions of

concern are "What needs will exist in the future?" and "How can systems be invented and designed to meet those needs?" These problems, then, are essentially long-range "planning" problems. Development problems share the characteristics of management problems, but in more acute form. The factors involved are numerous, uncertainty about the future is great, time phasing is critical. However, here developing objectives *is* the problem. So also is the invention of alternatives. That is, since development problems are concerned with systems which presently do not exist, a key task of the analysis is to set appropriate objectives and to "invent" alternative system designs.

Most often quantitative techniques will not be helpful to either the definition of objectives or the creation of alternatives. Qualitative techniques, such as Delphi, scenario writing, and paradigm construction can be helpful. Further, when alternative systems have been developed, simulation techniques can be used to compare them. Finally, subparts of the systems designed may be subject to quantitative treatment.

Examples of problems in this category are: development of transportation, building, and other urban physical systems; and development of policies for education, health, welfare, public safety, and other governmental activities. Thus, developmental problems may focus on physical systems or on "systems of policy" which eventually result in physical actions in a specific context.

INTERRELATION OF POLICY ANALYSIS WITH DECISION PROBLEMS

Policy analyses of broader problems frequently include studies of narrower problems as components. A development problem analysis will usually include analyses of programming and operational problems. Often it is the completion of these component studies which absorbs most of the man-hours and makes the broader analysis possible. However, the solution of broad urban problems depends only in slight part on these component studies. This is so because the broader problems are concerned with the future, and as one looks into the future the number of factors increases, uncertainties multiply, and different kinds of objectives and criteria become important.

This is also true of the techniques used in policy analysis. Decisions regarding planning and programming problems do not invariably require different analytic techniques from those used for operational problems, but in most cases they do. However, though techniques may differ, the basic methodology of policy analysis remains the same.

THE NEED FOR A MIXED STRATEGY IN POLICY ANALYSIS

The problems chosen for analysis by a particular urban government will depend upon a variety of factors, including that government's past approaches to problem solving, its subjective conception of what a problem is as well as the objective reality of the problem, the nature of change in that government and its community, and the character of its decision makers. Some writers[9] argue for solving operational problems first. Doing so generally means that programming and developmental problems will not be addressed for some time. Yet the greatest potential benefit of policy analysis is in just those areas where the problems are most complex, the costs

and risks highest, the uncertainties greatest, and the results most likely to be seen only over an extended time period.

Over concern for any one of these types of problems seems inappropriate. If operational problems are unattended, their effects may be of considerable consequence in the aggregate. Similarly, inattention to major problems may negate all of the smaller improvements. Therefore, a mixed analysis strategy is needed. What this involves is comprehensive analysis of a system to determine areas in which more detailed analysis can be appropriately utilized. That is, detailed analyses should be conducted where there is a high likelihood that they will not be negated by broad changes in system design as a result of higher level policy analyses, and where the analysis of smaller problems may actually constitute component analyses for a higher level problem.[10]

For example, in their analysis of the Criminal Justice System (CJS) Blumstein and Larson[11] performed a comprehensive study of the court, police, prison, and probation systems. They identified "crime prevention" as a significant operation of the system and "police patrol detection" as a subcomponent of crime prevention. They then developed a mathematical model of the patrol detection operation. The model permits evaluation of alternative means for increasing the rate of detecting crimes in progress by patrolling police units. The costs and benefits of each alternative can be computed and an alternative chosen using an appropriate criterion.

Police patrol detection is an operational problem, and therefore the model has immediate applicability in the day-to-day activities of urban

governments. At the same time, it fits into the overall CJS analysis as a submodel.

Thus, a mixed approach provides a particular procedure for:

1. The collection of information: e.g., the overall CJS analysis pointed to crime prevention, which pointed to a police patrol detection operation, the model for which indicated specific factors influencing that operation.
2. The allocation of resources: e.g., police patrol detection was favored over other methods of prevention.
3. Guidelines for relations between resource allocation and information collection: e.g., resources should be allocated to the patrol detection model if the model and the information produced fit into the overall CJS analysis.

The mixed analysis strategy combines a detailed and quantitative examination of policy problems at the operational level with a broad and qualitative analysis of policy problems at the systems levels (management and development). The relative investment in policy analysis among these different problem levels depends on how costly it would be to ignore a problem or to be wrong in developing a solution.

RELATED TYPES OF ANALYSIS: SIMILARITIES AND DISTINCTIONS

Much of policy analysis is synonymous in concept and principle with a variety of approaches used to inform public policy decisions. Among these are systems analysis, policy research, policy planning, operations research, management science, systems engineering, economic analysis, regional analysis, cost-effectiveness analysis, and cost-benefit analysis. It is likely that any of the approaches implied by these terms may be applied to the three categories of decision problems identified. Review of the experience indicates that this has been the case. Why particular individuals choose to use one or the other of these terms to characterize their work seems to be related to the purpose of the analysis, the type of problem usually addressed, the context in which the analysis appears, tradition, disciplinary backgrounds, organizational affiliations, fashion, and a host of other factors.

The differences between these various types of analysis appear to be less in principle or concept than in application. The proponents of each type of analysis acknowledge the four approaches earlier described by C. West Churchman (see page 21) as characteristic of policy analysis. They espouse similar aims and objectives. While in practice the proponents may fall short of their professed principles and aims, sufficient examples exist, in each case, in which "good" analysis has been achieved, that is, in which the ideal and the actual practice constitute a good fit.

What is perhaps most common to these various approaches is a trend towards extending analysis to increasingly complex decision problems. In the process, greater emphasis is being placed on: (1) the nonquantitative methods, concepts, and approaches of the so-called soft sciences, (for example, sociology, political science, and anthropology); (2) ways of stimulating creative ideas; and (3) the social process in which analysis is performed and through which the results of analysis are implemented.

It may be that, sociologically, differences do exist between these types of analysis. Perhaps a carefully drawn sample of practitioners and their work would reveal important differences in background, skills, perspectives, concepts, approach, methodology, or technique. However, to my knowledge no such comparison has been made. Thus, it is difficult to say one should turn to the policy researcher rather than the systems analyst, or to the systems analyst rather than the operations researcher or management scientist.

Figure 3–1 is an inventory of various types of analysis. No attempt is made to distinguish one from the other or from policy analysis. Rather, the chart is intended to suggest (1) that policy analysis and many other kinds of analysis may be described by certain key characteristics and by an intellectual process of perception, design, and evaluation, and (2) that there exist bodies of theory and concepts, and methods, tools, and techniques, any of which may be used in the conduct of analysis.

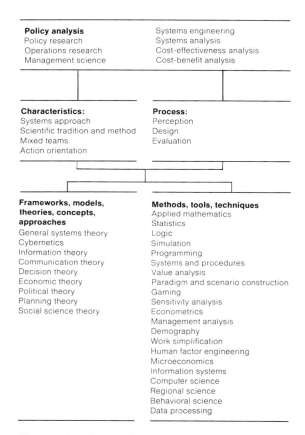

Figure 3-1. Policy analysis and related approaches to analysis.

....

Notes

[1] For a detailed discussion of various aspects of this definition in a different context, see Yehezkel Dror, *Public Policy-Making Reexamined* (San Francisco: Chandler Publishing Company, 1968), pp. 12–22.

[2] C. West Churchman, *The Systems Approach* (New York: Dell Publishing Co. [paperback ed., Delta Books], 1968), pp. 13–14. Copyright © 1968 by C. West Churchman. Reprinted by permission of Delacorte Press.

[3] Ibid., p. xi.

[4] See: Paul C. Obler and Herman A. Estrin, eds., *The New Scientist: Essays on the Methods and Values of Modern Science,* Anchor Books (Garden City, N.Y.: Doubleday and Company, 1962); F. S. C. Northrop, *The Logic of the Sciences and the Humanities,* Meridian Books (New York: World Publishing Company, 1963).

[5] Russell L. Ackoff and Patrick Rivett, *A Manager's Guide to Operations Research* (New York: John Wiley & Sons, Inc., 1963), pp. 23–24. Copyright © 1963 by John Wiley & Sons, Inc. Reprinted by permission of John Wiley & Sons, Inc.

[6] Ibid., p. 24.

[7] Ibid., p. 25.

[8] Ibid., p. 31.

[9] For example: Philip M. Morse, "Introduction," in *Operations Research for Public Systems,* ed. by Philip M. Morse and L. W. Bacon (Cambridge, Mass.: The M.I.T. Press, 1967), pp. 1–15; R. A. Ward, *Operational Research in Local Government* (London: George Allen and Unwin, Ltd., 1964).

[10] This is neither more nor less than avoiding the dual trap of incrementalism and rationalism in decision making. See: Amitai Etzioni. "Mixed-Scanning: A 'Third' Approach to Decision-Making," *Public Administration Review,* XXVII (December 1967), 385–92.

[11] See Alfred Blumstein and Richard C. Larson, "A Systems Approach to the Study of Crime and Criminal Justice," in Morse and Bacon, *Operations Research,* pp. 159–80.

The Process of Analysis

4

AN OVERVIEW[1]

The process of analysis can be described simply as involving three interrelated activities: perception, design, and evaluation. In the first, perception, the issues are clarified, the extent of inquiry is limited, and the objectives identified in a way that is helpful to picking an alternative. The second, design, involves identification of existing alternatives, design of new alternatives, and gathering of information for comparison of alternatives. Finally, in evaluation, the alternatives are examined for feasibility and compared in terms of their benefit and cost, with time and risk taken into account.

Analysis seldom proceeds in this simplified and orderly fashion. Often the objectives are multiple, conflicting, and obscure; the alternatives are not adequate to attain the objectives; the measures of benefit do not really measure the extent to which the objectives are attained; the predictions from evaluation models are full of uncertainties; and other criteria that look almost as plausible as the ones chosen may lead to a different order of preference. When this happens, a modification

of the above approach is required, for a single pass or attempt at a problem is seldom enough. In such an instance, the key to successful analysis is a continuous process of formulating the problem, selecting objectives, designing alternatives, collecting data, building models, weighing costs against benefits, questioning assumptions and data, reexamining the objectives, opening new alternatives, building better models, and so on, until a satisfactory solution is obtained.

In this chapter each of the major activities comprising the process of analysis is examined in detail. An attempt is made throughout to emphasize (1) the interrelatedness of each activity, (2) the notion that analysis is iterative and may involve working through each activity or the whole process several times, and (3) the fact that, while models and quantitative technique may be utilized extensively, the process of analysis is permeated with numerous judgments. The aim is not to provide a step-by-step procedure for performing policy analysis. Rather, it is to indicate in some detail the nature of the process and the kinds of considerations involved.

PERCEPTION

Analysis may start at any point in the policy making process. Usually, however, analysis is initiated by someone's perception of disparities or opportunities in the present scheme of things. Perception, as used here, refers to the apprehension of the existence of some situation requiring policy decision and action. It involves two steps: (1) problem formulation; (2) identification and clarification of objectives.

Problem formulation

"What is the problem?" is the first question to be asked. It may be satisfactorily answered only upon completion of the analysis. That is, most problems of any complexity can seldom be comprehended clearly at the start. The decision makers and analysts usually have some general notions about the problem, but as the analysis proceeds these notions may be revised or rejected. Additional information developed in the analysis may change their understanding of the situation, the alternative courses of action considered possible, or the objectives deemed appropriate. For example, in the East Lansing case study described in Chapter 5 the city manager and analysts gained a clear perception of the fire station location problem only after a first round of analysis had been completed.

Problem formulation involves an attempt to: (1) isolate the questions or issues involved in a situation; (2) fix the context within which the issues are to be realized (that is, define a system and its boundaries). This latter task may also involve an attempt to discover, in preliminary fashion, the variables operating in a situation and the relations among them.

Determining the issues. Not everything in the environment of an organization is relevant to decision and action. What is relevant are those things which aid or prevent the attainment of objectives, or which permit the adoption of new objectives and programs for their implementation. Issues are identified by perceived disparities or opportunities in the environment. Thus, someone perceives a need for low-income housing, improved police protection or garbage collection, or a better way of recruiting and selecting municipal employees. Or, perhaps, new revenue sources are discovered, a chance to attract a major industry develops, or a new federal program is enacted for training of the hard-core unemployed.

Which problems and opportunities are identified for decision and action is a matter of valuation. Such valuations are made continuously by people throughout government and the community. Some valuations are routine in that the issues or questions involved have arisen before and perceptions of what is important have been defined. Other valuations are ad hoc and require considerable investigation in order to determine whether a particular issue shall be the subject of analysis and decision.

For example, the reduction of crimes by juveniles is frequently identified as a problem. Preliminary fact-gathering may show that projected changes in age groups make it likely that the crime rate for the juvenile population may decline over the next several years. Thus, a situation initially seen as a problem may come to be regarded as neither urgent nor important for governmental action and will require no further analysis. Were the obverse the case, some unit within government might be required to take actions to reduce juvenile crime. Which actions can be taken becomes the subject of further analysis. The actions possible will depend in part upon the conceptualization of the system in which juvenile crime exists and the relationship of government actions to controlling it.

Conceptualizing a system. To proceed further in analysis, then, some area of activity must be conceptualized as a system. Systems are rarely known in advance. They are almost always contrived. That is, *system* is a mental construct which is applied to some entity. For example, an individual, an organization, or a community may be considered as a system. The advantage of the concept is that it provides a common language for communicating about the entity and a framework for analyzing it.

The following features are said to be characteristic of and essential to any system:

1. The system constitutes a whole set of related things or events;
2. The whole is seeking to fulfill a set of goals;
3. The whole is composed of differentiable elements or subsystems, and the elements or subsystems are integrated in a patterned or structured form;
4. The elements or subsystems are in interaction, mutually affecting one another;
5. The whole system exists within an environment which is distinct and definable from the system itself;
6. A boundary differentiates the system from its environment;
7. The system is in constant interaction with its environment, receiving inputs from the environment and producing outputs in exchange;
8. The system processes inputs into outputs through internal transactions in accordance with established needs;
9. The whole system seeks to maintain a state of dynamic equilibrium internally with its subsystems and externally with its environment. Feedback is the process by which the system maintains equilibrium and steers towards the system's objectives;
10. To maintain dynamic equilibrium, the system is in a state of constant flux or change;
11. The system has some mechanism for the control of its activities.

The task of conceptualizing a system, therefore, involves describing some existing activity in these terms and identifying the boundaries, goals and objectives, elements or subsystems, inputs and outputs and the relations between them, and those environmental factors which seem to affect the system in some important way. The task of analysis as it proceeds is to operationalize this conceptual model by developing symbolic representations for each of the important elements. As will be seen, this requires empirical observation and measurement of the elements and their integration into a mathematical, logical, verbal, or other model.

Defining system boundaries. In problem formulation one has to decide what seems to be part of the system under consideration and what does not. This is the boundary question. At the extreme, everything relates to everything else and therefore nothing can be isolated as a system. However, problems of global scope are never solved. Simplification is essential — both to highlight what is relevant and to reduce the complexity of reality to the scope of analytic ability. Further, it is inevitable that not all decisions can be made at the highest level or by one individual or group; some must be delegated to others. Decision makers and analysts usually must consider actions that pertain to only part of a problem. Other choices are set aside temporarily, possible decisions about some things being neglected and specific decisions about others being assumed. This process of breaking a larger problem into component parts for the purposes of analysis is referred to as *factoring*.

In setting boundaries for the system to be studied, three considerations are important:

1. Whether the boundaries encompass at least that area of activity where some knowledge of system relationships exists or can be readily determined
2. Whether the boundaries encompass all of the relevant elements (variables) under control of the governmental system
3. Whether the boundaries delimit a system that

can be effectively studied within the time and monetary constraints of the situation requiring decision and action.

In the case of juvenile crime the juvenile population, their families, the police, the courts, the welfare agencies, and the schools may all be said to constitute relevant parts of a system. Or, if such an all-inclusive definition seems beyond the scope of analysis or beyond the control of a particular governmental unit, the system may be defined to encompass only those parts over which that government has direct control. In this case the system might be defined as the juvenile population, the police, and the schools. The other factors would constitute the environment of the system and would be treated as factors outside any model developed.

Formulating as a system the interactions of activities considered to be vaguely related to each other in a way that permits useful analysis is a difficult task. It is probable that any initial formulation will change as the analysis proceeds. The city as a system is difficult to distinguish by a single boundary, as it can be characterized by numerous noncoterminous boundaries on the basis of, for example: natural or man-made features; homogeneity of some characteristics of the area or its population; service patterns of local service agencies (such as stores, hospitals, churches, telephone companies, schools); local governmental units; and felt sense of community identification. The boundary most often chosen by governmental analysts is the legal-jurisdictional one. When one deals with problems of the individual city as a functional entity this boundary is extremely useful. For example, municipal boundaries are often adequate for

problems of policing, fire protection, library service, and building regulation. They are probably inadequate for problems of waste disposal (but not waste collection), air pollution, transportation, and social welfare.

The San Francisco Community Renewal (CRP), discussed in Chapter 6, i point. As part of the CRP study t analysts developed a computer of the housing market and defin aries of the system modeled as the city and county of San Franc chose this boundary because th paying for the study and becaus the city could neither exert cont governmental units nor elicit the in the study. The San Francisco considered the environment of studied. When the system was this environment was treated as pressure creating certain dema straints on the San Francisco h the time the analysis began the demand was not known. Theref projections were developed. W jections were compared with th available in the region it becar planners and analysts that hou blacks, the poor, and the aged by suburban developments. As influx of the above groups was Francisco, which contained ho economic range and which alr high percentage of these grou population.

Because the analysts had limi boundaries to the city's jurisd limited to those alternatives which the city could itself influence in attempting to develop alternative courses of action. Many options less costly politically, socially, and economically were closed out. More important, the projections suggested an even greater division than already existed between black and white, rich and poor, central city and suburbs. From the standpoint of broad social policy, therefore, the system boundaries and governmental base for action were simply inadequate. Had the analysts extended the study boundaries to include the region, the resultant analyses could have produced information that would have indicated a greater range of possible action alternatives and made possible equitable means of handling the problem population.

Identification and clarification of objectives
The next step in formulation is identifying and clarifying objectives. Objectives are an operational specification of general goals, which in turn are an externalization of internal values and preferences held by individuals in the community. Values can be specified and ordered to various degrees. At one extreme they are specified only by such general terms as the public interest and are ranked only subjectively, often implicitly and inconsistently. At the other extreme they are reworked into fully operational objectives that have a clear order of priority and even have some quantitative basis for determining how various trade-offs might be made between them.

It is generally supposed that goals should, and can, be set independently of the plans to attain them. Yet there is considerable evidence that operationally significant objectives are often the result of opportunities that possible alternatives offer rather than a source of such alternatives. There are at least two reasons for this. First, it is impossible to select satisfactory objectives without some idea of the cost and difficulty of attaining them, and such information can only come as part of the analysis. Second, only some of the possible consequences of different alternatives can be anticipated before the analysis, and some of the consequences discovered may become goals. A chief characteristic of policy analysis is that solutions are often found in a set of compromises which seek to balance and to reconcile conflicting objectives and questions of value. It is more important to choose the right objective than it is to make the right choice among alternatives. The choice of the wrong alternative may merely mean that something less than the best system is being chosen. Choice of the wrong objective means that the wrong problem is being solved.

Objectives and their order of priority are determined largely by value judgments rather than by rational analysis. These judgments should be made explicit. And, they should be based upon examination of the consistency, social consequences, and feasibility of the objectives.[2]

Interrelation of perceptual activities
The process of perception involves an interrelation between defining the issues, conceptualizing a system, defining its boundaries, and identifying and clarifying objectives—all of which serve to clarify the problem. Which conditions in the environment are considered issues for decision and action is a matter determined in part by the values and objectives of the participants. Values and objectives also influence definition of the relevant system and the boundaries for analysis. In turn, objectives are partially determined by the problems and opportunities perceived in the environment, by the capacity of governmental systems to respond to environmental conditions, and by the boundaries that can or must be set.

The perception phase of analysis requires much interaction between policy makers and analysts. The frequent tendency of policy analysts is to accept the decision makers' original statement of the problem without much thought as to whether that statement is correct or how an answer to the statement will contribute to the decisions it is meant to assist. Because the concern of policy analysis is often with the future, the analyst's major job may be to decide what the policy maker should want to do.

On the other hand, policy analysts are seldom capable of defining problems alone. They may choose simplifications which are useful in bringing a problem within the bounds of analytic feasibility but which make the resulting analysis irrelevant to the real concerns of the policy makers. Initial attempts at analysis are frequently false starts resulting from wrong definition of problems. Some iteration of analysis is desirable in policy analysis, but that resulting from wrong problem definition is to be avoided. (For example, see the East Lansing case study in Chapter 5.)

But how are the policy maker and the analyst to know that their formulation of the problem is adequate? One answer is analysis. That is, the process of problem formulation should itself be subjected to analysis. With the use of the few facts and relationships that are known at an early stage and assuming others, an initial attempt can be made to solve the problem. This attempt will provide a basis for better problem formulation and permit preliminary testing of possible solutions.

Primarily as the result of discussion and intuition, the original effort to state a problem should suggest one or more possible solutions or hypotheses. As the study progresses, these original ideas are enriched and elaborated upon, or discarded, as new ideas are found. The process of analysis is iterative. Each hypothesis serves as a guide to later work — it tells us what we are looking for while we are looking. As a result, the final statement of conclusions and recommendations in policy studies usually rests on a knowledge of facts about the problem which the analysts and policy makers lacked at the start. In the early stages it is not a mistake to hold an idea as to the solution; the error is to refuse to abandon such an idea in the face of mounting evidence.

An example of the perceptual process

The following example illustrates several of the above points about perception. The decline of the central business district (CBD) is considered a problem in many cities. The traditional definition of the problem is in terms of deteriorated physical structures, lack of parking, congested streets, lack of pedestrian areas, lack of amenity, decline in retail sales, and the like. Recently, a group of planners and public administrators working in a Los Angeles community were asked to develop recommendations to solve the problem of the declining CBD. In approaching this problem, they looked at the entire economic system

of the community (particularly the business component), the population characteristics, tax policy, land use and housing trends, and the transportation network. The group found that the declining CBD was only an outward expression of a much more significant change taking place in the community. It was changing from an essentially suburban residential community of young families and a slight mixture of land uses to a more intensive and confined residential development pattern of older households, extensive industrial land use, and service-type retail stores. In addition, the imminent construction of freeways which would surround the community suggested a future reinforcement of the developing trend.

Thus, the initial definition of what was happening in the CBD was translated into a more fundamental change in the entire structure and functioning of the community. However, even this change could not be considered a problem until the community or its political leaders decided what they wanted the community's future to be (inasmuch as they could exercise control over that future). Several alternative futures were developed. The political leaders decided that they wanted to maintain the traditional image of the city as a suburban community. This then became the problem, and developing a CBD that would relate to their conception of a suburban community shopping district became one component of the overall problem. Other components involved attracting young families to the community, arresting industrial growth, building recreation programs and facilities, and initiating new tax policies. Had the political leaders chosen not to attempt to forestall the developing trend, the problem

might have been defined as that industry to further the demise of uses and to develop a strong se service business center to serve uses.

Several points are brought out b First, manifest problems are diffe problems. Very often the manifes only a symptom of a more basic Second, problems are not unitary. of the declining CBD was not sim relating to commercial business b volved issues of transportation, tax industrial development, and popula Third, a problem is not a problem ur defined as such. Until the decision n choose to make some objective conc subject of their attention, and desire t condition, it is not a problem. Thus, p definition is essentially subjective. The the policy analyst is to try to achieve correlation between objective and sub problems. Finally, in analysis, the prob remains static. Interplay between a gro understanding of what a problem invol and might involve in the future forces a redefinition.

DESIGN

The design phase is basically concerned finding alternatives and the data on whic their comparison is to be based. It is as portant to look for new alternatives (and data to support them) as it is to look for compare them. If there are no alternativ ideas about them, there is nothing to cc or to choose between. If a preferred co action is to be designated, it must be discovered earlier that such a course exists, even if the alternative is to take no action.

Finding alternatives
Usually, analysis is concerned with comparing an existing system with other systems. The purpose is to compare systems in a way that is relevant to a choice between them and that helps to decide which is better. Generally, only one of the systems compared will be an existing one, for the object is to try out innovations and new proposals in the comparisons. Existing systems may fail to meet the desired objectives in some way, or may be totally unacceptable. In other instances, existing alternatives may be suitable for the present but do not meet requirements predicted for the future. Or the problem may be to determine what the future might be and what it should be. Here the invention of alternatives becomes important. These, then, are design problems. Design in policy analysis is the process of inventing new elements and recombining known or existing elements in such a way as to produce a desired whole. A particular configuration of elements intended to accomplish a particular objective is an alternative.

Design is involved in a wide range of different types of human activity. The architect or engineer, for example, invents forms and occasionally structural methods and recombines rooms, spaces, and materials. These may all be regarded as elements. The final product of his efforts is judged as more satisfactory or less satisfactory according to the budget and program of his client and according to certain ill-defined canons of aesthetics and functional efficiency. In

the urban realm the city official, the city manager, or the department head may be regarded as policy designers. Their elements may be people, physical resources, financial resources, capital investments, modes of organization, laws, regulations, or taxes. Their problem in designing a coordinated set of policies is to maximize the overall quality of life in the community. On a smaller scale, the process of designing a budget involves inventing new elements and combining existing elements (in this case various programs) so as to maximize the quality of service in a community within certain financial limits.

Much of the process of design is intuitive and is the product of creative individuals. However, systematic analysis can assist the design process by helping the designer to order the elements logically and by allowing the designer to try out many possible combinations of the various elements and to test their impacts.[3] Simulation is a particularly useful tool here. If there is a model of a system, this model can be processed incorporating successive changes which correspond to alternative designs or combinations of the elements in the system. The influence of various designs on the desired objectives can be traced. The policy maker then has a basis for selecting the design which most effectively achieves the desired result or system output. This process was used with the San Francisco housing market model which is discussed in Chapter 6. The model was used to allow decision makers to compare existing public policies and various combinations of these policies in order to determine their relative impacts on the housing market. These impacts could then be related to the objectives of the decision makers as an aid to choice among the alternatives.

The possible number of alternatives in any problem is virtually unlimited. While it is technically possible in many cases to consider all possible alternatives and their impacts, the cost, time, and relevance of so doing is often prohibitive. And such an undertaking is not necessary. The policy analysts and decision makers generally have some basis for judging which alternatives seem more relevant than others. Real world constraints also limit the number of feasible alternatives to a few. The key danger, though, is that some important alternatives will be overlooked. One approach to this problem is to define alternatives in a series of stages, starting with a complete list, eliminating the obviously impracticable alternatives, developing new ones by combining those already known, eliminating still others and so on, until a reasonable set is obtained.

Finding the data
In some analyses the data needed for comparing alternatives are available or can be collected from existing records. This is often the case when comparing existing systems. For example, in a study to establish the optimum location of new fire stations to be built in the city of East Lansing, Michigan, the following data requirements were developed:

1. Estimated travel time for fire equipment over each block-long segment of the street network, including the ideal estimate and estimates under conditions of traffic congestion and other trip variables
2. The fire generation potential of each city block as indicated by the population density and by the structure type, density, condition, and use

3. The damage potential for each block, including the cost of damage in terms of life and property loss
4. The fire spread potential of each block.[4]

These data were unavailable in the form specified, but were obtained from existing records in the fire, public works, building, and planning departments.

Sometimes the data needed for analysis must be developed by experimentation, as when comparing new systems or when data on current systems are nonexistent. For example, in comparing alternative transportation systems data are needed on the implications of each system for users (e.g., accessibility, convenience, safety, cost), for nonusers (i.e., the opportunity costs), for the environment, for urban structure and functioning, and for an urban area as a whole. Data on users are available from transportation and related studies; so are data on opportunity costs. Data are scarce on such matters as the impact of various transportation systems on environmental factors of noise, air pollution, or water pollution. Still fewer data are available for the impact of transportation on urban structure and functioning (economic conditions, location patterns, and sociopolitical factors such as redistribution of population or the splitting of communities). Some of these facts can be collected through experimentation with parts of the overall problem. Thus, performance data on various transportation vehicles can be obtained through theoretical and empirical studies of the hardware. User reactions to new systems can be obtained through experiments which modify existing systems or which use prototypes. These same kinds of experiments can be used to test out environmental and other factors.

However, in still other cases the judgment of experts may be required. Expert opinion may be called on when it is necessary to use numerical data or assumptions that cannot be based on theory or experience. Experts may be helpful, for example, in determining the impact of various transportation systems on political and social structures. The Delphi technique is a method for obtaining the judgments of experts systematically and is described in Chapter 10.

The role of theory and empirical research. When theory exists, it provides a guide in looking for data. For example, in the fire station location problem, network theory was used. In the San Francisco housing market model, market theory provided a guide to data collection. The theory utilized may be highly formal (network and market theory), or it may be simply a hunch or a hypothesis—for example, that fire station location should be related in some way to the characteristics of the area to be served (fire incidence) and to the operational procedures of getting to a fire.

Whether theory exists or not, data collection is necessary. Where theory exists, the data provide a means of testing the theory. Both the theory and the data help to solve the problem. When theory does not exist, data collection may be necessary so that relevant theory can be built. The difficulty of achieving a balance between theoretical analysis and empirical research is indicated by D. M. Fort, who says that

the proper balance between theoretical analysis and fact-gathering depends on the problem. It is important, of course, to get the facts on the proper subject; a preliminary theoretical analysis can be very useful to this end, in pointing out what information is lacking and most needed. Much effort can be and often is wasted gathering the wrong data, for failure to do the necessary theoretical homework first. On the other hand, much effort is also wasted applying sophisticated analytical techniques to inadequate data, trying to make silk purses out of sows' ears. Physical experiments and data gathering in general are expensive; making plans and decisions in the face of uncertainty, even if aided by the best possible systems analysis, can also be expensive. A proper balance may well call for much more emphasis on fact-gathering than has been customary.[5]

Any analysis will be heavily supported by component studies of cost, engineering, human factors, and political and social considerations. Therefore, the data gathering phase of analysis will generally be the most time-consuming and costly. To assure adequate attention to all parts of the policy study, a balance must be struck between theoretical analysis and fact-gathering and between the design phase and other phases in the process of analysis. For example, extensive data gathering in the San Francisco Community Renewal Program (CRP) study left insufficient money and time to adequately evaluate the results of the housing market model. Evaluation and interpretation of the model results was completed after the CRP was completed. In this case the judgment and experience of the planners was utilized to make the CRP recommendations. When later tested with the aid of the model, the recommendations were found to be sound.

EVALUATION

As an intellectual process the evaluation phase of policy analysis involves predicting the consequences of selecting various alternatives as a basis for choosing from among them. It may simply require the judgment of an individual expert. It may involve using a single quantitative or formal model such as an elaborate computer program which combines in a single computation all the various submodels for determining dollar cost, environmental forecasts, and goal achievement. Or it may involve a variety of processes, including quantitative and qualitative models, political gaming, and intuition. What is common to all evaluations is that they are done with the aid of some kind of model which is used in an experimental fashion to try out various alternatives.

The role of models in evaluation

Models are used because the real thing often is not available for experimentation. Modeling involves ignoring many of the actual features of a problem under study and abstracting from the real situation certain variables and their interaction. The set of interacting variables makes up an idealized version of the real situation that concerns the decision makers. This idealization is called a model. The model is then operated on or experimented with. The aim is to obtain answers to specific questions, which will provide clues to aid in dealing with that part of the real world to which the model corresponds.

Modeling is used in policy analysis to provide a framework, a way of organizing the thinking and communicating about a problem. It is also a guide to data gathering and computation. Finally, modeling is an aid to the process of evaluation, that is, to examination of the implications and costs of various alternatives so that they can be compared. For many important problems, simple comparisons of outcomes without any indication of which outcome is best may be the most that can be done. This may be all that is necessary. Quantitative and formal models may not be

required or applicable. Usually evaluation can go beyond this minimum, although it may not be possible initially to abstract the situation to a mathematical model or series of equations. Nevertheless, some way can be found to represent the consequences that follow from particular choices.

A crude example

The following example is used to illustrate the role of models in analysis. Suppose the problem is to advise decision makers on alternatives to urban redevelopment in order to meet the housing demand of an increasing population in a central city. The analysis could take two forms:

1. Some level of housing supply is fixed and an attempt is made to determine the alternative which will attain the desired effectiveness at minimum cost.
2. The budget level is fixed and an attempt is made to maximize effectiveness, that is, to get the most housing for the least cost (assuming an existing mix of housing types, income levels, population groups, etc.)

Let us pursue the first form. For the analysis to be carried out, the environment must be forecast. This forecast includes the population increase expected over the time period in question and the housing demand generated by that increase. It also includes an effort to determine those factors which influence purchase decisions on the part of householders and those influencing private investment decisions in new or upgraded housing.

The second step is to model the interactions of supply and demand in the housing market: that is, "Under what conditions will householders,

choose various types of housing?" and "What is the likelihood of various types of housing being available under various private investment assumptions?"

The third step is to model the influence of public interventions (code enforcement, rehabilitation, tax policy, etc.) in the housing market and to develop a cost model which measures the relative amounts of public and private investment under various public interventions.

A fourth step might be to develop an analytic scenario (model) to describe political and social forces operating in the environment over the time period in question. The scenario would start with the present state of the world and illustrate, step-by-step, how, in one or more future situations, racial tensions might erupt, political power might be redistributed, the middle class might return to the central city, and similar changes might occur. The scenario will probably not provide a clear way of weighing consequences; nor will it indicate a preferred rating of alternatives. Rather, it will serve to bring factors to bear on the decision which could not be accounted for in the previous models but which might be relevant to the decision at hand and might otherwise be overlooked.

How then might these various evaluative steps be put together? From the quantitative models would come comparison of alternatives such as those indicated in Table 4–1.

However, individual decision makers might each choose different alternatives. And usually there are a number of decision makers. What is needed, therefore, is a collective judgment from these men and the analysts who advise them. One

Table 4-1. Hypothetical housing market outcomes for three alternatives for an urban redevelopment project.

Expected housing market outcomes	Alternatives		
	A	B	C
Private market residential investment (in millions)	$ 576	$ 200	$ 1,000
Number of substandard structures	36,922	70,000	10,000
Dwelling unit increase	24,000	15,000	70,000
Public investment in various programs (in millions)	$100	$40	$200
Household increase	70,000	70,000	70,000

Table 4-2. Sample form for evaluating decision makers' preferences regarding three alternatives for an urban redevelopment project.

Considerations	Rating of alternatives		
	A	B	C
Private market residential investment	_____	_____	_____
Number of substandard structures	_____	_____	_____
Dwelling unit increase	_____	_____	_____
Public investment	_____	_____	_____
Household increase	_____	_____	_____
Segregation	_____	_____	_____
Flexibility	_____	_____	_____
Growth impact	_____	_____	_____
Political desirability	_____	_____	_____

technique for pooling judgments is to ask each decision maker and analyst to fill in an array of alternatives such as that illustrated in Table 4–2. Each individual would then rate the various alternatives (using, say, a number between 0 and 10), indicating his preference or his conception of the worth of each alternative relative to the various considerations pertinent to the decision. A numerical measure could then be worked out which would indicate the decision makers' preferences.

This technique obviously leaves uncertainty as to the outcomes listed in the table. It fails to eliminate moral and value uncertainty as to which combination of outcomes would be preferable. But the simple act of displaying systematically the opinions and judgments of each decision maker for his own use is likely to be helpful to him. When the judgments of other decision makers are presented along with each one's arguments, the information may be more valuable. In fact, such feedback information may help bring about a consensus among the decision makers. Whether the group preference (as indicated by the scaled rating) is utilized or not (and sometimes it should not be, for the alternative which comes out on top may do so by default), the comparison is likely to be helpful.

The outputs of models and judgment
Assuming a study has been done properly, the analysis may still not be ended. The outcomes from a model must be interpreted in the light of considerations which may lie outside those incorporated in the model. The "state of the art" of policy analysis is not sufficiently advanced to include social and political considerations in the

formal evaluation models. Since major decisions in the field of public policy are part of a social process as well as an intellectual process, these must be accounted for in the analysis. Considerations other than those of cost effectiveness are important. Included here are custom, tradition, morale, aesthetics, and individual and organizational behavior. Some of these considerations may be treated in models. Generally, the integration of such considerations with the results of models is a task for the decision makers, and it is a task that is essentially a judgmental one.

Decision makers receive several aids in their attempt to interpret the results of policy analysis studies. The policy analyst supplies recommendations on the basis of what he thinks the study implies. However, it is important to distinguish between what a study actually shows and the conclusions or recommendations drawn by the analyst. That is, when new minds — particularly those of the decision makers — review a problem, they bring new information and insight. Even though results obtained from a model are not changed, recommendations for action based upon the results may be changed because of this review. For example, one experienced user of analysis in the military states the following:

Simply said, the purpose of an analysis is to provide illumination and visibility — to expose some problem in terms that are as simple as possible. This expose is used as one of a number of inputs by some "decision-maker." Contrary to popular practice, the primary output of an analysis is not conclusions and recommendations. Most studies by analysts do have conclusions and recommendations even though they should not, since invariably whether or not some particular course of action should be followed depends on factors quite beyond those that have been quantified by the analyst. A "summary" is fine and allowable, but "conclusions" and "recommendations" by the analyst are, for the most part, neither appropriate nor useful. Drawing conclusions and making recommendations (regarding these types of decisions) are the responsibility of the decision-maker and should not be preempted by the analyst.[6]

A model, even the most sophisticated mathematical optimizing model, is only an indicator. It is not a final judge. While an analysis may compare alternatives under a great many different assumptions, using various models, decisions are not made on the basis of these comparisons alone. This would hold true even if an immensely more complicated version of the study were to be carried out.

Notes

[1] A more extensive, slightly different, and excellent discussion of the process of analysis is E. S. Quade, "Principles and Procedures of Systems Analysis," in *Systems Analysis and Policy Planning: Applications in Defense,* ed. by. E. S. Quade and W. I. Boucher (New York: American Elsevier Publishing Co., 1969), pp. 30–53. In fact, the entire book is recommended reading for those interested in pursuing the subject further. For a different but equally important work, see Alfred J. Kahn, *Theory and Practice of Social Planning* (New York: Russell Sage Foundation, 1969).

[2] Various techniques for assessing preferences and various process approaches to determining goals are discussed in: Kahn, *Theory and Practice of Social Planning,* Chapter 4.

[3] Britton Harris describes three ways in which alternatives are presently developed and suggests ways of improving the process as well as ways of testing various designs (Britton Harris, "The City of the Future: The Problem of Optimal Design," *The Regional Science Association Papers,* XIX (1967), 185–95). See also: Christopher Alexander, *Notes on the Synthesis Form* (Cambridge, Mass.: Harvard University Press, 1966).

Two very useful works describing design considerations and ways of generating alternatives are: Selma Mushkin and Brian Herman, *The Search for Alternatives: Program Options in a PPB System* (Washington, D.C.: The George Washington University, 1968); and Kahn, *Theory and Practice of Social Planning,* particularly Chapters 5–8.

[4] East Lansing Project Team, "East Lansing: A Facilities Location Analysis," East Lansing, Mich., 1968. (Mimeographed.)

[5] D. M. Fort, *Systems Analysis as an Aid in Air Transportation Planning* (Santa Monica: Rand Corporation, 1966), p. 10; also cited in Quade and Boucher, *Systems Analysis,* p. 42.

[6] Glenn A. Keat, "On Analysis," *Air University Review,* XVIII (May–June 1967), 50; also cited in Quade and Boucher, *Systems Analysis,* p. 52.

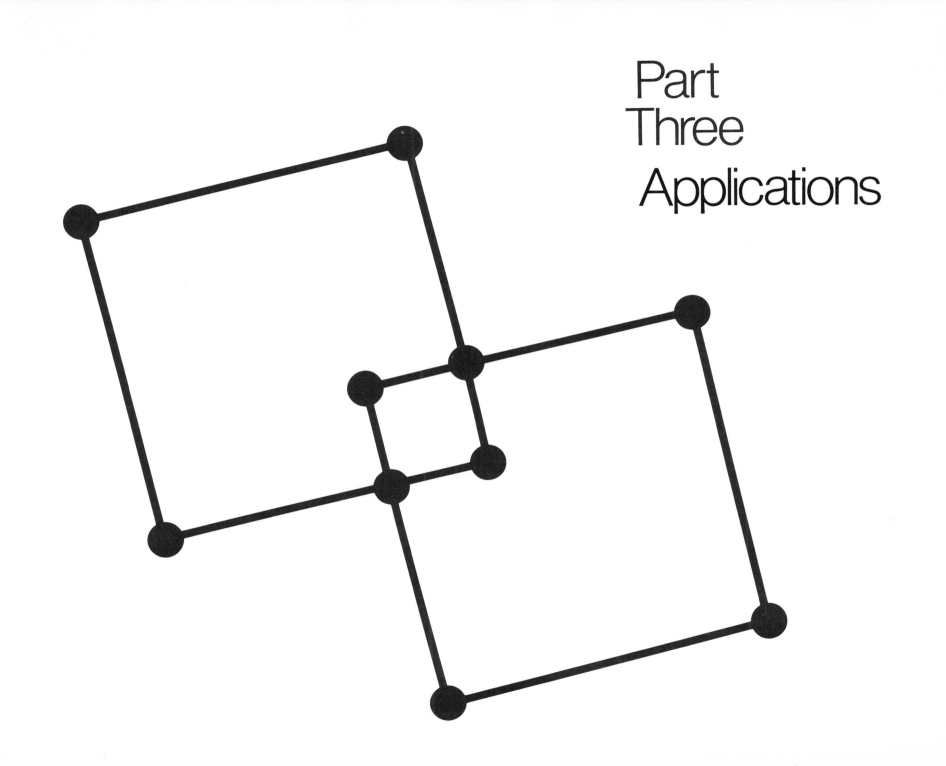

Part
Three
Applications

Operational Problems

Certain examples illustrating the use of analysis on operational problems will be presented here. Each example focuses on a different problem and involves the use of different techniques. Some of the analyses were used to inform decision makers in a real situation; others were developed after the fact but refer to concrete decision situations. The purpose of these examples (and of others which will appear in later chapters) is to permit a closer examination of the use of analysis on concrete problems. Such an examination is intended to provide a better understanding of policy analysis—the way it is conducted, the use of technique, the results, and the pitfalls which it may contain.

The three examples to be discussed now are: (1) the local tax impact of a new plant; (2) the Old Mint; (3) fire station location.

THE LOCAL TAX IMPACT OF A NEW PLANT

It is commonly assumed that the tax impact of a new plant locating in a community will be positive. That this is often untrue is a fact which

some cities have recognized only belatedly and some not at all. The present case study is drawn from work conducted by Stephen H. Sosnick[1] in Davis, California, as an effort to aid government decision makers in the development and application of industrial location policy.

The background

In 1957 residents of the city of Davis engaged in heated controversy over the prospective addition of a food processing plant (a cannery) to the community's economy. Debate centered largely around the economic and social advantages or disadvantages which might accrue to the small college–residential community—by the introduction of this plant specifically and by industrialization generally. Two referendums settled the issue in favor of the industry. It was apparent, however, that none of the parties in the controversy had very good information on which to base a decision. In the hope of preventing, or at least informing, such controversy in the future, the city took steps to develop a tool for analyzing the economic impact of specific plant locations that might be proposed at some future date.

The problem

The problem was to develop some way of determining how to predict the tax impact of a new plant, taking into account the principal direct and indirect effects, costs, and benefits. Cities often assume that a new plant will help to hold down tax rates. Actually, the impact on city and school tax rates can be positive or negative. It depends on whether the increase in local revenues outweighs the cost of providing public services and facilities to the plant and providing them for the additional population which the plant brings into the community.

The analysis

The approach to a solution was to develop a generalized model of the major variables involved in the tax impact question and then to obtain empirical estimates of certain of these variables for the Davis case. The analysis involved making certain assumptions about tax impact and school district arrangements, but these are amenable to modification where circumstances warrant varying from the assumed case.

The overall structure of the problem may be stated as follows: the average change in city-plus-school annual income, or N, will depend primarily upon four attributes of the new plant and certain relatively fixed attributes of the city related to each of the plant attributes.

The attributes of the new plant are:

1. Average permanent employment over the years, or J
2. Average annual payroll per permanent job, or W
3. Average investment in land and inventories per job, or V
4. Average investment in buildings and equipment per job, or $I - I$ needing multiplication by a depreciated factor, μ, to maintain comparability over time.

These attributes are critical because the increase in local population is related to J (number of jobs), the increase in local personal income is related to JW (annual payroll), and the increase in the industrial tax roll is related to $JV + \mu JI$ (average investment). Therefore, N can be expressed symbolically as a simple linear function of the four plant attributes:[2]

$$N = \alpha \, [JV + \mu JI] + \beta \, [JW] + \gamma J.$$

In the equation, α, β, γ, and μ are attributes of the city. They are variable constants or parameters. They will vary over cities and over time, but for any one city and starting time they are constants determined by the city's economic character. They are estimated from information about the city that is commonly available. Once they are empirically derived, these estimates can be used repeatedly by the city until the economic structure of the community changes sufficiently to warrant their reestimation.

Thus, the model developed is generalized and applicable to many other cities and to many types of plants. In application, the parameters must be estimated for the specific city in question, but this is readily done.

But what does the model do? Basically, it allows four kinds of predictions to be made: (1) the net tax impact of a new plant; (2) the minimum plant investment per job that is needed if existing taxpayers are to break even; (3) the share of a representative homeowner in the total tax gain or loss; and (4) the income that a man who will commute to a job in a different city must earn if existing taxpayers are to break even from the arrival of his household.

These predictions can be used to rate potential establishments from a tax viewpoint. They can also be used in negotiating with new prospects. A city that seeks to attract a new plant by making concessions in assessments, depreciation schedules, or service charges can use the equations and their predictions to estimate how much net income would be left after concessions of various amounts. Finally, the predictions might be used in connection with other information. For example, if a segment of a community's population is low-skilled and unemployed, and the city is seeking to provide employment for these people, it is likely that the net tax impact from a new plant that would employ this population would be a loss. The amount of loss could be estimated with such a model[3] and compared with the political, social, and economic costs and benefits of failing to provide such employment.

To illustrate the application of the model, Sosnick developed empirical estimates of the parameters for the city of Davis at its 1962 tax rates, levels of city and school services, and economic conditions. The result was as follows:

(1m) $N = 0.0147 \, JV + 0.0093 \, JI + 0.0207 \, JW - 278 J.$

That is, the change in average annual city-plus-school net income (N) is likely to be $147 for each $10,000 of average inventory and increased land value (JV), plus $93 for each $10,000 of building and equipment (JI), plus $207 for each $10,000 of annual payroll (JW), minus $278 for each permanent job (J).

For example, suppose a plant was contemplated that would have $1,000,000 of inventory and land appreciation, $3,000,000 of buildings and equipment, 55 permanent jobs, and $7,500 annual payroll per job—figures representative of a sizeable cannery. Substitute these figures into equation (1m), we obtain $35,824. In other words, the illustrative plant would increase average city-plus-school net income in Davis by an amount that is most likely to be about $36,000. The increase could be used to improve services or to reduce tax rates.[4]

Sosnick also developed other examples of the predictions possible, explained how the basic equation is modified for these other predictions, and indicated how numerical estimates of the parameters were derived.

Comment

The model developed by Sosnick is concerned only with the criterion of net tax impact. Other objectives and criteria may be important in making decisions about new plant location. These might include: (1) decreasing the number of people who must commute to other cities for work; (2) providing jobs for a particular group in the population; or (3) achieving a broad mix of types of industries and jobs in the city's economy. The model, however, provides information only about tax impacts. Other information (e.g., the value of decreasing commutation, increasing jobs for minorities, and achieving a balanced economy) would be important to the choice in the three examples cited above. Such information must be developed by analyses outside the model and used in conjunction with the model's predictions. In some instances the model itself would require modification to account for a finer characterization of the model elements. In other instances the tax impact model would have to be used in conjunction with other models.

For example, in the first instance cited above (decreasing commutation), all that might be required in addition to the present model output might be some evaluations of the value of decreasing commutation.

In the second instance—providing special jobs—the model itself would have to be modified and new information developed on the nontax costs and benefits of providing jobs for a particular population group. At present the model treats all industries, jobs, and people similarly. A finer breakdown, grouping these elements into classes, might permit discrimination of impacts among population groups from different types of jobs in different industries. The model output (still only tax impact, but at a finer level of analysis) could then be combined with cost-benefit information to aid final choice.

In the third instance (balance or mix in the economy) the tax impact model would have to be used in conjunction with an overall model of the community's economy, such as an input/output model. The input/output model could indicate the specific contributions of various types of industry to the economy, including the type in question. This information, combined with the tax impact information for the specific plant in question, may then provide a basis for choice.

Thus the tax impact model illustrates a number of points:

1. Models seldom provide a clear-cut basis for choice, unless the decision makers' objectives can be expressed by a simple criterion, for example, net tax impact. There is almost always some measure of discretion and judgment which the decision makers must bring to bear in choosing among alternatives.
2. In building such models the analysts also exercise judgment. There are numerous critical assumptions and uncertainties involved in estimating the parameter values for Sosnick's model which importantly affect the results and the uses that can be made of the results. For example, one analyst who reviewed the case considers the claims of what the model can be used for as considerably overstated and misleading.
3. For most decisions, the output of models must be combined with other information to assist choice among alternatives. Models generally represent only part of some larger problem. There are many aspects of any problem which are, or must be, omitted from the model. To include everything might require more money, time, and effort than the expected

results would justify. Quantification of some things may be impossible. Others may be better handled by analyses outside the model. Finally, some things are best handled by bringing to bear the experience and intuition of people familiar with a problem.
4. Models may be used in conjunction with one another: one model may provide input to another. Different models may account for different parts of a problem and may serve as a check on the outputs of each.

COST-BENEFIT AND THE OLD MINT

This study was conducted as an exercise in demonstrating the technique of cost-benefit analysis rather than as an aid to decision making in the particular case cited. The study, by Nathaniel Lichfield,[5] is one of three cases demonstrating the technique and utility of cost-benefit analysis in urban redevelopment. The actual decisions were reached without the analysis being available. However, as Lichfield points out, "The value of the studies is not thereby undermined for this lies not in the decisions they point to but in the opportunity to demonstrate the technique of analysis on concrete problems."[6]

The details of the computations are not reported here—only the background, the approach, and the results of the study.

The background
The Old Mint is the popular name for the former United States branch mint that occupies a one-acre city block within the San Francisco central business district (Figure 5-1). The building is rectangular in plan, approximately 160 by 270 feet, two stories in height over a high basement.

It was built by the federal government between 1869 and 1874, and soon became the principal mint in the United States. As the main federal depot for all gold and silver produced in the West, it played an important role in the economy of the growing West. The structure survived the earthquake and fire of 1906, but in 1937 its mint operations ceased with the construction of a new mint building on Market Street. The Old Mint was designed by Alfred B. Mullett, the foremost architect of federal government buildings in the post–Civil War era. Thus, the Old Mint had earned fame for historic and architectural reasons. Consequently, in 1956 the Advisory Board on National Parks, Historic Sites, Buildings, and Monuments reported to the secretary of the Interior that the building possessed national significance within the meaning of the Historic Sites Act of 1935. This act defines as national policy the preservation of "historic buildings of national significance for the inspiration and benefit of the people of the United States."

The problem
Since 1937 the Old Mint has been intermittently vacant or used sporadically by a variety of federal departments. At the time of the study it was largely vacant, and the General Services

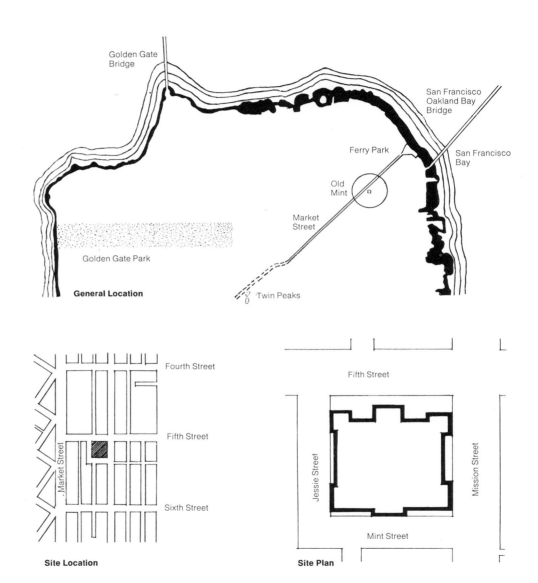

Figure 5-1. Location of the Old Mint, San Francisco. Source: Nathaniel Lichfield, *Cost-Benefit Analysis in Urban Redevelopment* (Berkeley: Real Estate Research Program, Institute of Business and Economic Research, University of California, 1962), p. 12 a-b.

Administration (GSA) of the federal government was concerned about its future. The GSA considered a number of alternatives but eventually focused on two. The first was to preserve the building because of its architectural and historic importance. The GSA found that they could retain the building, refurbish it at a cost of around $1 million, and rent the space to three units of the National Park Service which were then located in different parts of the city. At the same time the building could serve as a mint museum open to the public.

The second alternative was to demolish the building and sell the site for commercial use. The Old Mint constituted a valuable building site and the city of San Francisco was interested in having the federal noncontributing building torn down to make way for a commercial structure that would contribute to the city's tax roll. The three National Park Service units could be accommodated in the new Federal Office Building. The value of the cleared site was estimated at $1 million and the cost of demolishing the Old Mint at around $300,000, which would mean a net gain of $700,000 for the federal government.

The GSA, then, was faced with a choice essentially between its interest as a property owner and the interests of various publics. Included in these publics were the city of San Francisco; the National Park Service; nearby property owners, residents, and businesses; and individuals and organizations concerned about preserving historic structures.

The analysis
In his approach to the Old Mint case Lichfield first developed a framework or model. Basically,

Table 5-1. Model for a comparison of benefits and costs to producers and consumers, as prepared for the Old Mint case; two schemes are shown. Source: Lichfield, _Cost-Benefit Analysis in Urban Redevelopment_, p. 10a.

1	2	3		4		5	6	7	8		9		10
		Scheme 1		Scheme 2					Scheme 1		Scheme 2		
Item no.	Producers	Ben.	Cost	Ben.	Cost	Remarks	Item no.	Consumers	Ben.	Cost	Ben.	Cost	Remarks
1							2						
3							4						
5							6						

the model consists of a set of accounts. In one account are the "producers": individuals or groups who play a part in creating a particular service. In the other account are the "consumers": individuals or groups who use the services produced. Each producer or consumer group constitutes a separate entity. Generally, particular producer and consumer groups are linked, paired, or associated with one another. They can be conceived as engaged in transactions whereby the producer produces services for sale to the consumer. Each transaction results in producers and consumers incurring certain costs and benefits. These may be market or nonmarket, direct or indirect, economic or noneconomic, real or transfer costs and benefits. The result of each transaction for each pair of consumers and producers is then recorded in benefit and cost columns. Since at least two alternatives are always compared, the benefits and costs are

entered for each. Table 5-1 illustrates this basic model.

The next step is comparison of the alternatives. In simplest terms it involves subtraction of costs and benefits of one scheme from those of another and derivation of net benefit. The framework for this is Table 5-2. The basic model, then, was an accounting scheme which attempted to indicate the implications of each alternative in terms of costs and benefits to the various groups that would be affected.

The analysis conducted by Lichfield attempted to shed light on the Old Mint problem as manifested in 1960. It forecast the implications of each of three alternatives in terms of costs and benefits falling on various sections of the community. In tracing repercussions it was necessary to establish a cutoff point (that is, to define the

Table 5-2. Model for indicating net differences in benefits and costs as prepared for the Old Mint case; two schemes are shown. Source: Lichfield, *Cost-Benefit Analysis in Urban Redevelopment,* p. 10a.

Item no.	Producers	Scheme 1 minus Scheme 2		
		Ben.	Cost	Net
1				
3				
5				

Item no.	Consumers	Scheme 1 minus Scheme 2		
		Ben.	Cost	Net
2				
4				
6				

boundaries of the study). Lichfield decided that the analysis would not go beyond the costs and benefits which would flow from changes affecting the following properties:

1. The office premises then occupied by the three units of the National Park Service
2. The Old Mint itself
3. The new Federal Building
4. The properties immediately adjoining the Old Mint.

Table 5–3 presents the analysis by showing figures for conditions as they existed at the time of the study (Scheme 1), and then as they would exist under the two alternatives posited: Scheme 2 (Old Mint retained) and Scheme 3 (Old Mint demolished and site for sale). The following is an explanation of each item in Table 5–3 and is taken directly from Lichfield's original study.

1. *Federal Government as Property Owners:* For the purpose of this item, we regard the Federal Government as landlord of the National Park Service, meeting its cost of accommodation and receiving its rents.

   a. Existing National Park Service Offices. The Federal Government does not own these. The rent it pays equals the rent it receives from the Service. These would disappear under Schemes 1 and 2.
   b. Old Mint. Under each of the three schemes, past investment in the Old Mint can be regarded as a sunk cost, and therefore shown as nil. In Scheme 1, no benefit is being received from the unused property, but there remains an annual operating cost of $30,000. To restore the property for occupation by the National Park Service would cost $1 million. The benefit would then comprise the annual gross rents of $180,000, net of operating costs which would rise to $85,000. There would be no net benefit from visitors to

the building or museum, since fees would be calculated to balance costs. If the Old Mint were demolished the net benefit would be $700,000 as already noted.
   c. New Federal Building—National Park Service Section. If the Old Mint is retained no space for the National Park Service would be needed in the new Federal Building. If it is demolished, space would be needed. There would be no extra cost for land, since the building could be raised in height. Construction cost would be $1,350,000. For this the Government would receive gross annual rates of $225,000, but would pay extra operating costs of $100,000.

The reduction shows the net position of the Federal Government. At present the Old Mint costs $30,000 per year. If used by the Service it would show an annual benefit of $65,000. If it were demolished and the Service accommodated in the new Federal Building, the annual benefit would be $106,000.

2. *National Park Service:* The occupation benefits to the National Park Service would be greater in the Old Mint than in the present three dispersed offices, and greater in the new Federal Building than in the outmoded Old Mint. But for the greater benefits the Service would pay the larger rents noted in paragraph 1: $180,000 and $225,000 compared with the present $46,000. Since these rents are based on market values, it can be assumed that benefits would equal costs in all situations.

3. *Nearby Property Owners:* All sites in the immediate vicinity are covered by improvements. Their current use values would be affected by the alternatives. The effects could be forecast but have not been, so "M" entries are shown.

   First, the attraction of visitors and employees to the Old Mint would give rise to local trade and so enhance values more than costs. Visitors would increase under Scheme 2 (perhaps around 100,000 per year—see Item 9), but would disappear in Scheme 3. The number of employees would be greater in Scheme 3, for whereas the National Park Service would employ about 200 people a new commercial building would employ many more. Although no figures have been used we can forecast probabilities. Nearby property values would be higher in Schemes 2 and 3 than at present, and are likely to be higher in Scheme 2 than 3.

4. *Nearby Business Proprietors:* All that has been said with regard to nearby property owners can be applied to nearby business proprietors. But insofar as increased business is done in Schemes 2 and 3, it can be expected that rents of premises will eventually rise when contracts are reviewed. It is assumed that rising rents would then absorb rising proprietors' profits, and therefore that benefits would then be matched by costs.

5. *Other Property Owners:* The choice of the Federal Government will affect the value of other (than nearby) property which is suitable for commercial and industrial purposes, either as it exists or on redevelopment. First, the removal of the National Park Service to either the Old Mint or the new Federal Building will reduce the immediate demand for office space in other buildings. There will be an immediate vacancy, however short-lived, in the space now occupied by the National Park Service. Assuming that this small increase in supply will make no impact on price levels, the net effect can be seen by studying the result of the vacancy in the existing National Park Service offices. The owners of this space will lose their income of $46,000 in Schemes 2 and 3, but not save all their operating expenses. Of these, they cannot avoid $12,000—i.e., they *could* avoid $34,000. Their operating profit of $27,000 per annum would thus be transformed to an operating

loss of $12,000 per annum in the second and third situations. Secondly other property owners will be affected by the fate of the $1,000,000 potential development value, which can be said to be floating over the Old Mint site. If the building remains, the development value that could be realized on the site would accrue to other property owners at no cost, either in increase of established rents or on redevelopment. The value would not necessarily equal the value for offices of the Old Mint site but would approximate to it. If the Old Mint is demolished, these property owners would lose the development value. This would go to the Federal Government (Item 1). But as already noted, it would obtain only $700,000 and not the $1,000,000.

The reduction shows that other property owners benefit most in the current situation, having the net rent income from the Park Service lettings and also the development value. They lose the former in Scheme 2. They lose both in Scheme 3, being left also with operating costs on the current National Park Service offices.

6. *Other Commercial and Industrial Occupiers:* Potential occupiers of new buildings on the Old Mint site (Scheme 3) might have better or worse conditions should they go elsewhere (Scheme 2). Any difference would be compensated for by differences in rents, so that their position would be neutral. There will also be repercussions on current occupiers of other commercial and industrial buildings. These repercussions would be in the nature of price changes simply because of changes in the supply situation. For reasons given earlier . . . these pecuniary indirect effects are ignored.

7. *City Operation–Tax Revenues and Municipal Costs:* The repercussions will be traced in relation to each of the properties mentioned in Items 1 and 5 above.

a. Existing National Park Service Offices. The revenue and cost to the City will be the same in the three situations (m).

b. The Old Mint. The cost will be much the same in all situations (m). If retained the Old Mint earns no taxes, but demolished it brings the City an estimated $150,000 per year.
c. New Federal Building. The costs will be the same (m) and no taxes will be earned in any of the situations.
d. Floating Value. If the Old Mint is retained, it must be assumed that the City will earn taxes from the satisfaction elsewhere of the floating demand referred to under 5 above. This demand is likely to be met in increased values in existing buildings as well as in new construction. Since old buildings pay less taxes than new, something less will be earned than the $150,000 which will be obtained from a new building on the site of the Old Mint; so an "m" entry is shown. Against this must be set the operating expenditure on the shifted value for which an "m" is also shown.

The reduction shows the net effect in City revenue and operating costs, after omitting the many common items. If the Old Mint is retained there will be prospective tax revenue when the floating value settles as well as the associated operating costs. If the Old Mint is demolished, the floating value revenue of Schemes 1 and 2 will be replaced by the rather greater $150,000 which can be expected from the new development on the site.

Schemes 2 and 3 are likely to show a surplus of revenue over costs. The surplus would be greater in Scheme 3 for the revenue will be higher and the costs less. The City could pass on these benefits to the taxpayers, either in services or a reduction in the tax rate. The latter is assumed for the purpose of analysis. A tax adjustment is accordingly shown (a negative benefit) which leaves the City with benefits balancing costs.

8. *City Taxpayers:* The tax adjustment is shown as a negative cost, which is bigger in Schemes 3 and 2.

Table 5-3. Benefits and costs for alternative uses of Old Mint; existing conditions also shown. Source: Lichfield, *Cost-Benefit Analysis in Urban Redevelopment*, p. 14b.

Item no.	Producers	1 Conditions existing				2 OM for NPS offices				3 OM demolished and sold				Remarks
		Benefit		Cost		Benefit		Cost		Benefit		Cost		
		C	A	C	A	C	A	C	A	C	A	C	A	
1	**Federal government as property owners**													
	a) existing NPS offices		m_1		m_1									
	b) Old Mint—initial property restoration							1000		700				
	recurring income						180		85					
	operating				30						225	1350		
	c) new federal building, NPS section initial													
	recurring income								65		106		100	
	operating reduction:				30									
3	**Nearby property owners**													
	a) visitors		m_2				m_2+ m_3				m_3+ m_3+			
	b) Old Mint site employees reduction:		m_2				m_2+ m_3							
5	**Other property owners**													
	a) existing NPS offices		46		19				12	E				
	b) floating development value reduction:	1000	67			1000	28							
7	**City operation—tax revenue and costs**													
	a) existing NPS offices				m_4				m_4		150			
	b) Old Mint				m_5				m_5					
	c) new federal building				m_6				m_6					
	d) floating development value		m_7		m_8		m_7		m_8		150			
	reduction:		m_7		m_8		m_7				m_9+			
	adjustment: final reduction:						$\underline{m_9}$							
9	**City economy** tourists and student		m_{10}				$m_{10}+$							
11	**Fixed capital investment**													
	1b) Old Mint—restoration							1000				300		
	demolition											M		
	new building											1350		
	1c) new federal building							M— 1000				1650		
	5b) floating value							M—				M		
	Total													

Item no.	Consumers	1 Conditions existing				2 OM for NPS offices				3 OM demolished and sold				Remarks
		Benefit		Cost		Benefit		Cost		Benefit		Cost		
		C	A	C	A	C	A	C	A	C	A	C	A	
2	**National Park Service**													
	a) existing offices	i_1			46									
	b) Old Mint						i_2		180					
	c) new federal building										i_3		225	
	reduction:			•	•			•	•			•	•	
4	**Nearby Business Proprietors**													
	a) tourists		m_2		m_2		m_2+		m_2+		m_3+		m_3+	
	b) Old Mint site employees						m_3		m_3					
	reduction:		•		•		•		•		•		•	
6	**Other Occupiers**													
	reduction:		•		•		•		•		•		•	
8	**City Taxpayers**													
	reduction:								$\underline{m_9}$				m_9+	
10	**Public**													
	a) citizens, tourists, and students	i_4		m_{11}		i_4+		$m_{11}+$						
	reduction:	i_6				i_6								
	b) National Heritage	i_4		m_{11}		i_4+		$m_{11}+$						
	reduction:	i_5				i_6								

Notes to Table 5-3

1. All columns show absolutes.
2. All figures are in $000.
3. C is a capital (once for all) item; A is an annual (continuing) item.
4. M or m shows a measurable item which has not been measured, initial or annual respectively. In each item different numbers (m_1, m_2, etc.) indicate different figures.
5. I or i shows an intangible (nonmeasurable) item, initial or annual respectively. The numbering (i_1, i_2, etc.) is as for M items.
6. The entries which are underlined are negative.
7. The reduction shows the annual net benefits and costs under each item other than capital investment.

9. *City Economy–Tourist Traffic:* Visitors to the Old Mint would spend money in the City, boosting its economy over and above the trade they would generate in property near the Old Mint, which has already been covered in Items 3 and 4. From records of visits to other historic monuments it has been estimated that as many as 100,000 people per year might visit the building if restored. Local and out of town visitors, in San Francisco for diverse reasons, would spend money at the Old Mint. Their extra expenditure in the City would be difficult to measure, but an "m" is shown, indicating an increase in benefit in Scheme 2 and no benefit in Scheme 3. In passing it might be noted that the typical visitor to the City is estimated to spend $25 per day.

10. *The Public:* In the event of demolition, tourists and

students would lose the intangible benefits of association with a building of this character. In addition the nation as a whole would be poorer, for in the words of the Historic Sites Act, the Old Mint is filled with "significance for the inspiration and benefit of the [people of the] United States." Intangible benefits are reflected [in] the first two situations, but not in the third. The citizens and tourists who visited the building would incur a money cost in travel and admission in the first two situations which would in total be less than the benefit derived. There would be no money cost in the third.

11. *Fixed Capital Investment:* The Federal Government's new fixed capital investment would be $1,000,000 in Scheme 2 and $1,650,000 in Scheme 3 (new building plus the demolition of the Old Mint). In addition, in Scheme 3 there would be the new building on the Old Mint site. This would cost something more than the new building necessary to meet the floating demand in Scheme 2, which would be met in part by existing buildings. The new fixed capital in Scheme 2 would therefore be less than in Scheme 3. But note that as property owners and developers, the Federal Government makes a better financial investment in Scheme 3. Scheme 2 would earn $95,000 on $1,700,000 ($700,000 plus $1,000,000) or 5.5%. Scheme 3 would earn a net income of $115,000 on an investment of $1,350,000, or 8.8%.

Summation
[Table 5–4] summarizes [Table 5–3]. It outlines the differences in annual costs and benefits that arise if the Old Mint is retained and occupied by the National Park Service (Scheme 2) instead of being demolished (Scheme 3). Results are obtained by deducting the [Table 5–3] reduced costs and benefits of Scheme 3 from those of Scheme 2, keeping benefits and costs distinct, transferring the differences to [Table 5–4], and there striking a net balance.
    A study of the net column in [Table 5–4], and group-

ing of items, leads to the following conclusions about Scheme 2 as related to Scheme 3.

1, 3, 5. The Federal Government as property owners would lose $41,000 per annum. Other property owners would gain by about this amount, and nearby owners are likely to be better off.

7, 8. While in both schemes the City would have a surplus of taxes over operating costs to pass on to taxpayers, the surplus would be smaller in Scheme 2.

9. The City economy would benefit more in Scheme 2.

2, 4, 6. The National Park Service, nearby business proprietors, and other proprietors remain in a neutral position in both schemes.

10. In Scheme 2, citizens, tourists, students, and the nation as a whole would have the intangible benefits of the Old Mint. Although those visiting would have to pay, in total this amounts to less than the intangible benefits derived from the visits.

Totals. Since there are several M entries the probabilities must be evaluated to see whether the total net benefits exceed costs.

Consumers 2–10. In Items 2, 4, and 6 no net benefit or cost arises. Item 8 local taxpayers would have to pay more, but the amount is uncertain. While tourists, students, and the national heritage would have a benefit— the Old Mint—benefit would exceed cost.

Conclusion
In terms of the whole community it seems that the intangible benefit of retaining the Old Mint would be bought not at economic loss but at net economic advantage. Property owners as a whole would benefit as would the city economy; and would lose nothing like the amount of taxes that could be earned on the Old

Mint site if it were redeveloped. Furthermore, the net advantages in retaining the Old Mint would be obtained with a smaller investment in real resources. It would use an existing structure instead of providing a new one, and save the particularly heavy cost of demolishing the Old Mint.
    A final word needs to be said about the incidence of costs in saving the Old Mint. The Federal Government would clearly lose both in income and return on investment. And the lower municipal revenue would cause a redistribution of tax burden; the lower tax revenue from the buildings covered in the analysis would be made up by higher taxes from the remainder of the City taxpayers.[7]

Some comments on analysis of costs and benefits
The analysis of costs and benefits as conducted in the Old Mint study will in many cases be all that is necessary in a policy analysis study. That is, the problem, the objectives, and the alternatives and their impacts may be known or easily derived, and the bulk of the analysis may focus, therefore, on comparison of the alternatives. In other instances analysis of costs and benefits may be part of a broader analysis in which other techniques are utilized to structure and understand the problem and to identify objectives and alternatives and the consequences of various alternatives.

Although the Lichfield studies focused on problems of urban physical development, analysis of costs and benefits can be extended to other areas of concern as well. While it is generally easier to conduct studies in physical development, important studies have been carried out in such areas as taxation,[8] education, health, welfare, transportation, building regulation, and public safety.[9]

**Table 5-4. Difference in annual benefits and costs
if Old Mint were retained and occupied by National
Park Service instead of being demolished (summary
of Table 5-3). Source: Lichfield, *Cost-Benefit
Analysis in Urban Redevelopment*, p. 18b.**

Item no.	Producers	Scheme 2 minus Scheme 3		
		Ben.	Cost	Net
1	Federal government as property owners	41	•	41
3	Nearby property owners	m_2+ m_3 m_3+	•	m_2+ m_3 m_3+
5	Other property owners	28	12	40
7	City operation	•	•	•
9	City economy	$m_{10}+$	•	$m_{10}+$
	Total net			m_2+ m_3 m_3+ $m_{10}+$

Item no.	Consumers	Scheme 2 minus Scheme 3		
		Ben.	Cost	Net
2	National Park Service	•	•	•
4	Nearby business proprietors	•	•	•
6	Other property owners	•	•	•
8	City taxpayers	m_9 m_9+	•	m_9 m_9+
10	Public	i_4+ i_6	$m_{11}+$	i_4+ i_6 $m_{11}+$
	Total net			m_9 m_9+ i_4+ i_6 $m_{11}+$

Notes:

1. The benefits and costs shown are obtained by deducting the Table 5-3 reduced items in Scheme 3 from Scheme 2, keeping benefits and costs separate in the colums so headed. The net is then shown in the third column by deducting costs from benefits. A + benefits and − costs is +; and A − benefits and + costs is −.

2. Where M and I items do not permit arithmetical reduction in the net column, probabilities are forecast.

3. All quantities are in annual terms.

4. Figures are in $000.

Sometimes a straightforward analysis of costs without any attempt to discuss associated benefits can be a helpful tool for decision makers. Such an analysis was conducted by the Southern California Research Council[10] for local governments in Los Angeles County. The study was aimed at predicting population growth and estimating the cost of providing governmental services and facilities to the population over a twelve-year period. Since this growth was in many ways uncontrollable by the governments in question it would have a significant impact on how resources would be used, and the analysis provided important information for use in financial and land use planning decisions.

FIRE STATION LOCATION

In East Lansing, Michigan, an important case study was recently carried out as part of a HUD-sponsored technology application program. The program was conducted by the International City Management Association (ICMA) in conjunction with the Technical Analysis Division (TAD) of the National Bureau of Standards, the Fels Institute of Local and State Government[11] of the University of Pennsylvania, and, also, the American Society of Planning Officials (ASPO). The full program included case studies in two other cities as well. The sponsors and conductors of the study felt that the new body of decision-aiding techniques which had been developed in fields such as operations research, management science, and systems analysis seemed applicable to the problems of city management and planning. TAD had the technology, in the sense that it had people trained and experienced in the use of various techniques. The cities had problems and were interested in trying out new approaches to solving them. The International

City Management Association wanted to see what TAD and the selected cities, working together, might accomplish.[12]

The East Lansing case study provides a good illustration of the consortium's efforts.[13] The presentation here varies from that of the others in this chapter, however. It not only describes the analysis effort and its results but it also discusses some of the problems encountered and the issues raised. These problems and issues point out what decision makers may expect to encounter even on problems as relatively simple as facility location.

The background and discussion

A master plan prepared for the city of East Lansing (36,000 population in 1965) in 1967 indicated that the city needed four fire stations to service expected growth patterns in the community. This determination had been arrived at by the city planner in consultation with the fire chief. They used the traditional method of drawing circles on a map at a radius that represented the standard or accepted definition of what constitutes an appropriate fire service area. The number of circles defined the number of stations required.[14]

The city had two existing fire stations, one which was quite old and was located in the downtown area and another newer one located on the Michigan State University campus. The cost of building and equipping two new stations was estimated at about $500,000, and the annual operating cost for them was estimated at some $130,000. Faced with many other budget demands for capital construction and operation of services, the city manager was reluctant to build the two new stations.

Despite the fact that the need for two new stations had been determined by accepted methods, the manager questioned whether they were really needed. He felt that if the older existing station could be relocated perhaps only one new station would be needed. His knowledge of the city and his experience also indicated that the actual incidence of fire and the probability of fire occurrence were unevenly distributed across the community. Some areas of the city experienced more fires than others and were more likely to have fires because of physical, activity, or population characteristics associated with them. It seemed to the manager that the location of stations should be related to fire incidence and potential fire hazard.

As the study developed, the manager and his fire chief became aware of the fact that the question of the number of fire stations needed was closely related not only to where such stations would be located but also to something else—the fire response level that the manager and chief considered acceptable given the cost of alternative response levels. That is, in the end the manager and chief had to make a judgment about what level of fire response they were willing to accept. The analysis provided them with information which would aid their decision making, but it did not relieve them of the ultimate choice.

It must also be pointed out that the problem as just stated was not the problem which the analysis group started out to solve. As stated in an interim report on the project, the problem was originally defined as "that of finding the proper location of a new fire station."[15] There are several factors which may help to account for the difference in these problem statements:

1. Rarely is the nature of a problem understood when analysis is begun. If it were, there would generally be little need for analysis.
2. The East Lansing case study was intended to focus on the planning aspects of the problem, and these were translated into questions of location.
3. The TAD analysts were familiar with a computer program for dealing with the location questions and tended to force the problem into a form which could be handled by this existing technique.
4. The decision makers (manager and fire chief) were unclear about their objectives in having the analysis done, or were in conflict about objectives, or perhaps did not communicate their objectives clearly to the analysts; or all of the above difficulties may have existed.

These problems can be expected in policy analysis studies, and they are mentioned here to convey a sense of what is often encountered even under the best of circumstances. The remainder of the case description will deal with how the problem stated by the analysts was solved, how this led to a restatement of the problem in the decision makers' terms, and what was done to solve the new problem. Finally, some evaluative comments are made in addition to those implicit in the case description.

The initial problem and the analysis
As stated above, the East Lansing problem was initially seen as one of fire station location. It was felt that the most significant factors involved were fire hazard and response time. That is, various sections of the city represented greater or lesser fire hazards, and fire stations should be located to minimize response time to all hazards,

especially to the greater ones. The problem was then broken into two subproblems:

1. Determining what factors make up a fire hazard and rating locations according to hazardousness
2. Determining travel (response) times to all fire hazard locations. The notion here was that the city would be divided into links and nodes. Nodes were street intersections and links the street lengths between these intersections. Links would be described in terms of travel time so that, given a hypothesized fire station location and fire event location, the travel (response) time could be predicted.

Fire hazard rating. In order to determine what factors constituted fire hazards it was necessary to analyze fire history data.[16] Such analysis, it was felt, would indicate some clear relationships between structural, activity, or other characteristics of properties in the city so that predictions could be made about the probability of fire at various locations. The analysis (covering a ten-year period) "did not reveal specific findings concerning damage potential or fire potential because of structural type or because of the way the structure was used (activity)."[17] Since statistically significant correlations were not obtainable, the analysis group was forced to rely upon factors loosely related to the frequency of fires and their own judgment as to what constituted a fire hazard. After considerable debate, the factors chosen were: population, number of stories, construction type, age, area, and occupancy type.

The development of hazard ratings for each property in the community was the next task. This required gathering data on each chosen factor

for each parcel of property in the city and applying a weighting scale to each property based on those data. This application resulted in a hazard rating for each property. The equation used for the weighting scale was as follows:

$$\text{population} + \begin{array}{c}\text{number of}\\\text{stories}\end{array} + \text{construction type} + \text{age} + \text{area} = \text{sum} \times \text{occupancy type.}$$

Each of the variables in the equation could be given a range of weights and the range varied for each. In general, the weighting scheme tended to give greater consideration to population than to any other variable. This was because the fire history data had suggested a strong relationship (although not statistically significant) between population density and fire incidence, and because the analysis group chose to weight the number of people endangered above the other factors.

When each property was assigned a hazard rating, all of the properties in a particular block were combined and an overall hazard rating assigned to that block. Each block rating in turn was assigned to some predetermined node (street intersection). The purpose of this assignment was to simplify the tracing of paths to potential fire locations.

All of the data manipulation (addition, multiplication) was done on the computer, as was the tracing of paths. The input to the computer included the following:

1. The entire street network of the city, with travel time between nodes
2. A listing of nodes (i.e., block areas)
3. Structural data for each property

4. The weighting criteria
5. Hypothesized fire station locations
6. Hypothesized fire locations
7. Data which represented future growth patterns in 1975.[18] All of the other data were based on existing conditions. The idea of including the growth variables was simply to permit a crude estimate of whether the locations selected based on existing conditions would hold under future conditions. Since only two variables were used (population and construction type),[19] the test was crude indeed.

The computer program. The basic program used in the study was one which traced minimum time paths between points in a network—a very common application in transportation studies. The points in this case were hypothesized fire station locations and potential fire locations ("potentiality" being determined by the hazard ratings assigned to each node). The way the program worked was as follows:

1. Choose a fire station location.
2. Calculate the travel time from the chosen fire station location to all nodes.
3. Calculate the weighting function (hazard) for all nodes.
4. Multiply (2) × (3) for each node.
5. Sum up the products of the above.
6. Repeat this operation for each chosen fire station location.

The output of the program is the sum of the products. Since each hypothesized station location has a different sum of the products, the locations can be compared. The preferred location is the one with the smallest sum. What the smallest sum says in essence is: here is the location which minimizes travel (response) time to potential fire locations, taking into account the fact that some locations are more hazardous than others.

The model works very well when you have only one station. When there are several, it is necessary to manually establish fire districts. The model can then be used to determine the preferred location within the district boundaries. By working back and forth between setting district boundaries by hand and running the model for each set of boundaries, it is possible to improve upon the location of boundaries. In East Lansing, the first setting of boundaries was a simple north–south division which placed the university (the biggest single hazard) entirely in the southern district. Eventually, a three-way division was arrived at which resulted in a triangular division of the city, again with the university entirely encompassed by one district.

But how did the analysts arrive at the three-way division? Somewhere in the process someone must have decided that three fire stations were needed.

Restatement of the problem

As the output from the analysis was developed the city manager realized that the study was not getting at the question of how many fire stations were needed. He therefore indicated what he wanted from the analysis, and the group set about producing it. At this point, the only way information could be developed to answer the number question was by rerunning the program assuming two stations in one run, three in another, and four (or five, or six) in another. The results of these runs would indicate what overall travel (response) times could be expected assuming two (then existing), three, or four stations. By comparing the response times under each alternative and the cost of building and operating new facilities, the decision makers could have some basis for choosing among the alternatives.[20] They chose three stations.

Comments on the study

Three qualifications seem in order before raising several further issues about the study. First, the study was experimental. It was the first time the city personnel had engaged in an analysis of this type and it was one of the first TAD experiences of working on city problems. It was also the first time anyone had tried a new approach to fire station location. Second, the matters of time, money, distance (East Lansing to Washington, D.C.), and data availability and quality were factors which greatly inhibited the analysis group's effort. Third, despite these limitations and the problems encountered, the group feels optimistic about the experience and is working to improve the model.

The East Lansing study provides a background for discussion of five important issues in policy analysis: (1) the relation between analysts and decision makers; (2) the formulation of objectives; (3) the selection of an approach to problems; (4) the exchange of information; and (5) the cost of analysis.

The role of analysts and decision makers. The East Lansing case clearly indicates that analysts and decision makers must work together at every major phase of a project. Experience with this project and others indicates that analysts have a tendency to fit problems to techniques rather than vice versa. In this case, because the analysts approached the problem with a preconceived notion of how it should be solved, alternative approaches were overlooked, as were data which might have been useful. For example, the East Lansing Project Team commented as follows:

It was the City's experience in this study that the . . . experts had a tendency to want to fit the project needs to an already established [computer] program rather than to build a program to fit the needs of the study at hand. Certain data was not utilized because it did not fit the existing program to be used; therefore, certain questions have gone unanswered.[21]

Elsewhere they stated:

An additional drawback was due to the predetermined computer approach—a much broader program of mathematically calculating percentages of fire probability could have been extremely helpful in determining a rating system. Further inquiry into the probability of fires occurring simultaneously and forecasts from these probabilities applied to the future growth of the City would have allowed the City's team to determine a breaking point in the range of the rating system which would indicate the number of fire stations necessary to avoid serious undercoverage of the City's fire potential. This and other similar kinds of shortcomings, mechanical and otherwise, were found with the program.[22]

Further, numerous value judgments are involved in the technical aspects of the work, and unless the decision makers are involved and understand what is being done the models, criteria, weightings, etc., will reflect the analysts' values rather than those of the decision makers. In the East Lansing case, because city experts (city planners and the fire chief) were working jointly with

operations research analysts, many of the value determinations were made in concert although with considerable debate. As the fire chief was one of the key decision makers as well as an expert, some representation of the decision makers' values was included. However, the limitations here are brought out by the next point.

Determination of objectives. The case clearly points out the importance of beginning with the right statement of objectives. While the initial objective of the study was optimum station location, as had been stated by the city planner and the fire chief, the objective of the city manager was to determine the number of stations needed. As mentioned earlier, a number of possible factors may have accounted for the discrepancies in objectives and problem statement (see pages 54–55).

Stating one's objectives clearly is not without its drawbacks. One consequence of a clear statement of objectives is the potentiality of generating conflict. The literature of management theory continually stresses the importance of stating one's objectives. The literature on organization behavior is filled with warnings of what happens when you do. The need for a clear statement of objectives in policy analysis is obvious, and such a statement must be made with recognition of its consequences. One can avoid the issue for some time, but if the decision makers' true objectives are to be attained, they must be stated at some point—hopefully before the wrong problem is solved. This is not to say that only the top decision makers' objectives are to be achieved. Rather, it is to point out that the whole process of analysis—and particularly the determination of objectives—may in reality be an

arena for bargaining over just what the objectives will be. This is to be expected. The mere act of reaching a definite agreement on what will be done may be extremely useful in itself, regardless of any technical achievement.

Structuring the problem and the solution approach. The initial step in any policy analysis is problem formulation. This involves an attempt to state issues, define boundaries, determine the objective, structure the problem, and search for an approach to the problem. Problem formulation is not a step-by-step process of performing the tasks just listed. Rather, it involves going back and forth between each of these until satisfactory closure is achieved. And, as suggested by the East Lansing case, a fully satisfactory statement of the problem sometimes may be reached only when the study is near completion.

Problem formulation is as much an attempt to develop and consider alternative ways of approaching the problem as it is to clarify the problem. There is an interrelation between these two objectives. Stating a problem helps to suggest ways of approaching it. Alternative ways of approaching a problem help to define it. The greatest error is to approach a problem with a predetermined approach and try to fit the problem to the approach. (I use *approach* here both in a broad sense, such as in the four characterizations by Churchman which I have quoted earlier [see page 21], and in a narrow sense to refer to technique.)

Exchange of information. In a case where neither analysts nor decision makers are familiar with each other's worlds, time is well spent at the beginning of a project in simply getting a good understanding of the various environments involved. This is also the time to determine what the roles of analysts and decision makers will be and how each can be helpful to the other. It should be noted, too, that more than one type of analyst or expert may be involved, and there is need for exchange among these people. In the East Lansing case, for example, the city experts stated they could have benefited from TAD's experience in data collection and coding.[23] Finally, there is need to develop a plan for carrying out the work early in the study; this should include the way in which the work will be coordinated.

The cost of analysis. The East Lansing Team estimated the city's costs for the project at around $6,000. Estimated costs for TAD were

$10,000 and for ICMA (and the other organizations), $4,000. The organization costs were borne by the HUD grant. While the costs may seem large, it should be remembered that the study was a pioneer effort. Further, if one wishes to consider the savings from not building a fourth fire station the project cost appears a good investment. Finally, the cost of applying the model for an effort of similar size in another city may run only from $5,000 to $10,000, depending upon the availability of computer time, programming staff, data, and a few sound thinkers.

It should be clear, however, that policy analysis is expensive. Attempts to justify the cost by projected savings, while often necessary to get approval to undertake analysis, may be defeating in the end. The best illustration of this is in the closely related area of data processing, or

computerization. Clearly, the computerization and automation of routine clerical tasks results in savings of some kind. But the real payoffs from the use of computers and the information handling capability they provide come from improvement in decision making and, ultimately, from improvement in the way a city defines and carries out its functions in the community. This is also the case with policy analysis. The savings which analysis sometimes makes possible are important. But the final payoff comes from (1) the greater understanding that analysis provides about what the community's problems are, and (2) the way in which analysis contributes to the evolution of a way of defining problems, determining objectives, developing programs to meet the objectives, and facilitating program execution within a particular governmental entity.

Notes

[1] Stephen H. Sosnick, *The Local Tax Impact of a New Plant* (Davis, Calif.: Institute of Governmental Affairs, University of California, 1964).

[2] Ibid., pp. 3–4.

[3] However, the model would have to be modified to account for a finer breakdown of jobs and industries. That is, jobs in different industries would need to be specified as skilled and unskilled (at minimum). The constants would also need to be reestimated on the basis of this division.

[4] Sosnick, *Local Tax Impact,* p. 4.

[5] Nathaniel Lichfield, *Cost-Benefit Analysis in Urban Redevelopment* (Berkeley: Real Estate Research Program, Institute of Business and Economic Research, University of California, 1962). For a similar application see: James C. T. Mao, "Efficiency in Public Urban Renewal Expenditures through Benefit-Cost Analysis," *Journal of the American Institute of Planners,* XXXII (March 1966), 95–107.

[6] Lichfield, *Cost-Benefit Analysis,* p. viii.

[7] Lichfield, *Cost-Benefit Analysis,* pp. 14–19.

[8] For example, Sunnyvale, California, used an analysis of benefits to property owners from government improvements (e.g., water, sewer, parking, street lighting) as a basis for determining how the cost of providing such improvements should be distributed among various classes of residential, commercial, and industrial properties. Although the actual analysis was nowhere as sophisticated as that done by Lichfield, the case illustrates a novel application of the concept. See: City of Sunnyvale, *Benefit System vs. Tax System of Financing Public Improvements* (Sunnyvale, California: City of Sunnyvale, 1962).

[9] The following works contain particularly good illustrations and involve investigation of a wide variety of problems, from the cost or benefit viewpoint or both: U.S., Department of Commerce, National Bureau of Standards, *Notes on the State-of-the-Art of Cost-Benefit Analysis As Related to Transportation Systems,* by Joseph D. Crumlish, Technical Note No. 294 (Washington, D.C.: Government Printing Office, 1966); Walter Isard and Robert Coughlin, *Municipal Costs and Revenues* (Wellesley, Mass.: Chandler-Davis Publishing

Company, 1957); Lichfield, *Cost-Benefit Analysis*; James C. T. Mao, "Public Urban Renewal Expenditures"; Clarence E. Ridley and Herbert A. Simon, *Measuring Municipal Activities* (2nd ed.; Chicago: International City Managers' Association, 1943); Julius Margolis, "The Demand (Benefit Measure) for Urban Public Services," in *Issues in Urban Economics*, ed. by Harvey S. Perloff and Lowdon Wingo, Jr. (Baltimore: The Johns Hopkins Press, 1968), pp. 527–65; Werner Z. Hirsch, "The Supply of Urban Public Services," in *Issues in Urban Economics*, pp. 477–525.

[10] Southern California Research Council, *The Cost of Metropolitan Growth* (Los Angeles: Southern California Research Council, 1958).

[11] Now the Fels Center of Government.

[12] For further information on the East Lansing study and the other case studies, see International City Management Association and U.S. Department of Housing and Urban Development, *Applying Systems Analysis in Urban Government: Three Case Studies* (Washington, D.C.: International City Management Association, 1972).

[13] The project also involved a training program. ICMA, TAD, and the Fels Institute held several seminars for city managers and planners to introduce them to the systems approach, systematic analysis, and some of the newer decision-aiding techniques. The case applications developed out of the initial seminar and have been used as case materials in later seminars.

[14] This is a simplification, in that the actual process is somewhat more complicated and the resultant districts are usually irregular. See, for example: Frank S. So, "Governmental and Community Facilities," in *Principles and Practice of Urban Planning*, ed. by William I. Goodman and Eric C. Freund (Washington, D.C.: International City Managers' Association, 1968), pp. 222–27; American Insurance Association, *Fire Department Standards: Distribution of Companies and Response to Alarms* (New York: American Insurance Association, 1963). The broader context of the whole problem is set by the AIS grading schedule: American Insurance Association, *Standard Schedule for Grading Cities and Towns of the United States with Reference to Their Fire Defense and Physical Conditions* (New York: American Insurance Association, 1956; Amendments, 1964).

[15] East Lansing Project Team, "East Lansing: A Facilities Location Analysis," East Lansing, Mich., 1968, p. 1. (Mimeographed.)

[16] The data collected were as follows: node number of the fire location (assigned); date, day, and hour of the fire; station first responding and distance of station from the fire; fire direction; number of persons endangered; fire cause; structure occupancy type; number of stories; year structure was built; structure fire rating; damage to structure and contents; address of fire.

[17] U.S., Department of Commerce, National Bureau of

Standards Project Team, "East Lansing Fire Station Location," Washington, D.C., 1968, p. 6. (Mimeographed.)

[18] At some point data were also used to represent continuation of existing trends, assuming the master plan might not be achieved.

[19] Estimates of future population and building construction type were obtained on the basis of expected population growth and the holding capacity of various land use areas as defined by the master plan. These figures were then substituted for present conditions in the 1975 run.

[20] The choice was not this simple, however. There were many other considerations which the model did not include and which the decision makers had to bring to bear. Among these were: the existence of mutual aid agreements; the response capability of each unit at a station; the relation of response capability to other activities of the firemen, e.g., fire prevention; and the cost-benefit of building one or more stations in relation to their effect upon the city's American Insurance Association rating.

[21] East Lansing Project Team, "A Facilities Location," p. 8.

[22] Ibid., p. 7.

[23] Ibid., p. 9.

Programming Problems: The San Francisco Housing Market Simulation Model

Following is a discussion of an illustration of the use of policy analysis on a problem of considerable complexity, belonging to that class of decision problems described in Chapter 3 as programming problems. The illustration focuses on the development of the San Francisco housing market simulation model. The model was constructed as part of that city's Community Renewal Program (CRP) study by the consultant firm of Arthur D. Little, Inc.[1]

The San Francisco model-building effort was chosen for presentation because:

1. It represents one of the most sophisticated attempts to use model-building in local government.
2. It illustrates (although in limited scope) the concepts, elements, and process of analysis described in Chapters 3 and 4.
3. It illustrates the state of the art of policy analysis and the difficulty of achieving the theoretical model of the analysis process.
4. It illustrates some of the present problems and present limitations in the conduct of policy analysis.

Although the model-building effort was part of a renewal planning project, the illustration focuses on programming rather than policy formulation. That is, the simulation model was developed primarily to assist in scheduling existing public actions over time to bring about a more effective use of public and private resources to provide for the housing needs of San Francisco's population. To some extent goals and objectives were given, although they were not operationally specified. The means of achieving goals were also given. The means were limited to those policies, programs, projects, services, and actions currently available to the city. Finally, although the CRP study and the model were developed in a long-term context (eighteen years), the action recommendations were for a mid-range time period (six years) with specific actions programmed on a year-by-year basis.

The chosen illustration is an incomplete and imperfect example of the model of the policy analysis process presented in Chapter 4. This lack of completeness is partly due to the author's lack of detailed information about various aspects of the case. However, much is due to the fact that many decisions and actions related to the case were implicit rather than explicit, representing shared understandings rather than formal agreements, and were based on intuition, judgment, and experience rather than on formal analysis. These conditions are often simply facts of life in dealing with problems of such complexity. But they are also a result of the failure of the analysts to be concerned with "process" because of overemphasis on the particular problem being solved. It is likely that the social histories of studies such as the San Francisco CRP may be more instructive and useful to the conduct of future analyses than the models and the results of the studies themselves. This conclusion seems warranted because current understanding of the urban system is so limited, because existing methods of representing it are inadequate and incomplete at best, and because policy analysis is still more art than science.

The illustration is incomplete also because the model-building effort was limited to evaluation of alternative courses of action for one part (housing) of a larger problem (community renewal programming). Further, the evaluation model and process were incomplete in that the model was limited to forecasting consequences of the alternatives largely in terms of their impacts on the private housing market. The model could not be used to provide cost and benefit comparison of the alternatives, or any other comparison which would help the decision makers to choose among various courses of action. These analyses had to be conducted outside the model itself; but, as it turned out, they were not developed. Despite these limitations, the process of developing the CRP model illustrates much that is instructive about policy analysis.

THE SAN FRANCISCO HOUSING MARKET MODEL

The background
The Housing Act of 1959 established the Community Renewal Program as a new device in urban renewal planning and programming. Previously, local governments typically attacked renewal problems on a project-by-project basis, looking at only one aspect of their overall problem at a time. As a result, traditional renewal activity was often inconclusive, inadequate, and, at times, harmful. Through the CRP, however, local governments were to focus their efforts on achieving a broader and more coordinated approach to renewal. They were to combine many of their existing programs with some new tools and programs and plan them in an integrated manner on a time-phased, priority basis. Moreover, both public and private actions were to be coordinated on a city-wide basis. That is, the underlying philosophy of the CRP (and earlier renewal programs) was that a city should be able to provide for its housing needs through

actions of the private sector, limiting public actions to those which would facilitate private efforts.

All of this assumed that planners, administrators, urbanologists, and others knew considerably more than they did about the urban system and about ways of representing it which would be helpful to the development of such comprehensive and integrated programs. Planners, and others who were aware of the limitations in knowledge and methodology, felt that a key weakness lay in the inability of conventional methods of data analysis and forecasting to identify and measure accurately the consequences of various public and private actions on the urban system. It was impossible, with conventional methods, to allow for the fact that actions aimed at one part of the environment affect other parts, that programs aimed at physical environment often affect the social environment, that programs aimed at one geographical area affect other areas, and that planning aimed at short-term goals affects the long-term equilibrium.

A combination of developments in the early sixties seemed to offer a way of improving planning methodology so that such interrelations might be tractable. Among these were: the increased computational capacity of computers; the 1960 census, which made available a large data base on urban housing and population characteristics; the acquisition of skills and techniques in model-building from such fields as operations research, management science, and economics; and a better understanding of the key factors determining land use patterns in urban areas. These developments gradually led

to a number of projects in which large-scale analysis and model-building were employed in an attempt to simulate the operations and interactions of a mass of variables relevant to planning and the urban system. The first major effort of this type was in conjunction with the Penn-Jersey Transportation Study;[2] it was followed by models developed for renewal planning in Boston,[3] Pittsburgh,[4] and San Francisco.

The San Francisco CRP effort, like the others, involved more than simply model-building. The modeling effort was conducted in conjunction with other CRP studies, methods, and activities and was to be employed primarily as a means of testing the impacts of various action programs which would be developed by more conventional methods. Nevertheless, it is the modeling effort which is the major focus of this case illustration.

The problem
The overall objective addressed by the San Francisco CRP effort was the development of a comprehensive, integrated program of public and private actions aimed at improving the living environment of the city. A central problem in doing this was to develop some way of accounting for the effects of each individual action on the community environment. That is, a coordinated action program could be developed only when the combined effects of separate policies and actions were understood. Such understanding could be achieved only if the whole problem were conceived in such a way that the individual parts could fit into some logical framework which would represent the system under study.[5] This realization by the city's planners and the consultants led to the idea of constructing such

a framework or a model. As stated by the consultants:

The fundamental objective of the CRP is its programming function, that is, the establishment of a schedule of actions, both private and public, on a time phased basis. Such programming requires an overall view of the system being programmed—that is, the City and its interrelated elements—so that the renewal planners can have reference at all times to the state of the system and to the changes in that state which will be occasioned by individual program actions. The systems concept, utilizing a mathematical model adapted to electronic computers, offers the most promising method of dealing with the complexities involved.[6]

Initially, a model-building program was considered that would comprehend the entire spectrum of city processes related to renewal planning and programming. After some discussion, it was decided to concentrate the effort on development of a model of the housing market. One reason for this focus was the limited knowledge and methodology mentioned previously. Another was the massiveness of even this limited task. Most important, however, was the fact that housing was regarded by law and tradition as the key target of renewal action.[7] Further, preliminary analyses of population and housing trends in San Francisco indicated that the city faced severe problems of housing its people, and these problems would be exacerbated if projected trends continued.[8]

Thus, the problem addressed by the model-building effort was that of developing a framework which could be used to "test the effects of various public policy programs upon the supply of housing in the city—quantity, quality, general location, rents, prices, etc.,—in relation to the demand for that housing."[9]

Implicit in this statement of the problem were two other statements:

1. That a key objective of the CRP was to achieve some kind of adjustment between the needs of the city's people for housing and that housing which the private sector would normally provide. The adjustment mechanism was government action. That is, government was to stimulate the private sector to provide needed housing; or, if this were not possible, to provide housing directly through public action. Thus, the aim was to achieve some kind of overall balance in total housing supply and demand. However, "balance" was not defined.

2. Because balance was not defined, the model would be constructed and used as an instrument for hypothesis testing. In other words, if the city officials had certain housing objectives, and if alternative action programs directed towards these objectives could be developed, then the model could be used to project the consequences of these hypothetical public action programs on the housing market and, thereby, on the character of the housing supply. The model output, then, would be a statement of the change in the housing stock effected by each set of government actions. When compared with housing demand, this statement would help the decision makers[10] to obtain some idea of the balance that could be achieved between supply and demand. However, it would not tell them what level of achievement to choose. For this purpose an estimate of the costs and benefits of achieving balance would be needed. This estimate would have to consider the economic costs and benefits to govern-

ment, the social and economic costs and benefits to various groups in the community, the political costs and benefits to various decision makers, and similar valuations. In short, the kind of analysis conducted by Lichfield for the Old Mint case (see Chapter 5) would be required, but on a much larger scale. Even then, as in the Old Mint case, the judgment and intuition of the decision makers would be required to evaluate many of these considerations and to choose a course of action. The planners and model-builders (hereafter referred to as analysts)[11] were aware of these limitations but felt that constructing the model was the best they could do and was considerably more than had been done in the past.

The analysis

Selection of an approach. The first task facing the analysts was selection of an approach to the problem. Each of the major models built previously had focused on some key element(s) as the prime determinant in the system under study and each had been built for some specific setting and immediate need.

In the case of San Francisco, our philosophy [approach] was established through consideration of the actions which it was feasible for a city government to take. Although an appreciable fraction of the total area of the United States is owned by the Federal, State and Local governments, the majority of urban area ownership is in private hands and is subject to only limited control. A city can effect zoning laws, restricting the type of construction which can take place in given localities; it can exert varying degrees of building code enforcement; it can build parks, roads, and other amenities; [etc.]. . . . However, the large majority of actions affecting a city's stock of housing will still be controlled by the activities of the many individual owners of property. Under these conditions, it seemed most appropriate to consider the operations of this private market in detail. Possible activities undertaken by the city government could then be studied in terms of their influence on the private market in an effort to determine the extent to which public activity can provide leverage to move the over-all system in a desirable direction.

This approach was based on the particular circumstances facing the City of San Francisco. It is obviously not the only possible approach, and it may not be the best approach for all cities. . . . For the moment we are at a point where considerable variety is necessary, and each model must be tailored to immediate needs.[12]

Constructing a framework. The task of analysis, then, was to develop a framework which adequately replicated the operation of the private housing market and the effects of public intervention in it. To do this, the analysts needed some sort of theory which would help them determine which elements of the housing market were most important and, of these, what the interactions were among them. They borrowed market structure generalizations from economics, in particular from the theory of the market for urban land.[13] However, additional hypothesis testing and development were required to select operating characteristics or rules for the decision-making variables replicated within the model. These operating characteristics were symbolically expressed to replicate the behavioral and economic motivations of the decision makers who interact in the real world housing market. These operating characteristics were determined by empirical research.

Thus, by bringing together existing theory and empirical research, the analysts developed a

theoretical or conceptual framework which represented the structure and functioning of the key elements in the San Francisco housing market as illustrated in Figure 6–1. The elements were basically four: the housing stock, or supply of housing; households, or demand for housing; investors, sellers, or suppliers of housing;[14] and government actions (e.g., code enforcement, urban renewal, tax policy, zoning, etc.).[15]

The basic interaction in the housing market was postulated as that between households and investors. The interaction was over the price (rent) of various kinds of housing in various locations. At any given time, the supply of housing could be described in terms of its key characteristics relevant to the market. Similarly, households could be described in terms of characteristics relevant to their preference for one type of housing versus another and by a price (rent) budget. Finally, investors or sellers could be described as preferring the highest possible price (rent) for their housing units.

Thus, various households seeking various types of housing would come together in the market and engage in price competition for the available housing supply. Transactions would be negotiated between buyers and sellers, and the sellers would choose the highest bidders. Some people, usually those who could pay what the traffic warranted, would get what they wanted. Others would have to sacrifice quality, location, or some other preference in order to meet the market price. Some people simply would not find what they wanted or could pay for in the market. At any rate, all of these transactions would result in a modification of where people lived and under

what conditions (housing and housing-related conditions).

This, then, was the basic set of interactions in the framework—that between buyers and sellers. However, another set of interactions had to be considered—that which explained how changes in the privately produced supply of housing came about. The idea was that changes in the amount or quality of housing occurred when households, because of an increase in their number or in their ability to pay, created a pressure for certain types of housing. In time, a high pressure would cause prices (rents) to rise. Investors or suppliers of housing would then evaluate this condition. If making a change would be financially profitable, investors would change the supply of housing to meet the pressure of demand. Profitability would be determined by comparing the cost of making the change with the anticipated future yield.

If changes were made, new housing units (of a type to meet demand and to bring profits) would be added to the city's housing stock and a number of older units subtracted from the stock to make way for the new ones. The housing changes would also result in changes in total construction investment and assessed value in the city.

This was the second set of interactions in the framework. The first and second together represented a basic cycle which was repeated over and over in the housing market and which largely determined who got what housing at what price, when new investment would be made, and what the overall quality and quantity of the housing supply would be. Each cycle represented some time span (two years was used).

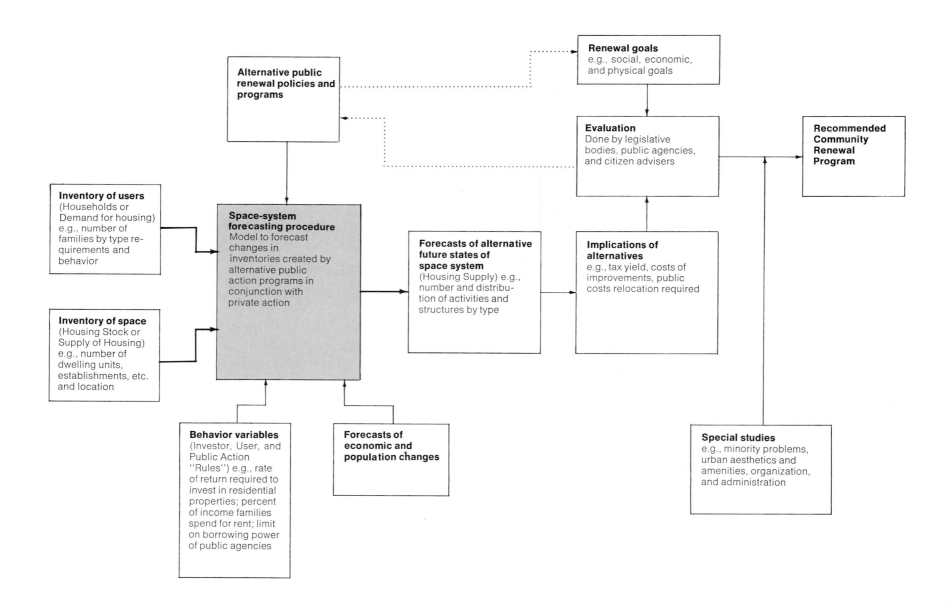

During that time, a number of changes could occur independent of, but not unrelated to, the basic interactions. Overall population could increase or decrease and change in character, older housing could become obsolescent, and the conditions under which investors would invest and buyers buy could have changed. Therefore, these and similar external factors had to be considered at each cycle, and they modified the basic interactions.

This, then, is a simplified version of the conceptual framework used by the model-builders to account for how the housing market operated without public intervention. However, government can and does intervene. Through various public action programs and policies, government may affect the market by interfering with, influencing, or controlling its operation.[16] This, in fact, was the whole point of the model: to account for the effects of government intervention so that, by various public actions, the market could be controlled (either directly or indirectly) to affect the relation between housing demand and supply. The next step in developing the framework was to indicate the relations between various public actions and the other elements of the model.

Figure 6-1. Type of conceptual framework developed to simulate the key elements in the San Francisco housing market and to postulate interrelation with the policy-making process. Adapted from: Cyril C. Herrmann, "Systems Approach to City Planning," *Harvard Business Review*, XLIV (September-October 1966), 74-75.

Figure 6–2 indicates some of the relationships investigated. This task involved developing rules that specified the impact of particular actions on the character and quality of the housing stock (for example, how capital improvements and city services affected the quality of the neighborhood environment; how code enforcement affected housing quality), on households (how rent supplements affected household budgets), and on investors (how tax abatement affected the cost of taxes; how land clearance affected the cost of land). When this was accomplished by the analysts, the framework was complete.

Constructing a model. The foregoing description is the conceptual framework used to describe the operation of the San Francisco housing market. When this framework was operationalized and translated into a computer program it became a computer model.[17] Constructing the model meant that each of the elements had to be specified in terms of some operating characteristics and all of the input elements empirically measured. It also meant that each of the various interactions had to be started in all of its complexity using all of the rules that had been developed to describe the various behaviors postulated. It further meant that since it was not feasible to describe each individual housing unit or the characteristics and behavior of each household or each investor, some way of aggregating the elements had to be found.

Getting numbers for the model. The next task, after specifying the elements of the model, was to gather the data which described the things to which the elements referred. Suffice it to say that between 12,000 and 15,000 items of

input data were used for each run of the model. Each run was a nine-period simulation of the housing market—each period representing two years for a total eighteen-year forecast. The majority of these data did not change from one run to the next, so they could be used repeatedly. Since any single run represented a different set of government actions, the data representing these actions were the major changed input data.

Theoretical use of the model. Use of the model depended upon the existence of alternative policies and their implementing action programs. These would be prepared independently of the model by conventional methods. Then, each alternative course of action would be fed into the model along with certain information representing existing and projected conditions about housing supply, consumers, and investors. The model would operate on these inputs in a way that simulated the operation of housing market processes. It would output information that represented the outcome of the particular alternative under the basic conditions assumed. Each different alternative would require a separate run of the model.

In addition, a base run under the assumed basic conditions but without the chosen public interventions would be required. Once completed, this run would be compared with numerous alternatives. The purpose of the base and intervention runs would be to determine whether public intervention achieved better results than no intervention. The purpose of running alternative courses of action, of course, would be to have some basis for comparing outcomes in order to determine which intervention alternative

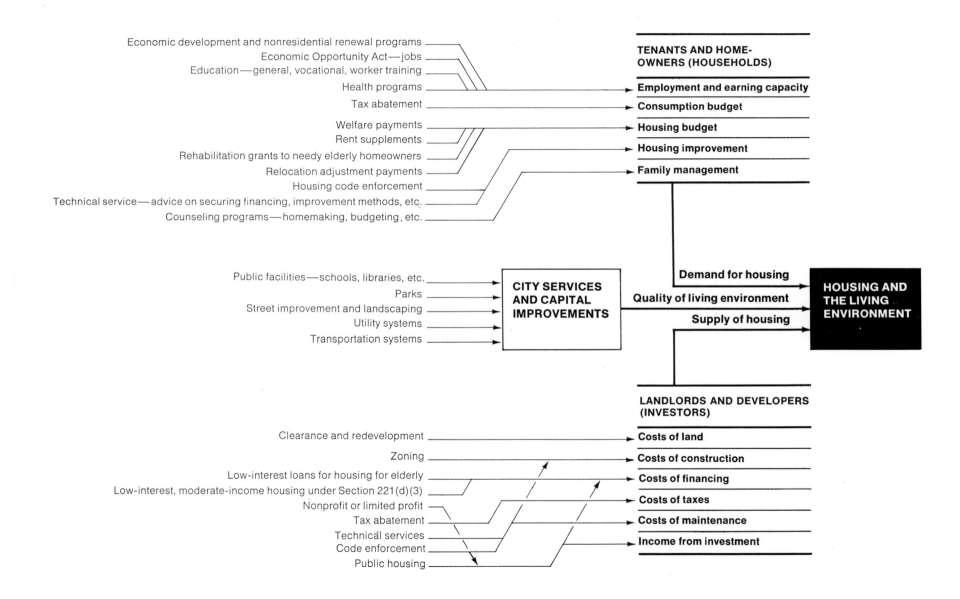

Economic development and nonresidential renewal programs

Economic Opportunity Act—jobs

Education—general, vocational, worker training

Health programs

Tax abatement

Welfare payments

Rent supplements

Rehabilitation grants to needy elderly homeowners

Relocation adjustment payments

Housing code enforcement

Technical service—advice on securing financing, improvement methods, etc.

Counseling programs—homemaking, budgeting, etc.

TENANTS AND HOME-OWNERS (HOUSEHOLDS)

Employment and earning capacity

Consumption budget

Housing budget

Housing improvement

Family management

Public facilities—schools, libraries, etc.

Parks

Street improvement and landscaping

Utility systems

Transportation systems

CITY SERVICES AND CAPITAL IMPROVEMENTS

Demand for housing

Quality of living environment

Supply of housing

HOUSING AND THE LIVING ENVIRONMENT

LANDLORDS AND DEVELOPERS (INVESTORS)

Clearance and redevelopment

Zoning

Low-interest loans for housing for elderly

Low-interest, moderate-income housing under Section 221(d)(3)

Nonprofit or limited profit

Tax abatement

Technical services

Code enforcement

Public housing

Costs of land

Costs of construction

Costs of financing

Costs of taxes

Costs of maintenance

Income from investment

was better. However, the outcomes would have to be compared by the decision makers, who would bring judgment and intuition to bear in an effort to choose one alternative. Figure 6–3 illustrates the model use procedure.

Actual use of the model. The model was not finished in time to assist directly in the development of specific renewal plans and programs. Thus, in a sense, the model made no major direct contribution to the planning process.[18] However, indirectly the thinking and work involved in producing the model contributed immensely to the decision processes of the analysts. The very process of constructing the model forced the analysts to make their assumptions explicit, to clarify their thinking, to search for insight into the key factors at work in the housing market, and to continually check their hypotheses and assertions by reference to the real world. Even before the model was completed, then, it provided a framework for discussion and debate. As such, it was of great value as an aid to the judgments that the professional city planners had to make in completing the CRP study.

In addition, the model was used to verify the plans, which of necessity had been prepared by

Figure 6-2. How public services and improvement programs influence housing and the living environment. Adapted from: Herrmann, "Systems Approach to City Planning," 79.

more conventional means.[19] The run used to verify the recommended Community Renewal Program is described below.

Because the model's strength lay in its ability to suggest the relative impact of public actions, two runs were required for verification: one with and one without public intervention.[20] The base run (without intervention) assumed a continually increasing population slightly higher than the target population listed in the CRP report and with a somewhat higher income distribution, and it simulated only those public actions, including zoning and renewal projects, that were already in force or approved. The public intervention run was identical to the base run, except that it included a simulation of the types of code enforcement, zoning, clearance, and public housing actions that were recommended in the CRP report. The public actions were simulated to test the efficacy of the recommended Community Renewal Program on the housing market (that is, the program's ability to promote additional private improvement in the quality of housing available to San Francisco).[21]

In general, the results of the verification run lent support to the housing-related recommendations of the Community Renewal Program. Specifically, after much interpretation and evaluation of the computer output, the following were among the major findings:[22]

1. If the population income distribution projected proved an accurate forecast, then the private sector of the economy would be capable of providing most of the new housing needed without public intervention. That is, population was expected to increase by 16

percent between 1960 and 1978, and the model output indicated that the private housing market would increase net housing by a corresponding 14 percent over the same period. Public intervention would not increase net housing over nonintervention (see Table 6–1).

2. While the net increase in the number of housing units did not differ significantly in the two runs, there was a significant difference in the number of substandard units in the housing inventory (see item 3, below, and Table 6–2).

3. The overall effect of the CRP was to encourage some 5,000 units to be upgraded from substandard to standard housing. During Periods 3 through 6, although the total number of housing units was increasing in both runs, the public action run indicated that the recommended code enforcement program would *reduce* the number of substandard units by approximately 9 percent, while the nonintervention run *increased* the number of substandard units by 3 percent.

4. Comparison of private investment in the two runs indicated that code enforcement would encourage a private investment in rehabilitation at a rate 40 percent higher than it would be without such a program (see Table 6–3).

Subsequent development of the simulation model

In 1965 the CRP study and modeling effort came to an end. However, the performance of the model was judged sufficiently promising by the San Francisco Department of City Planning to warrant further development aimed at bringing it to a more fully operational status. In August 1966 work was begun on several areas of improve-

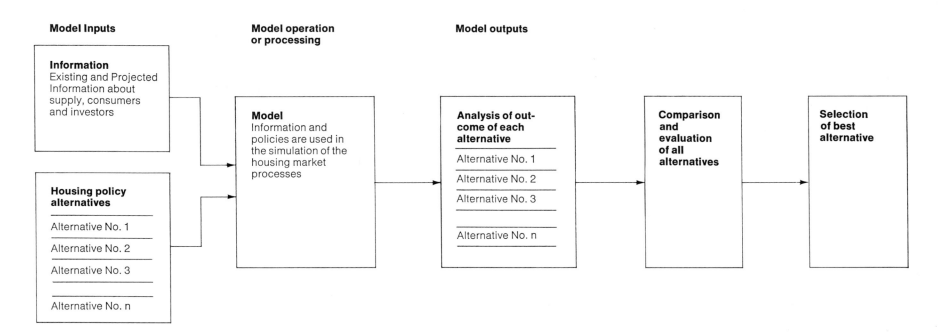

Figure 6-3. Procedure for use of San Francisco housing model. Source: San Francisco Department of City Planning, *Status of the San Francisco Simulation Model* **(San Francisco: Department of City Planning, 1968), p. 3.**

ment: simplifying the vast amount of detail in the model, shortening the operating time (from two hours to one hour), making the data input operation simpler, improving the readability of the output, and changing the basic neighborhood unit to the generally used Census Tract.[23]

Following these improvements, work was done to evaluate the mechanical operation, reliability, and utility of the model. It was concluded that, while mechanical operation was satisfactory, the model had not yet proven to be a reliable simulation and was cumbersome to use and understand. As a result, the planning department recommended that "further operations with the model be terminated at this time in the interest of other work programs of the Department."[24] However, other recommendations were made: (1) to begin collecting data which could be used to update and improve the model; and (2) to seek funds for further improvement work at some later date.[25]

COMMENTS ON MODEL-BUILDING AND POLICY ANALYSIS

The CRP model-building effort illustrates a number of problems encountered in policy analysis and in developing models to assist the analysis. It also illustrates the limitations and possibilities of such models once devised. Some of these problems, limitations, and possibilities will be discussed here.

The clientele and problem formulation

I don't want to know a God Damn thing about the future. I can't take that stuff into the future until I understand where the hell I am . . . that bit about the consequences of your decisions, that the model will tell you policy decisions, is three-quarters bull shit. . . . I just want to understand my world and the hell with the model. . . . [But] no, they didn't do that. They had to have a big God Damn model.

> City Official
> San Francisco, California
> Personal Interview, July 22, 1969[26]

Although the language of some of the official reports suggests that the CRP model was developed for the top political and administrative decision makers in San Francisco, in reality it was developed for professional city planners. The problem addressed by the model was formulated by the city's and the consultant's planners—not by the planning commission, the administrative leaders of the city, or the city's elected officials. As a result, the problem stated was essentially a technical one and that statement had much to do with the choice of a model-

ing approach. It was the renewal planner's problem that was being solved, by planners and model-builders, with the planners' assumptions and rationale.

What is important about the San Francisco case is not that the planners—and not the board of supervisors or someone else—were the client. It is that whoever is considered by the analysts to be the "decision makers" (client) fundamentally influences the whole process of analysis. This determines how the decision problem will be stated, whose objectives will be sought, which alternatives will be considered, how evaluation will be conducted, what choices will be made, and which actions will be implemented.

The importance of this point cannot be overestimated for a number of reasons:

1. The question of who is the client is in large part a question about the decision latitude being assumed. If the city planner is the client his decision latitude is considerably more limited and constrained than that of the city council, for example. If the client is the council, they, too, are constrained, but in different ways from the planner. Further, while the planner may be able to approximate the council's objective latitude (legal, financial, jurisdictional, and similar constraints), he cannot interpret its subjective latitude—that is, which objective constraints the council feels it can change and which it must accept. This is difficult even for the council to decide.

In the CRP study, for example, the consultants assumed the jurisdiction of the city of San Francisco as the system boundary. It

Table 6-1. San Francisco Community Renewal Program estimate of increase in households and in net dwelling units between 1960 and 1978. Source: Arthur D. Little, Inc., *Model of the San Francisco Housing Market* (San Francisco: Arthur D. Little, Inc., 1966), p. 41.

Period	Exogenous household increase (%)	Dwelling unit increase: base run (%)	Dwelling unit increase: public action run (%)
1960–62	1[1]	1.75	2.24	2.24
1962–64	2[1]	3.50	4.80	4.80
1964–66	3[1]	5.25	7.62	7.62
1966–68	4	7.00	9.81	9.84
1968–70	5	8.75	10.93	11.19
1970–72	6	10.50	12.40	12.57
1972–74	7[1]	12.25	13.33	13.21
1974–76	8[1]	14.00	13.74	13.63
1976–78	9[1]	15.75	14.22	14.36

[1] Note that the base run and public action runs were identical in terms of the public actions that had been programmed into the computer before Period 4 and after Period 6. Thus the first and last three periods indicate a simulation of the results that follow a cessation of the additional (Community Renewal Program) public actions that were simulated in the public action runs during Periods 4, 5, and 6.

Table 6-2. Condition of structures in San Francisco community renewal surveys in 1966 and 1972. Source: Little, *San Francisco Housing Market*, p. 42.

| | Period 3 (1966) | | Period 6 (1972) | | | |
| | | | Base run | | Public actions run | |
	Number of units	Percent	Number of units	Percent	Number of units	Percent
Condition 1[1]	118,774	37.2	131,714	39.6	137,132	41.1
2[1]	163,388	51.2	163,584	49.0	163,680	49.0
3[2]	24,690	7.7	21,822	6.6	18,046	5.4
4[2]	12,232	3.8	16,124	4.8	14,908	4.5
Total	319,084	100.0	333,244	100.0	333,766	100.0
Substandard (Conditions 3 and 4)	36,922	11.5	37,946	11.4	32,954	9.7

[1] Standard [2] Substandard

Table 6-3. Simulation model of private market residential investment in San Francisco found in the two runs (millions of dollars). Source: Little, *San Francisco Housing Market*, p. 43.

| | Base run | | | Public action run[1] | | |
Periods	New construction	Rehabilitation	Total	New construction	Rehabilitation	Total
1–3	457.8	118.2	576.0	457.8	118.2	576.0
4–6	450.3	89.9	540.2	450.6	124.9	545.5
7–9[1]	279.7	71.4	351.1	262.2	46.4	308.6

[1] No Community Renewal Program in public action run

is possible (though perhaps not probable) that if the board of supervisors had been aware of the limitations set by this choice of boundary the board would have opted for the metropolitan region as the study boundary and would have initiated action to secure an organizational capacity to deal with the housing problem at this level. (See the discussion on pages 71–72.)

2. Generally, analysts (model-builders, planners, other professionals, etc.) do not face problems as other decision makers must face them. They tend to ignore two things. First, they ignore many decision options which other decision makers would regard as important. Second, in considering this limited set of options they fail to consider many pros and cons that these other decision makers cannot ignore. Two obvious illustrations in the CRP study are political cost and benefit and the preference of whites, particularly lower income families, for segregated housing.

3. The latter illustration suggests another point. The expression "the decision makers" is misleading at best. *The* decision makers are not only political leaders and government professionals. They are the householders, the investors, the landlords, the businessmen, and all others who importantly affect whether decisions made at one level will be translated into the actions which higher level decision assumes or specifies. For example, the CRP study noted that one of the barriers to improvement of the living environment was limited concern for housing quality:

Census information indicates that many occupants of low-rental housing pay a relatively low proportion of their income for rent. A significant number of these occupants probably could increase their rent to obtain standard housing and still not suffer financial hardship. The reason they do not is . . . that many people have limited concern for the quality of the physical environment and hence may pay comparatively little for housing. This limited concern hinders a continued improvement of the housing stock.[27]

Elsewhere, a study recommendation says that code enforcement should be used as a means of housing improvement in neighborhoods where, among other considerations, "Present tenants can afford to pay higher rents to sustain adequate maintenance."[28] In other words, the analysts noted that some low-income renters spent proportionately less of their income for housing than did other low- and other-income renters. They implicitly decided (for these people) that these people could afford to pay more and also decided that the value of the housing improvements brought about by code enforcement were worth the higher rentals which would result. Thus, the policy recommendation assumes that the householders in question will see the error of their ways and spend a higher proportion of their income than previously for an improved housing stock. They may; but then, again, they may not.

The implication of this example is that the analysts need to be aware of the fact that various decision makers value things differently and that these valuations may be contrary to their own valuations or their inferences about the valuations of others.

In addition to sharpening their own awareness about such valuations, the analysts need to increase that of the decision makers whose responsibility it is to decide for others.

4. The foregoing point intentionally implies that everyone is a decision maker. In any particular instance, however, many people affected by actions which flow from higher level decisions have no real decision power of their own. For a variety of practical reasons they are unable to exercise whatever influence they have, whether that influence is a vote or a bid in the rental market. Nevertheless, the analysts and decision makers must consider these people if they are serious about analyzing the impacts of public decision and action. Here, perhaps, the analyst is justified in speculating about valuations. But, whether he can speculate or not, he can project what the impacts will be and on whom they will fall.

Selection of a system boundary
The analysts chose the legal-jurisdictional territory of the city of San Francisco[29] as the boundary of the system under study. They felt that the nature of the assignment dictated this choice.

Our charter for work applied to the City of San Francisco only, and we could not legitimately devote significant effort—or count on necessary assistance—in analyzing the region surrounding the city.[30]

However, they also felt that this circumstance was an unfortunate one because it meant that many important factors influencing the future of the city had to be treated as beyond the control of the decision makers. These factors were the result of metropolitan or regional forces, and forces beyond the region itself.

What this meant to the analysis effort was that these outside forces had to be handled by analyses outside the main model, or input to the

model as limitations, constraints, or forces limiting what the decision makers could decide. It meant, for example, that if the decision makers chose to make any substantial improvement in the quality of low-cost housing within the city, this could immediately result in a migration of low-income families from nearby surrounding areas. The movement of population into the city already consisted mainly of low-income families and was increasing. At the time of the study, more than 20 percent of the population of San Francisco was nonwhite. At the same time, there was a substantial movement of middle-income, largely white, families to the suburbs. Thus, improving the quality of low-income housing, an avowed aim of renewal efforts and one of concern to the city planners, meant a likelihood of increasing the city's proportion of low-income, nonwhite families, and the concomitant social and economic costs associated therewith. In essence, it pointed to the possibility that the central city (San Francisco) would increasingly have to bear the costs (political, social, economic) of providing for this population without the additional resources required to do so. The surrounding cities, which had the resources, would be relieved of the problem. In terms of broad social policy, this signified the likelihood of further increasing the segregation between blacks and whites, the split between central city and suburbs, and the uneven distribution of burden or costs and of resources.

Thus, if the boundaries had been set at the level of the whole region, in theory, at least, all major factors could be accounted for in the model. However, in practice it may have made little difference, for there was no single governmental entity at this level with the necessary powers to act or to induce the cities of the region to act on whatever regional policies might be decided. As a result, plans developed for the suitable political unit (the city) would be greatly weakened by what they left out, while plans developed for the natural social unit (the region) could not be implemented because of a lack of political cohesiveness.

This dilemma is typical of what analysts and decision makers alike face in setting the boundaries of the system to be studied. In some cases they have no choice but to live with the situation and to recognize it as an important barrier to the development of solutions. In other cases it may be argued that these limitations are so great that, before any analysis can be done, arrangements must be made for dealing with the organizational barriers to effective decision and action.

It should be noted that these problems do not occur only at the level of cities and metropolitan areas or regions. They also occur within the government organization itself, among agencies or departments or among these agencies and their subunits. Thus, the organizational setting in which analysis occurs has a significant impact on the possibility of conducting analysis and using its results. Therefore, the organizational context of a problem is as much a part of any analysis as are the substantive and intellectual issues surrounding the problem. Unless this fact is recognized and steps are taken during the process of analysis to handle these organizational factors, the likelihood of achieving concerted action aimed at improvement is seriously limited.

Finally, these organizational factors should not be viewed, as they often are by analysts, as perverse conditions which limit what can be done. They are in fact part of the real world conditions in which decision and action must take place. As such, they are subject to analysis and solution in the same way as the conditions surrounding substantive issues. If these organizational constraints are recognized and handled, the effort may well lead to more simplified and effective solution of the substantive issues which generate the whole analysis activity. In practical terms, this means that the types of analysts selected to work on a problem should often include not only model-builders and experts in the issue areas involved, but also organizational and behavioral scientists who understand the social and institutional context in which decision is arrived at and action eventually carried out.

Goals, objectives, and criteria

The goals and objectives of the CRP effort and its model-building component were discussed earlier in the Problem section (see pages 61–62). The purpose of establishing goals is to provide some basis for developing criteria for choosing among the alternatives in terms of their relative contribution to goal achievement. This is a difficult task. The city is a complex social organism with a wide mixture of goals which are often inconsistent and contradictory as expressed by the inhabitants. Furthermore, the political representatives may not be of much help. As two of the CRP model-builders have put it:

The political authorities for whom the work is being performed tend to be rather incoherent when discussing this subject [goals]; most typically they talk at a level of generality which is analytically meaningless, and one that all too often incorporates severe internal contradictions.[31]

In such cases, what does the analyst do? In the San Francisco CRP, the model-builders described their approach as "one of *avoidance*" [italics mine.]:[32]

We believe this tactic is sound both conceptually and in practice. Our model was developed to study the *implications* of possible civic actions, but did not aim to incorporate judgment as to which of a given set of implications was most desirable. We regard this general problem of goals and objectives as an educational problem, and one in which simulation models can play a most important role. Once sets of implications resulting from different feasible civic actions are made available to the political authorities, they must be forced to make the final evaluations; this is both their right and their responsibility. The very process of examining the implications of feasible civic actions and then making a selection will, in itself, assist in the development of a rationale from which goals and objectives may eventually be defined and subjected to analysis. At present, there are too few mechanisms for determining the feasibility of achievement of apparently desirable objectives, and thereby restricting those examined to a meaningful set; this process must be the starting point, and was one toward which our work was directed.[33]

In essence, they were saying that "if the city has certain housing objectives or needs, then the model would project what the consequences of public policies and public and private actions would be in relation to those objectives or needs."[34] This is a deceptively simple and logical statement. It implies that the diversity of interests involved can be formulated as a single public interest (i.e., if the city had certain housing objectives). More importantly, it suggests that the structure of the model accounts for the major factors involved in rational choice among alternative courses of action. But what kind of rationality does the model structure represent? Basically, it is economic rationality. The model simulates the existing structure and functioning of the urban housing market and economic behavior in it. The outputs of the model are largely the economic consequences of alternative public actions. This is not unimportant, and is considerably more information than is usually available to decision makers. Further, by using this information judgments can be made about the broader social implications of one alternative versus another. But this is the point: these social implications must be supplied by the decision makers (or other analysts) and so must any political implications which may derive from either economic or social consequences. Thus, of what use is the model to the political decision makers? The answer, presently, is very little or none. This should not be surprising, for, as the model-builders suggest, the model was not built for these people. It was built for professional city planners, by other planners and model-builders, with the planners' objectives and rationality in mind.[35]

It is clear that planners and other government professionals need such tools to improve the basis for their recommendations to political and top administrative decision makers. However, if these tools of the professionals ignore the political, social, and organizational realities which other decision makers cannot ignore, then the professionals should not be surprised if their plans are not accepted, or, if they are accepted in principle as a good thing, are never carried to fruition.

One implication of these facts for political and top managerial decision makers is that if model-building — or any other part of an analysis effort — is to serve their needs, they must be heavily involved in the whole process. Another implication is that, given the limited state of the art, sophisticated tools such as the CRP model may be less effective from the nonprofessional's standpoint than simpler tools or more conventional ones would be.

Presently, the ability to handle problems with technique can be characterized by three realms. In the first realm lie a small number of simple problems in which solutions are known or easily derived by a relatively straightforward application of technique. In the third realm lie a small number of extremely complex and insoluble problems in which technique is probably almost useless. In between these two realms lie the vast majority of problems which local governments face and for which little technique exists, or in which technique may be only of partial aid in arriving at solutions. Given this state of affairs it seems likely that the most important thing that can be done is to establish a close dialogue between the decision maker and the analyst through which each gains the benefit of the other's perspective and in which each acts as the protagonist of the other's viewpoint. In the debate which ensues and continues, information developed from detailed analyses may be brought to bear. However, now it is not the information, the detailed analyses, or the models used to create the information that is important, but it is the continuing debate between decision makers and analysts. If this sounds like Churchman's statement about *the* systems approach, which has been discussed here earlier, in Chapter 3 (see page 21), it should, because the point is the same.

Selection of a modeling approach
As indicated earlier, the housing market model was confined to the city of San Francisco and was tailored to that city's environment. Therefore, with the exception of the conceptual framework, few aspects of the model can be transferred directly to another city. This limitation characterizes most of the large urban and regional models developed in the United States. At present there is no easy way of extending, improving, and broadening the applicability of these models. As a result, we are developing a library of computer programs built at great expense but with limited potential usage.

One way of handling this problem is to greatly simplify the whole modeling operation. In essence, the idea is that instead of building one massive model which encompasses the totality of some system, one should build a series of smaller models — a family of models — each dealing with some aspect of the overall problem.[36] The links between the models can then be made manually, or they can be programmed to fit the specific environment modeled. This is essentially a modular approach and is one which greatly increases the possibility of transferring at least part of the family of models to other situations.

Another approach is to engage in research and development specifically aimed at development and application of generalized models useful for many cities. These may be of the massive simulation type, or families of models. In either case the effort would be divorced from the need to produce plans in some specific environment on a time schedule geared to other operations. While specific cities would be used as reference points for hypothesis-testing, data collection, and verification of the models, the environment and the model's characteristics would be independent for any single city. If the family of models notion were utilized, as one moved down the hierarchy from the general to the specific there could be provision for simulation or other replication in the context of a specific environment.

Models and reality
One of the problems frequently encountered in modeling efforts is that the model-builders themselves come to believe that the model represents reality. And, consciously or unconsciously, they tend to convey this impression to the unwitting decision makers. For example, Wolfe and Ernst speak of the San Francisco model as reproducing "in an abstracted form the *actual* [italics mine] interrelationships that occur, or might occur, in the market for land and building space in the city."[37] Elsewhere they speak of the model as a teacher. In general terms they say:

In each run there are apt to be certain "surprising" results. Most of these can be explained rapidly, almost by inspection—one looks and says, "I never thought about it that way, but the result does make sense." A smaller fraction of these surprises take rather elaborate tracing of the logical relationships to determine the interactions which were responsible. This process in itself is both educational and rewarding,

and in almost all cases the explanation for the unusual results contributed significantly to an understanding of the processes at work.[38]

More specifically they state:

The model has had enormous educational impact. The first evidence of this impact was on the participants in its development themselves. For example, the young junior planner assigned by the City of San Francisco to the project acquired a level of knowledge and understanding of the operation of the city which has led to his receiving a promotion and rapid growth in status. In fact, although he is still responsible for liaison with regard to the model he has become very difficult to talk to—simply because the knowledge he has acquired has made him almost invaluable for handling a host of matters in other areas which are the concern of the City Planning Department. His participation in the model has greatly improved his status in a valid way—by providing him a unique experience and fund of knowledge which has wide-spread utility.[39]

Models are analogies. They are, at best, an incomplete, coarse, and crude representation of the thing being modeled. Yet there is an almost universal tendency to suppose that a model, once built or formulated, is more than it is. Further, models do not teach us anything. At most, by following the exact steps we have programmed into them, they produce results which may show up fallacies in our thinking about a problem. However, if the same thinking that goes into trying to figure out "surprising results" went into the construction of the model, the surprising results would not occur, or at least they would not be surprising.[40]

This comment is less a criticism of the quoted statements than an attempt to suggest that

decision makers should approach model-builders, their models, and their results with some skepticism. Critical questioning of assumptions and results by decision makers will aid in sharpening their own thinking and that of the analysts who serve them.

Understanding the limitations of models
Related to the previous point, one of the most difficult things for decision makers to understand is the limitation of any particular model developed for them. For example, there were a number of technical limitations (computer operation, accuracy, usefulness) in the San Francisco model which eventually led to its tentative abandonment. However, the greatest limitation was with regard to what the model could do even if these other problems were solved. The model could not take a set of input values and convert these into a specific plan of action. If a specific plan were fed into the model, it could not even determine whether or not this was the best possible plan for a given set of circumstances. At best, the model could be "a tool to assist experienced planners in evaluating results that might be achieved through following a given course of action."[41]

There is also a possibility that the model could be used to assist decision makers in determining what their realistic objectives (as contrasted with their ultimate aims) will be. If a range of alternatives were analyzed with the model, the outcomes would suggest what is achievable under each alternative. The array of analyzed alternatives would suggest what the range of outcomes might be like. These outcomes might fall short of what the decision makers desire to achieve, but they would provide some indication of what could be achieved (under the assumptions of the model and the input data). Since what is desirable is always limited by what is achievable, the model outcomes could help the decision makers to decide what goals they will seek to achieve and what they will consider an acceptable level of achievement. Thus, particular goals and achievement levels could be settled upon. If these differed from the specific outcomes of the completed analysis but were within the range of outcomes, the initial alternatives could be modified and new outputs generated. In this way, through a process of working back and forth between objectives and alternatives, the decision makers could better decide what their objectives would be.

Conflicts among the analysts

Three major groups of people were involved in the model-building task: persons trained in city planning, persons trained in operations research and systems analysis, and representatives of the planning activity in the city of San Francisco. Inevitably, conflicts developed—primarily between the first two groups.

These [conflicts] were largely due to the fact that teams with this mix of interests and talents had seldom worked together previously; they required an educational period before cohesiveness could develop.[42]

The most important and most severe practical problems were of a different nature, however. They involved conflict over

the different levels of detail desired by the different participants to support their normal pattern of work and interest. The city planners, for example, maintained insistence on a level of detail which bordered on im-

practicality, in terms of input data requirements and output analysis. This was largely due to the current capabilities of simulation techniques. The operations research personnel wished to retain simplicity in the initial model, even at the cost of possible loss of validity and utility of results. Experience with the use of simulation in other fields had indicated a consistent pattern wherein initial models were found to be over-detailed, and successive versions were almost invariably made more aggregated. However, this process would presumably result in a model which could not answer all questions of interest to the planners—such as the areas of a city to which a specific population group would move if their current dwellings were taken over for redevelopment—although it would provide considerable data for analyzing such problems outside the main model. The compromise finally reached probably satisfied neither party. The level of detail incorporated led to an enormous burden of data acquisition, processing, editing, etc., and produced outputs at a level of detail which led to extremely lengthy requirements for output analysis.

The fundamental problem here is more a short-term than a long-term one. Over a period of time there is no reason why any desired level of detail cannot be incorporated—provided suitable input data can be found. But from the analytic point of view, there are enormous gains to be achieved through starting on a relatively simple and not too ambitious scale, incorporating greater detail only as its potential utility is clearly recognized. [This is the family of models notion.][43]

Cost, completion time, and use

Generally, policy analysis is expensive, whether it involves model-building or not. In commenting on the Penn-Jersey, Pittsburgh, and San Francisco models, Wolfe and Ernst state:

1. Each has cost far more to produce than was originally planned!
2. Each badly overran the original planned completion date!

3. Not one has yet received effective use for the purpose which inspired their original design![44]

The original model-building effort in San Francisco, for example, cost around $800,000 out of a total $1.2 million CRP budget. Data collection was the most expensive part of the effort, although the data were required in part for purposes other than simply modeling. Computer time was also costly, but not unduly so. In addition to data collection, the really time-consuming task was development of the model and analysis of its results. In terms of time, the model-building effort spanned approximately eighteen months of the twenty-six-month CRP study. Despite the time, money, and effort expended, the San Francisco model was not completed in time for use in developing and testing alternative CRP programs. The most that was achieved was a verification run after the CRP was completed.

Is this what decision makers and analysts can expect when dealing with such complex problems? To a great extent, the answer is probably yes. There are a variety of reasons for this:

1. Present knowledge of the urban system's structure and functioning is extremely limited. As a result, much time and effort is required to gain the necessary understanding, and many false starts are likely to be encountered. Data collection and skilled personnel account for the major costs. Regardless of cost, the conduct of research is time-consuming and there are limits to how much the whole process can be speeded up.
2. Even when the research has been conducted and the models built, problems are always

encountered in operating the model. Sometimes these problems are mechanical, having to do with computer and programming operations or calculation. At other times the problems arise when operation of the model reveals false assumptions, conflicting rules, or other inadequacies in its basic structure.

3. Further, even when these problems are solved there may be difficulties in interpreting and evaluating the results of the model in a way that will be useful to the decision makers.

It should be noted, however, that many of the

problems encountered in model-building arise because the modeling efforts are overambitious in scope (i.e., subject matter encompassed) or in level of detail sought. These problems can be ameliorated by giving careful attention to various problem approaches and comparing the costs and benefits of each.

Notes

[1] The illustration is based largely on published materials from the CRP study and papers subsequently written by various people connected with it.

[2] Henry Fagin, "The Penn-Jersey Transportation Study: The Launching of a Permanent Regional Planning Process," *Journal of the American Institute of Planners,* XXIX (February 1963), 9–18; John Herbert and Benjamin J. Stevens, "A Model for the Distribution of Residential Activities in Urban Areas," *Journal of Regional Science,* II (Fall 1960), 21–36.

[3] Donald M. Hill, "A Growth Allocation Model for the Boston Region," *Journal of the American Institute of Planners,* XXXI (May 1965), 111–20.

[4] Ira S. Lowry, *A Model of Metropolis* (Santa Monica: Rand Corporation, 1964).

[5] San Francisco Department of City Planning, *Status of the San Francisco Simulation Model* (San Francisco: Department of City Planning, 1968), p. 1.

[6] Arthur D. Little, Inc., *The San Francisco Community Renewal Program—Purpose, Scope and Method: A Progress Report to the San Francisco Department of City Planning* (San Francisco: Arthur D. Little, Inc., 1963), p. 21.

[7] San Francisco Department of City Planning, *Simulation Model,* p. 1.

[8] Harry B. Wolfe and Martin L. Ernst, "Simulation Models and Urban Planning," in *Operations Research for Public Systems,* ed. by Philip M. Morse and L. W. Bacon (Cambridge, Mass.: The M.I.T. Press, 1967), pp. 52–53.

[9] San Francisco Department of City Planning, *Simulation Model,* p. 1.

[10] The decision makers in this case were the consultant planners, the city's planners, the planning commission, and, ultimately, the city council. As it turned out, the decision makers to whom the model was most directly addressed were the planners—including those of the consultant agency—as well as the city.

[11] The model-building team consisted primarily of city planners, economists, operations researchers, and computer programmers. These people were assisted by a number of consultants in other fields. Within the team, the city planners and the economists were the urban experts; some economists, the operations researchers, and the computer programmers were the model-

builders. The separation of these roles was not always distinct, but such a separation did exist, and, as will be seen later, was an inevitable source of conflict within the team.

[12] Wolfe and Ernst, in Morse and Bacon, *Operations Research,* pp. 54–55. All quotes from Wolfe and Ernst are reprinted by permission of The M.I.T. Press, Cambridge, Mass. Copyright © 1967 by The M.I.T. Press.

[13] For a good explanation of the theory and its modification for the model, see: Ira S. Lowry, *Seven Models of Urban Development: A Structural Comparison* (Santa Monica: Rand Corporation, 1967), pp. 5–13, 38–44.

[14] Represented in the framework by a set of rules about the conditions under which investors would sell (rent) and invest (in construction of new housing or improvement of old housing).

[15] Government actions were also represented by a set of rules which specified the effects of particular actions on the private housing market.

[16] Government may, for example: initiate zoning actions prohibiting certain changes in the use of space (e.g., refuse to allow high rise development in certain areas); introduce changes in space use through code enforcement and renewal projects, as when profitable private

development conditions do not exist; provide cost subsidies or rent supplements to householders; provide mortgage guarantees to investors; install public improvements which alter the relative attractiveness of neighborhoods and thus affect the demand for housing; or give favorable tax treatment to investors who improve their properties.

[17] The model and the various input/output routines required some 30,000 to 35,000 individual computer instructions.

[18] Wolfe and Ernst, in Morse and Bacon, *Operations Research,* p. 78.

[19] Ibid.

[20] "Without public intervention" really meant without *further* public intervention. Certain public actions were already in effect and therefore constituted part of the base conditions.

[21] Arthur D. Little, Inc., *San Francisco Community Renewal Program: Model of the San Francisco Housing Market* (San Francisco: Arthur D. Little, Inc., 1966), p. 36.

[22] Ibid., pp. 36–43.

[23] San Francisco Department of City Planning, *Simulation Model,* pp. 7–11.

[24] Ibid., p. 27.

[25] Ibid., pp. 11–27.

[26] Quoted from: Gary D. Brewer, *Evaluation and Innovation in Urban Research* (Santa Monica: Rand Corporation, 1970), p. 11.

[27] Arthur D. Little, Inc., *San Francisco Housing Market,* p. 8.

[28] Ibid., p. 101.

[29] San Francisco has a consolidated form of government, i.e., the same unit performs both municipal and county government functions. The legislative body is the board of supervisors.

[30] Wolfe and Ernst, in Morse and Bacon, *Operations Research,* p. 53.

[31] Ibid., p. 56.

[32] Ibid.

[33] Ibid.

[34] San Francisco Department of City Planning, *Simulation Model,* p. 1.

[35] This could be all right, actually. The problem is only that the planners customarily ignore much of the problem.

[36] For a discussion and illustration of this idea, see: Norman C. Dalkey, *Families of Models* (Santa Monica: Rand Corporation, 1965).

[37] Wolfe and Ernst, in Morse and Bacon, *Operations Research,* p. 57.

[38] Ibid., p. 78.

[39] Ibid., p. 79.

[40] For an excellent discussion of these and related points, see: Alphonse Chapanis, "Men, Machines, and Models," *American Psychologist,* XVI (February 1961), 113–31.

[41] Wolfe and Ernst, in Morse and Bacon, *Operations Research,* p. 58.

[42] Ibid., p. 55.

[43] Ibid.

[44] Ibid., p. 51.

**Developmental Problems:
Three Urban Futures
in Paradigm Form**

As noted in Chapter 3, since development problems are most often concerned with systems that do not presently exist, a key task is to set appropriate objectives. But objectives rarely can be set without consideration of the means of achieving them. Means almost always influence what is or can be sought. Some objectives can be achieved only by means which are unacceptable when exposed to examination: thus the goals themselves become unacceptable. Other objectives are unattainable with present or foreseeable means. Sometimes the means themselves (e.g., new inventions) suggest new objectives. Thus, ends and means are closely interrelated. While this condition exists regardless of the type of decision problem, in development problems the interrelation of ends and means is often *the* critical issue of analysis. This chapter focuses on an illustration of such analysis.

ANALYSIS OF ALTERNATIVE FUTURES

The problem illustrated is that of analyzing alternative urban futures, which are presented in terms of the alternative value sets they embody and the related means of achieving these values.

The primary purpose of the case analysis was to aid formulation of and choice among competing values, goals, and objectives. For each competing value set, only one set of means was included in the analysis. This was done because the purpose of specifying means was to permit exploration of the actions that various value sets implied as a basis for choosing among values rather than choosing among alternatives. But the case illustration was also meant to show the interrelation of ends and means, to point up the fact that different values imply different means, and to point out that the means available may determine, in whole or in part, what values can be sought and achieved.

"Means of livelihood and ways of life"
The illustration is taken from the book *Communitas: Means of Livelihood and Ways of Life,* by Percival and Paul Goodman.[1] A significant feature of this book is that although the analysis was done in the late 1940s the method of analysis and the specific models presented are relevant today. In fact, while several partial analyses have been attempted since the Goodmans' none has been as clearly set forth, as

comprehensive in scope, or as rich in manner of development.

Although the Goodmans' entire book is an illustration of policy analysis, the focus is on three paradigms developed therein. The paradigms represent three alternative futures for society and for cities which the Goodmans saw in trends developing during the post–World War II period. But their work involved far more than simple projection of these perceived trends. The Goodmans analyzed past theories, concepts, plans, and practices of city building, primarily in twentieth century America but also drawing on earlier American and European history. The aim of this analysis was to expose to philosophical examination the important issues in community planning and the city building schemes that had been suggested over time by planners, pragmatists, and utopians. In their examination the Goodmans asked: "What is socially implied in any of these schemes as a way of life and how does each express some tendency of modern mankind?" The aim of this questioning was to test whether the various schemes which were proposed considered the ends and means implied, and whether or not they were, as a way of life, absurd.

This, then, was the method the Goodmans pursued: philosophical questioning and exposure of the social implications of various schemes, and examination of the logic of ends and means explicit or implicit in each scheme. The three paradigms were an application of this method of logical thinking to the construction of urban futures. However, the particular futures developed were less important to the Goodmans than the clarification they provided about ends, means, and the relation between the two in each paradigm.

A note on paradigms

Since paradigms have not been discussed previously, a brief explanation seems appropriate. A paradigm is a structured set of assumptions, concepts, propositions, and questions about a subject. It brings these together in a compact form, thereby permitting simultaneous inspections and evaluation of the set. The paradigm does not represent a set of categories introduced *de novo,* but rather a codification of those concepts and problems found in existing theory, research, and experience related to a particular subject. The purpose of constructing the paradigm is to expose the underlying logic of the ideas as a basis for correction, improvement, or choice among them. In *Communitas* the subject was "means of livelihood and ways of life" (i.e., ways of organizing society and urban communities). The material being codified was the literature of philosophy, economics, political science, sociology, city planning, architecture, and other fields addressed to this subject. Since thinking about this subject was diverse, as it generally is on any

complex and value-laden subject, the material was organized into different sets of logically related ideas. The purpose of this explicit and simplified organization was to permit examination of each particular set and comparison among sets as an aid to logical thinking and, ultimately, as an aid to choice among alternative ends and means of community organization. Table 7–1 is an abstracted statement of the underlying assumptions and propositions of the three paradigms.

The paradigms developed by the Goodmans provide an interesting contrast to recent future scenarios developed by several groups of city managers in conjunction with analysts from the Brookings Institution.[2] The scenarios were aimed at predicting present trends in the American city and the manner in which these trends will extend and intersect in the immediate (1969–75) and long-range (1975–85) future. The scenarios can be viewed as a prelude to the construction of paradigms like those of the Goodmans. The above-mentioned city managers' scenarios were essentially forecasts of the significant controllable and uncontrollable forces or factors which will affect the future of cities over the next decade. In constructing their paradigms the Goodmans did something similar. However, they went beyond forecasting. They chose certain features of the present and the future and organized these into related sets of ends and means relevant to exploration and analysis of alternative urban futures. In this way, they made explicit the values implied by each urban future and indicated how the community could be organized (in political, social, economic, and physical terms) to achieve the assumed value set. The value sets themselves were extrapolated from various political, social,

and economic philosophies extant or emergent in society. The importance of this additional step (paradigm construction) was that the analysis was pushed several levels beyond the prediction of single events. That is, the analysis: (1) treated the forecast events as interrelated and hypothesized certain relations; (2) selected some events for further consideration and eliminated others; (3) made the selection on the basis of a hypothesized and explicit set of values; and (4) linked values, events, and means to create a unified portrayal of the total selected set.

The problem

In its broadest terms, the problem which the Goodmans addressed was that of trying to gain insight into the making of choices about the use of technology and about the things which its use makes possible in modern society. Their basic point was that modern technology makes possible an almost endless variety of ways of life. Given this technology of free choice, the problem is to conceive of purposes for and ways of using technology that are consistent with one another.[3] The Goodmans state the problem as follows: "How to make a selection of modern technology? How to use our surplus? How to find the right relation between means and ends?"[4]

The analysis

Given the foregoing statement of the problem, the next task was to develop a way of approaching the problem:

We have chosen to present our thoughts in the form of three community models of our own. Given the complex and incommensurable factors of the subject, this seems to us the simplest as well as the liveliest

Table 7-1. Basic assumptions and propositions of the three paradigms.

Scheme I **The city of efficient consumption**	Scheme II **The new commune**	Scheme III **The subsistence city**
1. Modern society's productivity is higher than actual production. **2.** Actual production is higher than consumption capacity. **3.** For technical efficiency: a) actual production must be increased to capacity; b) consumption must be increased to match production. **4.** The key to technical efficiency lies in: a) concentration of production and consumption to form large markets and to reduce non-productive and nonconsumptive distribution and servicing activities; b) planning of the city to support a); c) advertising, or the artificial creation of demand; d) product obsolescence, changing fads, variety in style. **5.** The ideal of work under mass production conditions is not work itself, but the things which working allows the individual to do away from the work situation through leisure time, money, etc. **6.** This split between working and living means the city must also be split between places of work and of living (suburbs, open spaces, etc.). **7.** The total social fabric of the city must be in concert with the aim of technical efficiency.	**1.** Men like to make things, to handle materials, to see them take shape and come out as desired; men are proud of their products. **2.** Men like to work and be useful. **3.** Productive work is a kind of creation; it is an extension of the human personality into nature. **4.** Capitalist (private or state) production and machine industry have destroyed the instinctive pleasures of work so that most people dislike economic work. **5.** Mass production, breaking down the tasks of labor into small steps and distributing the products far from home, destroys the sense of creating anything. **6.** The division of the economy (and society) into production and consumption as two opposite poles means that working and living are also split. **7.** A way of life requires merging the means (work) with the end (living) so that work is a continuous process of satisfying activity—satisfying in itself and in its useful end. **8.** The model of such a society in the past was that of handicraft in a limited society, where the relations of guilds and small markets allowed a craftsman a say and a hand in every phase of production, distribution, and consumption.	**1.** Elementary subsistence and security are basic political needs of a society, prior to economic needs. **2.** The traditional method of providing security by subsidizing the full productivity of the economy is inefficient (e.g., unemployment insurance) and involves the danger that subsistence needs will not receive sufficient attention. It also requires substantial government intervention in the economy. **3.** A direct solution is to divide the economy and provide the subsistence directly, without jeopardy, without having to underwrite the rest of the economy, and without government intervention in the whole economy.
Query: How can society (the city) be organized under conditions of mass production and consumption to be useful for creating magnificence?	**Query:** How can this model of working and living be recreated under modern conditions? What are the implications of such a community?	**Query:** How can society (the city) be organized as a dual economy to provide subsistence needs and still allow for free provision of luxury needs?

method of presentation: to give typical important value-choices as if they were alternative programs and plans. None of these is presented as our own point of view. In fact, we should probably prefer to live in the second or middle scheme, and we don't make much effort to conceal our bemusement about the first, which is similar to New York in 1960. *Nevertheless, these three models are not plans, they are analyses* [italics mine]; they refer to no site; they have no style, which comes only in building something concrete; and most important, there is no population that purely makes these alternative choices as we present them. People in fact want a mixture of the three, in varying proportions depending on their traditions and circumstances.

Gunnar Myrdal, a great sociologist and a philosophic man, has said:

Value premises must be explicitly stated and not hidden as tacit assumptions . . . Since incompatible valuations are held in society, the value premises should ideally be given as a number of sets of alternative hypotheses.

This is exactly what we try to do. We present three alternative models of choices with regard to technology, surplus, and the relation of means and ends, and we ask what each formula gives us in economics, politics, education, domestic standards, popular and high culture, and other functions of the community. These are regional schemes for:

A. *Efficient Consumption.*
B. *Elimination of the Difference between Production and Consumption.*
C. *Planned Security with Minimum Regulation.*[5]

Construction of a model. Underlying each of the three analyses conducted by the Goodmans was a basic framework that can be described as a simple matrix. Along one dimension were assumptions about ends, means, and relations between the two. Along the other dimension were various functions and structures of the community which would be affected by any particular ends–means set. The cells of the matrix were the outcomes of the particular ends–means set on community structure and function. The basic framework, roughly completed for Scheme I, is shown in Table 7–2.

Getting data for the model. The data used by the Goodmans for filling in the basic model and constructing the paradigms were the writings of economists, philosophers, planners and architects, social reformers, and others throughout history. They chose ideas from these writings which pertained to one or more aspects of community life and combined them in order to present a unified scheme. Their bibliography for each of the three schemes is shown in Figure 7–1.

THREE COMMUNITY PARADIGMS

Scheme I: the city of efficient consumption

This scheme was drawn from the tastes and drives of America most obvious on the surface—its high production, high standard of living, artificially induced demand, and busy full employment. These features had been criticized by moralists as useless and unstable. Society was skimping on public goods, whereas production of frivolous goods was unbridled. The superabundance of private goods without the leavening of public goods (education, social services, wiser use of land, etc.) was destructive of the satisfaction of even the private goods. The aim of Scheme I was to answer such complaints—to make a useless economy useful for something great—namely, magnificence.[6]

The basic idea in this paradigm is that modern production has far outstripped people's ability to consume and that greater efficiency in consumption is required to match productive capacity. In order to increase consumption efficiency, the city is built like a gigantic department store. Everything within the city is organized to contribute to efficient production and consumption of goods and services. The city is large, on the order of several million people, to provide a concentrated market for mass production. Production is oriented to a variety of styles and changing fads to encourage consumption. Consumption is not primarily individual in its motivation, however. It is social, for it is social imitation and emulation that produces a lively demand. Services, whether public or private, are minimized by the planning of the city, because they play only an indirect role in a consumption economy. The heart of the city is the great department store. Here all things are available according to desire, and are on display in order to suggest the desire. The city's streets are the corridors of the department store.

The city is zoned into four large regions according to acts of buying and using up of goods (see Table 7–3 and Figure 7–2).

In the city center (a half mile in radius), work and market activity are concentrated under one roof, in one immense container (Figures 7–3, 7–5, and 7–6). What were formerly streets now assume the functions of promenade and display—they are the aisles of the great department store. The population at the busy hours is about 2.5 million. The city center is zoned as follows:

The materials and products of light manufacturing go via the freight routes in the basement or the cargo

Table 7-2. Basic model for the paradigms (partially completed for Scheme I).

Ends and means	Community structure and function					
	Economics	Politics	Social interaction and social structure	Popular and high culture	Aesthetics and physical form	Education
Ends: Emphasis on physical ends magnificence of physical plant and goods maximum production and consumption minimization of distribution and service activities **Means:** Maximum exploitation of physical means mass production of goods mass transportation mass housing **Ends-means relations:** Technical efficiency physical production at capacity consumption to match production	Free market economy Luxury goods Induced demand through advertising Installment buying Money economy Appeal to transient consumers	Voting in the market for "brands" of goods Governance by a corporate board of technologists, merchandisers, and semi-economists Voting for board members is a vote for a different "brand" of goods	City of 5 million people 2.5 million daytime population Social emulation and imitation Annual carnival Neighborhood is the basic social unit Mixture of classes in neighborhood to sharpen emulation Class structure based on style of goods that can be purchased Social relations fairly formal Older population resides in city; families with children reside in country Work is not a basic source of self-fulfillment; consumption of goods and leisure time is	Illustrated weeklies Mass entertainment and leisure Museums and exhibitions like industrial fairs Theatre and arts dramatize consumption	City zoned according to acts of buying and using up goods City like a giant department store Physical planning of city minimizes service and distribution requirements Mass-produced uniform housing space Uniform neighborhoods City and country visually separated Transportation designed to facilitate access to goods Ten acres of open space per 5,000 people	Higher education a commodity, and tends to be faddish Some conflict between university and rest of community Other education a process of socialization in the acts of consumption Other education conducted in the country; sharpens appetite for the city

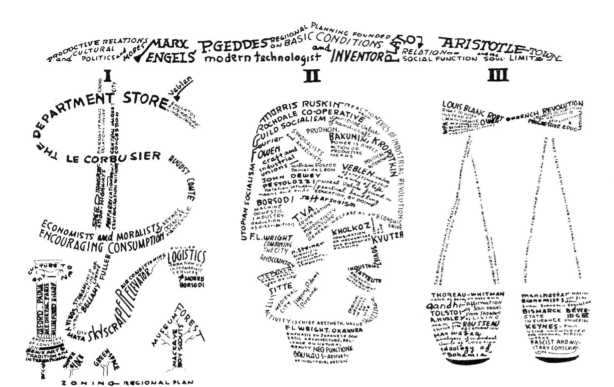

Figure 7-1. Bibliography for three ways of life today. Source: Percival and Paul Goodman, *Communitas: Means of Livelihood and Ways of Life* (2nd ed.; New York: Random House-Vintage Books, 1960). Copyright 1947, 1960 by Percival and Paul Goodman. Reprinted by permission of Random House, Inc.

planes that alight on the roof: the heart of industry is about in the middle. Business and administrative offices are in the upper and outer regions. The lower stories— most immediately available to the citizens who come by bus or car—house the stores and popular entertainments. In the outer envelope and in projecting spokes, with natural light and a good natural view, are the hotels and restaurants, opening out, on the ground floor, into the park of the university. Convenient to all is the roof airport and the basement levels of parking and transit [Figures 7–3 and 7–5].[7]

In planning and decoration the city center is like a great fair. Every aisle (street) displays the products that make it worthwhile to get up in the morning to go to work and to work efficiently in order to have at the same time the most money and the most leisure. The key to this permanent fair is advertising. The function of advertising is to suggest to the public the need for products, whether absolute necessities or not, by appealing to various human instincts. The idea is to create a ravenous demand that continuously recycles as new products are produced for consumption.

Next to the city center, extending in a mile-wide ring around it, is the university (Figure 7–4). It consists of theaters, opera houses, museums, libraries, lecture halls, and laboratories of liberal arts and sciences, and everything that belongs to these, set in a gigantic park. This zone "is the field of a deadly internecine strife: between those who would integrate [the creations and discoveries of the university] into the culture of the center and those who fear that this integration corrupts everything into hogwash."[8] The strife exhibits itself in many ways. For example, there are disagreements as to: whether to locate among the university's humanities the

Table 7-3. The four large zones of the city.

Zone 1	Zone 2	Zone 3	Zone 4
The market	**Arts and sciences**	**Domestic life**	**Open country**
Produced goods which are consumed in enjoyment of them	Produced goods but not consumed in enjoyment of them	Goods are consumed in enjoyment but they are not produced by men; they belong to nature	Goods which are neither produced nor consumed
Physical comforts, popular arts, medicine	Current fashionable ideas in the arts and sciences	Social and sexual intercourse, domestic life, and everything pertaining to the primary environments, or parents, children, friends	The stream of life itself, and the permanent things of nature
The great department stores, hotels, restaurants, popular arts, terminals	The university	Neighborhoods with their residences, schools, hospitals, shops, garages	Open country, camps, forest preserves, junior colleges

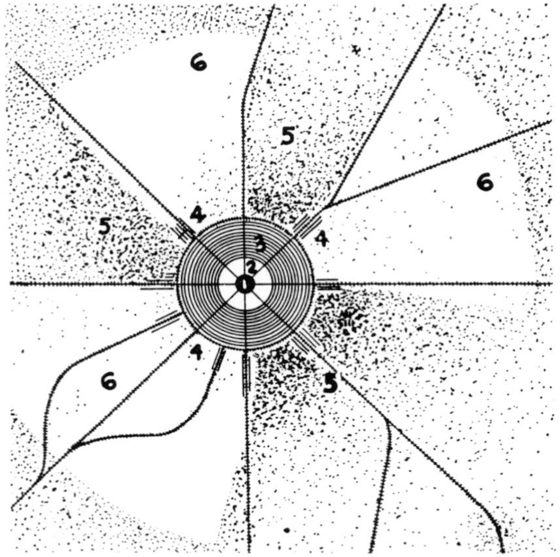

Regional plan. 1. Market, light industry, offices, entertainment, hotels, and terminals. 2. Culture, universities, museums, zoo. 3. Residences, schools, hospitals. 4. Heavy industry, terminals, long-distance airports. 5. Forest preserves, vacationland, 6. Agriculture.

Figure 7-2. The city zones. Source: Goodman, Communitas, p. 135.

popular humanities of higher merchandizing — or should these be placed in the city center as trade schools; whether to permit the reading of the classics in the arts and sciences, since they do not contribute to expanding production, are not consumed in enjoyment, and injure the solid economic value of illustrated weeklies produced in the city center. These and similar problems may be thrashed out in places provided in the park.

The style of the university is dictated by whatever concepts, ideas, discoveries, methods, tools, or techniques are in fashion among its inhabitants.

The zone next to the university consists of residential neighborhoods of the city. The neighborhood is the primary unit of emulation:

It is in the end unsatisfactory and indelicate to emulate, or to impute economic inferiority to, one's family and friends; on the other hand, to do so with total strangers is pointless. Therefore, at least for domestic display, the unit of emulation and so forth must be the neighborhood. Residents of one's neighborhood take notice, judge one's clothes, see that the lawn is clipped; they are not so well known that one is embarrassed to show off to them; they do not know us well enough to see through us.[9]

Each neighborhood consists of around 4,000

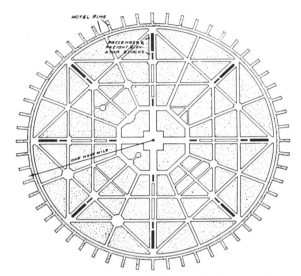

A street floor in the air-conditioned cylinder: one mile in diameter, air-conditioned, brightly lit, flexible space; transportation vertical, horizontal, and diagonal; continuous interior show window. The perimeter is for hotels and restaurants, air-conditioned but naturally lighted.

Figure 7-3. Cross-section of the city center. Source: ***Communitas*, p. 137.**

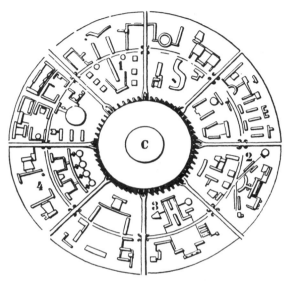

Plan of the university. C, the center; 1, natural history, zoos, aquariums, planetarium; 2, science, laboratories; 3, plastic arts; 4, music and drama.

Figure 7-4. Plan of the university. Source: ***Communitas*, p. 141.**

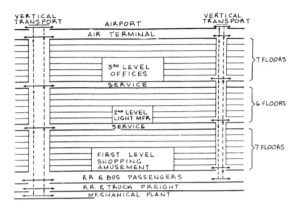

A section through the air-conditioned cylinder: twenty stories of continuous rentable area without courts or yards; four stories of passenger terminals for air, railroad, and bus; one story for terminals for light manufacture, with deliveries direct to vertical transportation; the lowest level contains the cylinder service (heat, cold, etc.).

Figure 7-5. A section through the center. Source: ***Communitas*, p. 139.**

people who live in a continuous apartment house around an open space of ten acres (Figures 7–7 and 7–8). Each neighborhood has its own shops, tennis courts, nurseries, and elementary schools, and each is a carbon copy of the next. The population contains a mix of classes (to stimulate class competition in emulation) and is composed largely of older persons (medicine increases longevity; young families flee the city). Within each apartment house, the family unit is

an empty shell without partitions and (for the rich) two stories high completely serviced with light, conditioned air, water, and similar basic necessities (Figure 7–9). Thus each family is free to choose how the unit shall be made livable and to buy livability at the great department store.

The final zone, open country, marks an abrupt break with the city. It is a forest wilderness

dotted with parks, camps for children, adolescents, and adults, junior colleges, and similar transitional mechanisms. The primary purpose of this zone is to provide for the initiation of the young and the reinitiation of the old into the city culture. For example:

The adolescent, given to rebellion, is encouraged, by a more animal existence in the open country. And we know that as his longings settle into habitual desires,

Figure 7-6. Street scene in the center. Source: ***Communitas,*** **p. 140.**

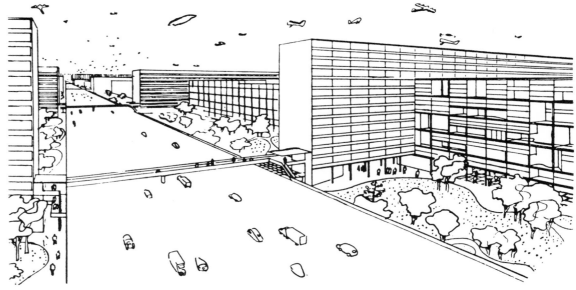

Figure 7-7. A residential zone. Source: ***Communitas,*** **p. 142.**

it is the environment of adult achievement that seems attractive to him; he has been away from it, and "nothing increases relish like a fast." In hundredfold strength the impressions of childhood have him in grip. Then the university, the school of adults both young and old, glorifies the values of the city in its popular humanities . . . .[10]

In its politics the city is uncomplicated. There is no need for political initiative for either central or neighborhood policy, as the economy is run by

a corporation of technologists, merchandizers, and semieconomists. Periodic elections are like other sales campaigns—to choose one or another brand of a basically identical commodity. People do exercise a powerful influence, however, in their choice of buying or not buying a product and in their choice of being employed in this or that factory or office.

Finally, in order to use up production inventories, there is a carnival season in the city every year.

During this season production activity comes to a halt and the ultimate in consumption ensues.

Not only are inventories wastefully used up but the contents of the housing shells are burned or otherwise destroyed. Even installment debts are forgiven. All of this serves a useful purpose, for now the department store shelves can be filled with the newest fashions and people can begin again to fill their shells with these goods, start-

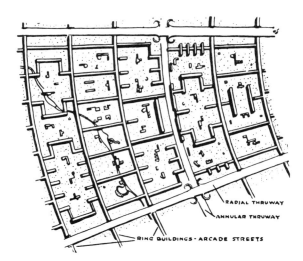

**Figure 7-8. Street plan in a residential district.
Source: *Communitas*, p. 145.**

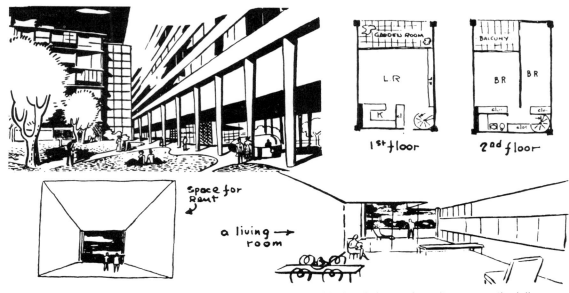

*At the left, a corner of a residential block showing an arcade and its local shops; above it a pneumatic delivery
system operating from the city center (for packages up to a yard in diameter). The rest shows a typical apartment
space, rented as a bare loft and made livable and/or expensive according to individual taste and/or fancy.*

**Figure 7-9. Residential space. Source: *Communitas*,
p. 146.**

ing with a clean slate on their installment payments.

Scheme II: the new commune
Whereas Scheme I posited a basic conflict and
division of working and living activities, this
scheme is an attempt to eliminate such conflict
and division. The basic idea in this paradigm is
that work should be integrated into man's total
way of life and be thought of as a continuous

process of satisfying activity — satisfying in itself
and satisfying in its useful end. To bring this
about the city must be organized along four
principles:

1. A closer relation of the personal and productive environments, making punctuality reasonable instead
of disciplinary, and introducing phases of home and
small-shop production; and vice versa, finding
appropriate technical uses for personal relations that
have come to be considered unproductive.

2. A role for all workers in all stages of the production
of the product; for experienced workers a voice and
hand in the design of the product and the design
and operation of the machines; and for all a political
voice on the basis of what they know best, their
specific industry, in the national economy.
3. A schedule of work designed on psychological and
moral as well as technical grounds, to give the most
well-rounded employment to each person, in a diversified environment. Even in technology and economics, the men are ends as well as means.

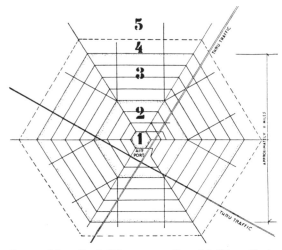

Zones of the city. 1, City squares. 2 and 3, Diversified farms accommodating all the children and their schools (the parents who work in the squares will generally live in the inner belt). 4, Industrialized agriculture and dairying. 5, Open country, grazing, etc.

Figure 7-10. The town and its environs. Source: Communitas, p. 158.

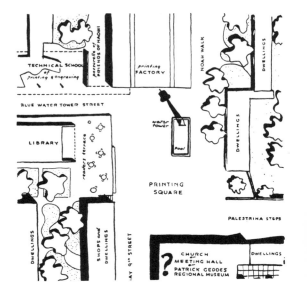

Figure 7-11. A town square. Source: Communitas, p. 163.

Figure 7-12. A busy square. Source: Communitas, p. 164.

4. Relatively small units with relative self-sufficiency, so that each community can enter into a larger whole with solidarity and independence of viewpoint.[11]

The city is now relatively self-contained, self-sufficient, and small—around 200,000 people. Diversified farming is the basis of self-subsistence. However, economically the city is part of a larger region of similar cities. Each city produces some specialized products for the region and the nation, based upon the particular natural advantages and resources of city and region, and in this way participates in broader economic life. The city is zoned (Figure 7–10) between urban and farm production, the latter divided between industrialized and more diversified farming. The difference between all these zones is not great; it is more a matter of degree, and in some areas zones blend into one another.

At the center of the city is the public square or plaza (Figure 7–11). The square is not a trafficway but a place where people remain, a place of leisure and a place for social interaction. Place of urban work and home are close at hand. On one side of the plaza is the factory; on another a small library; on still another an outdoor cafe (Figure 7–12). In the plaza, there is a clock with bells—a reminder rather than a tyrant; there are also a fountain, pigeons, musi-

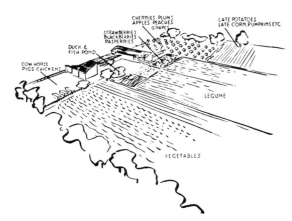

Disposition of farm production. The principle of the diversified farm is symbiosis, with a minimum of artificial fertilizer; city sewage, enriched by the products of the farm, is piped back to fertilize the land.

Figure 7-13. The city's farms. Source: *Communitas*, p. 167.

cians. On another side of the plaza is an apartment house, where a family is preparing a meal:

They go about this as follows. The ground floor of the building is not only a restaurant but a foodstore; the farmers deliver their produce here. The family cooks upstairs, phones down for their uncooked meat, vegetables, salad, and fixings, and these are delivered by dumbwaiter, cleaned and peeled—the potatoes peeled and spinach washed by machine. They dress and season the roast to taste and send it back with the

message: "Medium rare about 1845." The husband observes, unfortunately for the twentieth time, that when he was a student in Paris a baker on the corner used to roast their chickens in his oven. Simpler folk, who live in smaller row houses up the block, consider this procedure a lot of foolishness; they just shop for their food, prepare it themselves, cook it, and eat it. But they don't have factory jobs: they run a lathe in the basement.[12]

Surrounding the city center, extending in a ring some four or five miles wide, are diversified farms (Figure 7–13), accommodating all the children and their schools. This is the primary environment for children and is organized to meet their needs:

The best society for growing children, past the age of total dependency, is other children, older and younger by easy grades. It is a rough society but characterized at worst by conflict rather than by loving, absolute authority. These children, then, no longer sleep with their parents, but in a dormitory.[13]

The children's parents, who work in the factories and shops of the city, may live in small houses on the farms; that is, they may live at the homes of their children. If the parents choose to live in the city center, their children go to school on the farms. The children may visit their parents in the city or be visited by their parents at their farm homes.

Whether on the farm or in the factory, work is integrated so that each worker has a total grasp of all the operations involved in making a product. Work and education are also integrated. Farm and factory are not only centers of production, but they serve as centers of learning as well:

There must be a school of industry, academic and not immediately productive, connected with the factory. Now let us distinguish apprentices and graduates. To the apprentices, along with their schooling, is assigned the more monotonous work; to the graduates, the executive and coordinating work, the fine work, the finishing touches. The masterpiece that graduates an apprentice is a new invention, method, or other practical contribution advancing the industry. The masters are teachers, and as part of their job hold free discussions looking to basic changes.[14]

Providing for this integration of work and education requires the development of a schedule of activities for members of the community, and the schedule must in turn be related to the overall structure of the community's economy. An example of such a schedule worked out for one year is shown in Table 7–4.

Political life is also integrated with economic and social life. The city is organized as an economic democracy on the basis of productive units. Each of these productive units, relying on its own expertness and the bargaining power of what it has to offer, cooperates with the whole community. Thus the political system is one of syndicalism—a town meeting of small economic units.[15]

Finally, since work itself is satisfying and offers endless opportunity for invention, creativity, experimentation, and self-fulfillment, the city is not characterized by pursuits of mass leisure activities. The artisan shops and factories are the museums and cultural fairs; the public squares, the stages and concert halls; the farms, the zoos and arboretums. Leisure pursuits are, therefore, simple and integrated into the daily life of the individual.

Scheme III: the subsistence city

The basic notion in this paradigm is that society's present method of social insurance as a way of providing for elementary subsistence and security is an inefficient, and to some extent inhuman, solution. The paradigm posits a society (and a community) where the economy is divided into (1) government regulated production to provide for some uniform standard of subsistence for everyone and (2) unregulated private production to provide for luxury goods and services. This divided economy has several distinct advantages:

1. It directly provides for subsistence needs (which otherwise are in jeopardy).
2. It restricts government intervention to the subsistence sphere of the economy.
3. Every person can know that the work he does for a living is unquestionably useful and necessary, and unexploited.
4. The separation of subsistence from the values and demands of the rest of the economy gives the wage earner a new security, a breadth of freedom, and the possibility of choice.

In this scheme, subsistence needs are provided by direct government production under a system of universally conscripted labor. The subsistence production centers are run as government monopolies and pay not money but their own scrip, which is exchangeable only for subsistence goods. Luxury goods are provided by private enterprise. These enterprises are run and worked in by people who have completed their period of conscripted labor, where they learned basic production and organization skills, and who have a desire for obtaining money, wealth, or luxury items not obtainable in the subsistence

Table 7-4. Typical schedule of activities for a community (numerals equal months). Source: Communitas, pp. 161-62.

Basic work	Master workman	Apprentice workman	Farmer	Farm family	Ages 6 to 14	Ages 15 to 18
Factory	8(a)	6				1
Industrial agriculture		3(d)	2(d)	X		1
Diversified agriculture			8	X	X	
Domestic industry			8	X(e)		1
Formal and technical learning		2(b)				1(b)
Technical teaching	1(b)	1(b)				
General education					X	5
Study and travel						2(f)
Individual work (c)	2					
Unscheduled (g)	1	1	1	1	X	1

Notes on the schedule

(a) The factory work of the master workman and workwoman includes executive and fine work.

(b) The time of technical education runs concurrently with the working period.

(c) Graduate work at one's own time and place could be in a traveling trailer or country cottage; could comprise designing, drafting, assemblage of hand-assembled wholes (e.g., radios or clocks), finishing operations (lens-grinding), etc.

(d) Master farmwork in industrial agriculture includes supervision and maintenance and is divided co-operatively to spread over the year. The more mechanical work at peak seasons is done by the factory apprentices.

(e) Farm family industry includes the making of parts for the factories, co-operation with industrial agriculture (e.g., field kitchens), educational care of boarding city children.

(f) The spread of activity of the youth over many categories, including two months of travel, gives them an acquaintance with the different possibilities.

(g) Activity at one's own fancy or imagination: vocational, avocational, recreational, etc.

(X) Activities engaged in as occasion arises.

economy. Money is the medium of exchange in this economy.

The standard of minimum subsistence provided every individual is as follows:

1. Food sufficient in quantity and kind for health, palatable but without variety.
2. Uniform clothing adequate for all seasons.
3. Shelter on an individual, family, and group basis, with adequate conveniences for different environments.
4. Medical service.
5. Transportation.
but *not* primary education which is a public good taxed from the general economy.[16]

To achieve this standard, one year of work in every four or five years is required. Over a lifetime, each individual would serve a span of six to seven years in the national conscripted labor force, spaced out as convenient—with some choice as to the years in which to serve.

As the economy, medium of exchange, and work activity are divided between subsistence and luxury production, so is the city. That is, some cities are mainly subsistence production and consumption centers, isolated and apart from luxury production and consumption. Other cities combine subsistence and luxury production and consumption (although the subsistence centers are discrete entities) and form large metropolises. Thus, a major choice facing the individual is whether to live in the small, isolated production center or in the metropolis. In the latter, there are additional costs of living brought about simply by the concentration of population and luxury goods. The individual, therefore, must choose whether he wishes to pay the extra cost

for direct access to these luxury items or forego them for some time period (e.g., until all or part of his conscripted labor time is completed).

The subsistence cities are designed to be highly efficient production centers. In these centers space, production facilities, social services, etc., are utilized to maximum capacity, sometimes on two and three shifts. The centers are relatively small (50,000 people) and are decentralized to facilitate distribution and to take advantage of regional resources. The zones of a production city are shown in Figure 7–14.

Within the metropolis, production centers would be located near the outskirts of the city and may be as small as 5,000 in population (Figure 7–15). They are located there because land, housing, utilities, and social services are cheaper there than in the city center and can be provided under the subsistence standard.

In the subsistence community the major problem faced by people is a moral and psychological one—to discover what they want to do with their lives, rather than to follow widely advertised suggestions.

We are asking, in the framework of this model proposal, an intensely realistic question about the actual situation in our country. For indeed, in our surplus economy, millions really are technically unemployable—there is no necessary work for them to do, no man's work. If automation were allowed its full headway, these millions would become many many millions. *Because* they are really economically unproductive, they have no culture and no resources of leisure, since culture grows from productive life. At the same time, each one of these people, no matter how he hangs around or perhaps

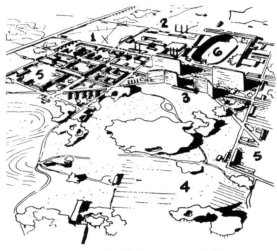

A production center for 50,000 workers. 1, Airport. 2, Heavy manufacture. 3, Light manufacture. 4, Industrialized agriculture. 5, Housing. 6, Sports and social center.

Figure 7-14. A production city. Source: Communitas, p. 205.

spends his time in getting quasi-visceral "kicks" or being "cool," must also feed his face and come in out of the rain. *It is this actuality that our scheme of a divided economy addresses and draws in black and white: we provide the subsistence part in an efficient, honorable, and compulsory way; and we leave open the horrendous question: then what?* [Italics mine.][17]

COMMENT

The paradigms developed by the Goodmans have counterparts in many of the urban and regional planning studies conducted in recent years.[18] However, these studies generally are limited to one aspect of community life—the physical setting and its form. They tend to start with physical form and draw out the broad social and value implications of physical form as side comments, if at all.[19] Thus, attention is focused on the forms presented rather than on the value choices implied by each form. The Goodman's technique would lay bare such values.

Finally, the writings of various utopians[20] and science fictionists[21] often contain paradigms, scenarios, or both. Sometimes these are serious attempts at analysis; at other times they are merely an attempt to project bizarre events to a logical or illogical conclusion. Nevertheless, they are frequently useful in exposing value choices and the implications of technology or other means to achieving ends. They are always useful as stimulation to thinking.

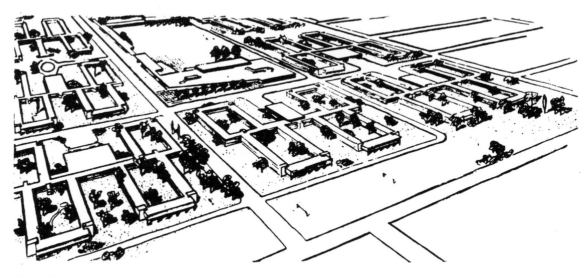

Figure 7-15. A production center for 5,000 population within a city. Source: *Communitas*, p. 204.

Notes

[1] Percival and Paul Goodman, *Communitas: Means of Livelihood and Ways of Life* (New York: Vintage Books, 1960 [paperback]; first published in hardback, New York, Random House, 1947). Copyright 1947, 1960 by Percival and Paul Goodman. The material quoted in this chapter, together with Figure 7–1 and Table 7–4 (plus the material on which Tables 7–1, 7–2, and 7–3 are based) are reprinted by permission of Random House, Inc. Figures 7–2 through 7–15 are reprinted by permission of Professor Percival Goodman.

[2] "Predicting the Future of Cities," *Public Management*, September 1969, pp. 2–23.

[3] Technology is often assumed to be neutral, but nothing could be further from the fact. In physical terms it probably is neutral. But technology always has non-physical implications and impacts, and very often it has indirect physical impacts. The technology of the automobile is a case in point. Since the first Fords rolled off the assembly line, political, social, and economic institutions have been built up around the automobile and have worked overtime to shape the form of our cities, the air we breathe, and our very perceptions of ourselves as individuals.

[4] Goodman, *Communitas*, p. 119.

[5] Ibid., pp. 119–20.

[6] Ibid., p. 219.

[7] Ibid., p. 138.

[8] Ibid., p. 140.

[9] Ibid., p. 143.

[10] Ibid., p. 147.

[11] Ibid., p. 155.

[12] Ibid., p. 165.

[13] Ibid., pp. 166–67.

[14] Ibid., p. 157.

[15] Within the larger society, the political system operates in a similar manner, but now the political unit is the city. Cities, in turn, form into regional political units on the basis of economic interdependency, and these regional units bargain with one another over national economic policy.

[16] Goodman, *Communitas,* pp. 200–201.

[17] Ibid., p. 213.

[18] U.S., National Capital Planning Commission and U.S., National Capital Regional Planning Council, *A Policies Plan for the Year 2000: The Nation's Capital* (Washington, D.C.: Government Printing Office, 1961); Northeastern Illinois Metropolitan Area Planning Commission, *Combination Evaluation of LRCA* [Long Range Conceptual Alternatives]: *Based on Design and Environmental Evaluation, Memo No. 19* (Chicago: Northwestern Illinois Planning Commission, 1965); Detroit Edison Company, Wayne State University, and Dosiadis Associates, *Emergence and Growth of an Urban Region: The Developing Urban Detroit Area,* Vol. II: *Future Alternatives* (Detroit: Detroit Edison Company, 1967); Twin Cities Metropolitan Planning Commission, *Selecting Policies for Metropolitan Growth* (Minneapolis: Twin Cities Metropolitan Planning Commission, 1967).

[19] The Washington metropolitan area plan (i.e., *A Policies Plan for the Year 2000,* above) is a typical example. Various metropolitan futures were sketched in terms of the layout of the physical plant, and then certain advantages and disadvantages of each layout were discussed. Underlying each of the layouts were certain biases of the planners: (1) scattered development is inherently evil; (2) open space must be preserved; (3) a strong central business district must be maintained; (4) the journey to work should be reduced; and (5) people desire a wide range of choice in types and locations of dwellings. These biases were never stated explicitly. The alternative futures were never discussed in terms of the broader value choices they implied. Since these broader choices were not a part of the planners' thinking in developing the various futures, this is not surprising. For other criticisms, relating to evaluation of the alternatives (means) rather than of ends, see: William L. C. Wheaton, "Operations Research for Metropolitan Planning," *Journal of the American Institute of Planners,* XXIX (November 1963), 250–59.

[20] See: Glen Negley and J. Max Patrick, *The Quest for Utopia* (New York: Henry Schuman, 1952), and Thomas A. Reiner, *The Place of the Ideal Community in Urban Planning* (Philadelphia: University of Pennsylvania Press, 1963).

[21] See, for example: Isaac Asimov, *The Caves of Steel* (New York: Doubleday and Company, 1954); B. F. Skinner, *Walden Two* (New York: Macmillan Co., 1948); Ayn Rand, *Anthem* (New York: New American Library, 1946); Bryan Aldiss, *Starswarm* (New York: New American Library, 1964); Walter Moudy, *No Man on Earth* (New York: Berkley Publishing Corporation, 1964); F. Pohl and J. Williamson, *Undersea City* (Hicksville, N.Y.: Gnome Press, 1958).

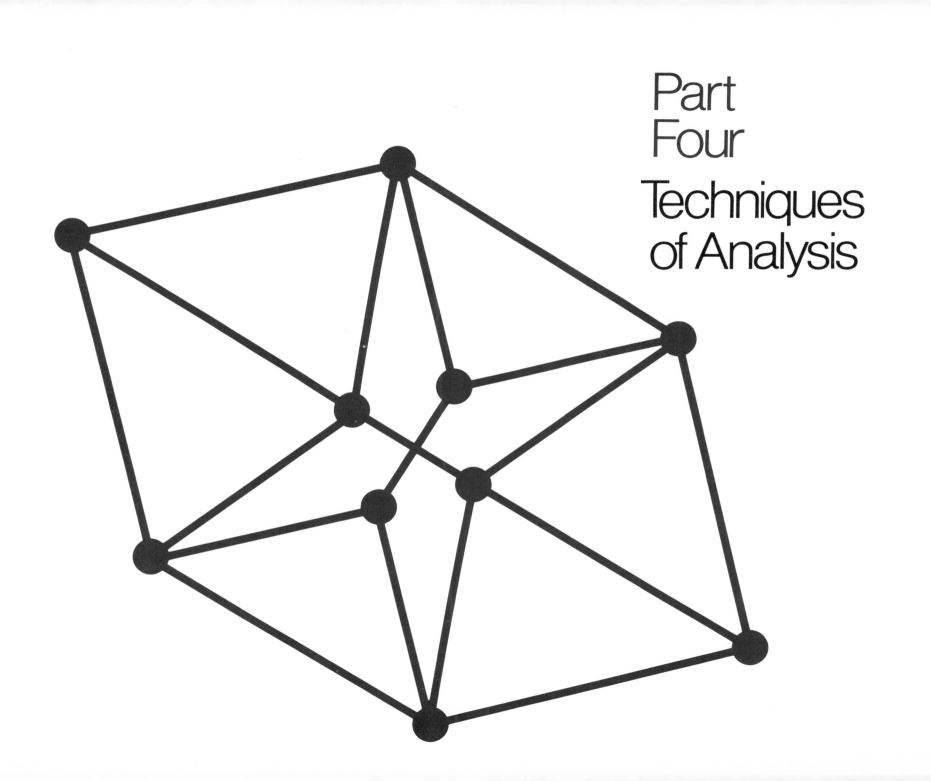

Part
Four

Techniques
of Analysis

Models

8

Models are a critical element in policy analysis. They are a central feature of all phases of analysis and are particularly important in the evaluation phase. All techniques of analysis employ some type of model (or models) in their application to decision problems.

Here we will discuss the nature of models and describe different types of models. First, the concept of a model is defined, and then models are distinguished as physical or symbolic as related to their manner of representing real world phenomena. Focusing largely on symbolic models, we depict the uses of models as description, prediction, and planning. Models are then viewed as black boxes in the total structure of policy analysis; this is followed by an attempt to look inside the black box to make explicit the basic structure of all models. Finally, a five-fold classification of models is presented which is based on the form in which the model is expressed. This classification scheme is then related to various techniques of analysis in the form of a map which indicates some of the territory to be covered in two subsequent chapters.

THE NATURE OF MODELS

Models defined

A model is an idealization, an abstraction, a simplification of real world phenomena. As indicated earlier, the phenomena of interest to local government policy makers and analysts are our cities, governments, or departments, the activities carried out in them, and the relations between these activities and desired improvements. To emphasize the wholeness and interrelatedness of these things we conceive them as systems. A model is a representation of the structure of such systems. And it is generally an incomplete representation of the real system — as the British mathematician Richard Stone says, "a slice of life."[1] However, this incompleteness is both a virtue and a necessity. The complexity of most real systems is so great that the total structure can be represented only in the actual system itself. In model-building the aim is to reduce this complexity, to identify the key elements in the system, and to understand the relations between or among these elements so that decisions can be made about those elements which the policy makers can control.

A model, then, is an imitation of reality. It is made up of those elements that are relevant to a particular situation and the relations among them. Questions are asked of the model (in experiments), and the answers hopefully provide some clues, some hints, which serve as guides in dealing with that part of the real world to which the model corresponds. This definition of a model would therefore include: a collection of mathematical equations, a program for a high-speed computer, a game, a scenario, an organization chart, a land use map, a city charter, a budget, or an architectural model. However, the models discussed here and in the following chapters will be those which utilize symbols (mathematical, logical, verbal) versus physical analogs to represent the real world.

Physical and symbolic models

A model is a representation of the structure of a system. Structure refers to the relationships between or among the elements, components, or parts of the system. In the language of model-building, these elements are referred to as variables. The representation used to depict relationships between or among variables may be physical or symbolic. The most common type of physical representation is the scale model, such as an architectural model of a building. However, a pilot plant or project (a school building or a low-income housing demonstration project) may also be a physical model in that it represents a small-scale version of some planned activity in which the aim is to try out various ideas as a means of deciding whether or not, and how, to implement some larger activity.

There are several important limitations to such physical models. Generally, the number of relationships that can be represented is limited; for example, the usual architectural model can show form, shape, mass, and some exterior detail, but cannot indicate the internal physical structure, room arrangement, support system flows (heating, cooling, lighting, water), or flows of people. If additional models were built to represent these things or if a pilot structure were built which encompassed all of them, the cost might be prohibitive. Even if the cost were not prohibitive, the number of items that could be varied or manipulated in any such pilot structure at any one time would be extremely limited. Thus, such experimentation would be slow and ultimately costly. Finally, there would be many activities and processes that could not be represented in such a pilot structure. For example, while it might be possible to have several families live in the structure and to observe their behavior to find out how well the structure meets their needs, there might be no reasonable way of studying how their needs change over time as they pass through various stages in the family life cycle. Similarly, there might be no way of studying the relations of this

family unit to its social community—to other people, to work, school, church, shopping, or leisure activity. The point here is that sooner or later one runs up against limitations in trying to carry out experiments with physical models. When this happens, another form of experimentation is needed.

Symbolic models are the major alternative to physical models. They are considerably more abstract but offer several important advantages: (1) the number of relationships that can be represented is greater and the relationships can be represented explicitly; (2) the elements or variables in the model can be manipulated and modified more readily, and therefore the number of things that can be tried is greater; (3) the experiments with such models can be conducted more rapidly; (4) the cost of such models is often far less than that of a counterpart physical model; and (5) the models can be used to represent and try out things that cannot be done using physical models.

The most common type of symbolic representation is that of mathematics, where various symbols are used to represent the elements and relationships in a system. Increasingly, however, the symbolism of computer programming is being used to represent relationships. Finally, words are an important form of symbolic representation.

Models and purposes
Models and purposes are interrelated. As the previous discussion suggests, the nature of a model depends on the nature of that part of the real world with which it is concerned. It also depends on the questions which decision

makers and analysts wish to ask of the model—the decisions to be affected by the model's results. Robert Specht illustrates this interrelation of models and purposes as follows:

If you are driving from Santa Monica to San Francisco and have not yet decided on a route, then an adequate model of this part of California may be a road map. If you are a trucker concerned about maintaining a schedule between here and San Francisco, then an adequate model may be a timetable that tells you, among other things, when you are due to pass Pismo. If you are a highway planner who must recommend a freeway route between the two cities, then quite a different model or set of models is necessary—road maps, topographic maps, maps of land use and value, traffic charts showing origin and destination, and a model, implicit and subjective, of the behavior of a population surfeited with taxes, attached to their real estate, and not altogether enchanted with freeways. Each is unrealistic in its own way, but each is useful when shaken well and taken as directed.[2]

The purposes of models may be classified as: (1) description, (2) prediction, and (3) planning.[3] Very often decision makers and analysts need a device to help them understand the forces at work in a system, develop theory about how the system works, or organize and short-cut fieldwork in efforts to test theory and find out how a system actually works. This is the aim of description—to lay out or describe the relevant elements or variables of a system and to indicate the form of the relationships between or among them. However, in description the relations between or among the variables generally are not made explicit and the resultant model cannot be manipulated to study the effect of changes in the variables. A geographic map, which can be prepared in whatever detail and scale necessary to convey an intended description, is an example of a descriptive model. Generally, all scale models, such as architectural models, blueprints, city plans, organization charts, and procedure charts, are descriptive models.

In other cases, decision makers and analysts are interested in the future state of a system if it continues as presently, or changes following some possible but uncertain event outside their control. This is the aim of prediction—to specify the future state of a given system. Prediction does not require understanding of why a system behaves as it does, but only that it behaves in this way rather than that under certain conditions. Thus, in prediction it is sufficient to note that two variables, X and Y, co-vary (e.g., that the variable Y has the value $5X$). A model with prediction as its aim would respond to questions in the form, "If X occurs, then Y will follow." The likelihood of X's occurrence may also be specified, as may other events which may reinforce or counteract the effects of the hypothetical change in X. Models to forecast city revenues, population, employment, traffic, or land use would be predictive models. The emphasis in predictive models is on forecasting the future state (level, amount, or other characteristics) of revenues or population and not on the reasons why revenues or population may increase or decrease. For example, the tax impact model described in Chapter 5 is an illustration of a predictive model. Basically, this model predicts the net impact on city and school tax rates that would result from introduction of a new plant in the community. The prediction is based on observed relationships between certain features or characteristics associated with the plant (employment, payroll, investment) and government revenues and expenditures related

to the plant and the employees it brings to the community.

In still other instances, decision makers and analysts are interested in making changes in an existing system. They not only want to forecast population, employment, land use, and traffic, but they seek greater understanding of the interrelation of these things to one another and to government action, so that they can develop policies, plans, programs, and actions designed to handle the forecast states of each of these sets of variables. In this instance they are seeking explanations. That is, they are seeking not only greater understanding of what the variables are or their future states, but how and why they interrelate with one another. They need a framework or a model in which they can manipulate the elements or variables representing the system in question so that they can try out in the abstract different ways of changing the actual system. Thus, the kind of model they seek is one which explicitly indicates the relationships among the variables in the system and which permits the decision makers and analysts to manipulate the variables. The San Francisco simulation model described in Chapter 6 is an illustration of a planning model. Briefly, this model replicates the behavior of the housing market. That is, it represents symbolically the interactions (1) between households and investors who buy and sell housing units, (2) between and among households, investors, and government actions— actions which are variously designed to improve the quality of the housing stock, the economic position of households, or the investment potential or opportunity of investors, and (3) between and among all of these elements and the outside world (i.e., changes in the number of people and

socioeconomic characteristics of the population in the larger area or region). Using this set of modeled interrelationships, decision makers and analysts can try out various mixes of government action programs (the controlled variables) and determine the impacts or outcomes of these programs on households, investors, and the housing stock.

THE STRUCTURE OF MODELS

Models as black boxes

A model may be viewed as a black box. It is designed to deal with a particular problem and is constructed to reflect the state of the world of which the alternatives available for solving the problem are a part. As illustrated in Figure 8–1, the analysts feed inputs (information about the alternatives) into the black box and from the box as outputs comes information about the effectiveness and the costs of each alternative. With the help of a criterion, the analysts or policy makers can then rank the alternatives in order of desirability and can select the optimum. However, as Specht points out, the black box

is simply a figure of speech to represent any device or process with which we can take into account, in a way as nearly logical as possible, the interrelations of the relevant factors. And the black box isn't really that color. If the analyst, the model builder, has done his work satisfactorily, the walls of the box will not be black; they will be transparent. The spectator and the user of the model will be able to see inside, will be able to understand and evaluate the structure of the model.[4]

Inside the black box: the structure of models

Since a model is a way of structuring a decision problem, and since the structure developed has

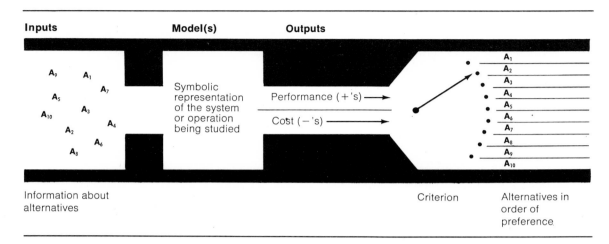

Inputs	Model(s)	Outputs

Symbolic representation of the system or operation being studied

Performance (+ 's) ⟶

Cost (− 's) ⟶

Information about alternatives

Criterion

Alternatives in order of preference

Figure 8-1. Models in the structure of analysis. Adapted from: E. S. Quade and W. I. Boucher, eds., *Systems Analysis and Policy Planning* (New York: American Elsevier Publishing Co., Inc., 1968), p. 13.

substantial impact on model outcomes, policy makers presumably should be interested in what goes on inside the black box (the structure of models). As indicated earlier, all mathematical models, for example, take the form of an equation in which a measure of the system's overall performance or benefit, P, is equated to some relationship, f, between a set of controlled elements of the system, C_i, and a set of uncontrolled elements, U_j. Expressed symbolically, the basic form of all mathematical and statistical models is

$$P = f(C_i, U_j).$$

This statement says that performance depends upon significant controlled and uncontrolled elements of the system.

In the language of modeling, elements are often referred to as variables. Some of the variables are control variables in the sense that policy makers are relatively free to specify them. They represent the things about which the policy makers can decide. Other variables may be considered as measures of performance, effectiveness, or objective achievement. These variables represent the outcomes resulting from alternative specifications of the control variables.

Still other variables may be uncontrollable in the sense that the policy makers must take them as givens. These are things that modify, limit, or constrain those things that the policy makers can specify. They therefore affect the performance variables or the outcomes possible under different choices about the control variables. Each of these types of variables merits further discussion.

The development of adequate measures of the systems performance may be a very difficult aspect of the analysis. Such measures must reflect the relative importance of, and conflict between, the multiplicity of objectives involved in every policy decision. These objectives are of two types:

1. Those which involve *retaining* things of value that are already available. The aim here is to minimize inputs where inputs are defined as expenditure, in the generalized sense.
2. Those which involve *obtaining* things of value that are not yet possessed. The aim here is to maximize outputs where outputs are defined as income, in the generalized sense.

The "things" involved may be resources (time, money, land, people), or states of the system (some per capita income level, employment level, community satisfaction, public support).

In developing *measures of performance* it is necessary, first, to develop measures of the degree to which each objective is obtained. These are called *measures of effectiveness*. Often the scales used in these measures may not be the same. For example, the scale used to measure the degree to which the objective to minimize cost is obtained may be monetary. The scale used to measure the degree to which the objective to maximize clientele service is obtained may be time. Sometimes it is desirable to find a way of expressing units on the different scales of effectiveness on some one common scale. The scale usually employed is a monetary one. However, there are many objectives in government which cannot be reduced to a monetary scale. Sometimes the most that can be done is to list various consequences and, perhaps, to rank them or to assign plus and minus values to them.

The *controlled variables* in a model may be such things as the type and frequency of services provided, the number of different services provided, the cost of each, departmental budgets, and the number of personnel employed. The values of each of the controlled variables can be set by the decision makers. The problem is to determine the values at which to set them.

Among the *uncontrolled variables* in the model may be such things as the cost of personnel and raw materials (the latter is usually not significant in the provision of government services), the location of the clientele, and the amount of demand for each service. These are factors which, at least within the context of the problem, are not subject to the decision makers' control.

The basic model may have to be supplemented by a set of statements which reflect *limitations* or *restrictions* or constraints on the possible values of the controlled variables. For example, the amounts allocated to departments in a budget cannot exceed the total amount available. Nor can the number and type of services provided to citizens be greater than the amount available.

These restrictions are expressed in a set of supplementary equations or "inequations" (i.e., statements involving the relationship "must be less than" or "must be greater than").

The following is a simplified illustration of these elements in the structure of models. Let us assume that a public works director in a small city (10,000 people) must choose between two vehicles for plowing out the city's streets after snowstorms. The first vehicle (let us call it x_1) will handle the average snowfall and is relatively inexpensive, say, $20,000. However, this vehicle cannot handle a large snowfall. The second vehicle (x_2) will handle even a large snowfall but is twice as expensive ($40,000) as the first.

From past records the public works director observes that in nine winters out of ten there are no big snowstorms. Thus he estimates that the probability is 1/10 that there may be a large snowstorm in a given winter. The director wants to minimize the total expected cost of snowfalls to the citizens, not just the cost of a vehicle for handling snow. In estimating the total expected cost associated with each vehicle he must include the value of the time lost by the citizens if a large snowstorm hits the city. If he chooses the second vehicle (x_2), he knows such time loss will not occur. If he chooses the first vehicle (x_1), he knows there will be some time loss and, therefore, he develops an estimate (C_T) of the value of the time loss in the event of a large snowstorm. Finally, he knows that, regardless of the vehicle chosen, the program or operating costs are the same since only one man would be required to operate either vehicle. Thus he chooses to disregard program costs in considering the two alternatives.

In order to systematize and make explicit his thinking about the decision problem, the public works director develops the following symbolism:

$$E = f(C, x, P)$$

where

- E = total expected cost of snowstorms to the citizens; this is the performance measure which the public works director wants to minimize
- C = c (annual amortized cost of each vehicle including initial capital outlay and maintenance costs) + C_T (value of time loss to citizens
- x = vehicle one (x_1) or vehicle two (x_2) [Note: c and x are the controlled or decision variables; that is, the public works director can choose either x_1 or x_2 at costs c_1 and c_2 respectively.]
- P = probability that there may be one or more large snowfalls in a given winter (p is an uncontrolled variable)
  $= p + p^2 + p^3 + \ldots (p = 0.1)$.

With this structure (model) of the decision problem, the public works director computes the expected cost of snowstorms as follows:

alternative 1 (vehicle one)
$E_1 = C_T [(0.1) + (0.1)^2 + (0.1)^3 \ldots] + c_1$
alternative 2 (vehicle two)
$E_2 = c_2$.

In the first equation the first number (0.1) within the brackets represents the probability (1/10) that there may be a big snowstorm in a given winter; the other terms within the brackets take into account the possibility of more than one large snowstorm in a given winter. In the second equation, there is no time loss (C_T) because vehicle two can handle even a large snowfall. If $c_1 = \$20,000$, $c_2 = \$40,000$, and $C_T = \$80,000$ per large storm,[5] then:

$$E_1 = \$80,000 \, [(0.1) + (0.1)^2 + (0.1)^3 \ldots] + \$20,000 = \$108,880$$
$$E_2 = \$40,000.$$

Thus, the public works director would choose vehicle two.

To this point, the example assumed there were no limitations or constraints on the amount the public works director could spend annually for the vehicle to be chosen. However, when he submits his proposal to purchase vehicle two to the council for approval, let us assume that the council sets a $30,000 limitation on the annual expenditure for snow removal equipment. What the council has decided, then, is to trade off the direct cost to government and the indirect cost to citizens in the event of a large snowfall. If we assume that the equipment which can be purchased for $30,000 is 50 percent better[6] than that which can be purchased for $20,000, the total expected cost of the third alternative would be:

$$E_3 = \$40,000 \, [(0.1) + (0.1)^2 + (0.1)^3 \ldots] + 40,000 = \$74,440.$$

Thus, by setting the $30,000 limit the council has chosen to trade off direct government expenditure and the indirect time loss to the citizenry. The additional $10,000 expenditure reduces the citizens' time loss by half but does not eliminate time loss. A comparison of the alternatives would appear as in Table 8–1.

Table 8-1. Comparison of alternatives E_1, E_2, and E_3.

Alternatives	Direct cost to government	Time loss to citizens	Total cost to citizens
E_1	$20,000	$	$108,880
E_2	40,000		40,000
E_3	30,000	44,400	74,440

Models and simulation

The derivation of a model by mathematical analysis fits many operational problems of urban governments. However, often the mathematics breaks down before the sheer complexity of many real life problems. Consequently, the policy analyst must find some way of experimenting in another abstract form. He must do so in such a way that there is a close relationship between the makeup of his experiment and the real life situation, so that the real life situation is not affected by the experiments. Such methods are called simulation.

Simulation is the process of imitating, without using formal analytic techniques, the essential features of a system or operation and analyzing its behavior by experimenting with the model. Simulation is a broadly inclusive term used to describe various physical or analog devices, such as a link trainer or a computer program. The method is explained by Ackoff and Rivett as follows:

Suppose we want to know the chance that a hand of cards at bridge will contain all four aces. In this particular case the problem is soluble mathematically, but if we assume that we have not got the mathematical equipment necessary to solve this problem theoretically the obvious thing to do would be to deal out a great number of bridge hands and find out how many of them contained all four aces. If we did this a sufficiently large number of times we would take the proportion of successes as being our estimate of the chance of four aces appearing.

Suppose now that we could not lay our hands on a pack of cards and were not able to solve the mathematics of the problem. One way of estimating the result would be to place 48 white balls and four black balls in a hat and take out four random samples of 13. If we then replaced the balls and carried on with this experiment we could take the proportion of times which we get four black balls as being the estimate of the proportion of bridge hands, which would contain four aces. As will be seen, we have now moved away from the direct experiment (i.e., taking the real life situation of a pack of cards and representing it by a bag of balls). In fact, we have simulated real life and carried out an experiment.[7]

By simulating a governmental decision-making situation (e.g., the budgeting process), we can determine those values of the controlled variables which optimize the performance of the system. Hence, however it is derived, whether by mathematics or by simulation, the basic form of quantitative models is:

$$P = f(C_i, U_j).$$

Nonquantitative models

The models constructed using mathematics and the all-computer models used in many simulations are generally highly quantitative. They require that the variables and relationships in the model be subject to fairly precise measurement. Often such measurement cannot be made, or is more difficult and costly than the decision problem justifies. For example, it is fairly easy to conceive of the programming problem involved in planning-programming-budgeting systems (PPBS) as a mathematical programming problem. However, given our present limited understanding of the urban system and of how various government programs affect the system we cannot develop the kind of information that would allow us to use mathematical programming to determine the optimum mix of programs. Further, it is extremely unlikely that we would be willing to state a single objective (e.g., minimize total cost) for determining which program mix is to be considered optimal.

Quantitative models, therefore, are often inadequate. Most existing quantitative models cannot take account of complex organizational, political, social, and economic factors, or they do so only under oversimplified and unacceptable assumptions. Thus, nonquantitative models and techniques are required.

The form of nonquantitative models is less easily described, but in essence it is the same as that of the quantitative models. That is, the purpose of the models is evaluation, and the relation between performance and controlled and uncontrolled aspects of a system still holds. However, it may be less explicit or may be only implicit.

Operational gaming, a form of simulation which involves role playing by human participants, is a case in point. The game structure (which is a model) furnishes the participants with an artificial, simulated environment. Within this environment they can jointly and simultaneously experiment, acquiring through feedback the insights necessary to make successful predictions within the gaming context. These experiments, therefore, provide indirect insights about the real world. A gaming model cannot indicate what an optimal response to an uncertain state of affairs might be. It can do much, however, to make the players aware of uncertainties and of the necessity for formulating plans in such a way as to cope with all foreseeable contingencies. Further, more than any other tool, gaming simulation permits the incorporation of political factors directly through the various roles and indirectly through the game structure itself.

TYPES OF MODELS

There are numerous ways of classifying models. Several have been used here already. The first distinguished between models which represented systems physically and symbolically. Focusing largely on symbolic models, a further distinction was made on the basis of model purposes—those of describing, predicting, and planning. Finally, models were classified generally as to whether they were quantified or nonquantified.

A fourth classification scheme is introduced here as a basis for developing a map of the techniques to be discussed in subsequent chapters. The scheme chosen is based on the form of the model, i.e., the way in which it is expressed.[8] The scheme also suggests the

quantitative nature of the models and how narrow or how broad a part of the world can be treated satisfactorily with the model. Table 8–2 depicts the classification scheme and gives examples of each. Five types of models are identified. From most quantitative to most qualitative, these are: analytical; all-computer; people; people and computer; and verbal models.

Analytical models

Analytical models take the form of sets of mathematical equations and are susceptible to "solution." They deal with generality not with specificity: that is, with all possible combinations in a decision problem versus a single combination. In this category are the models employed in the techniques of linear, nonlinear, and dynamic programming, queuing theory, network theory, game theory, and information theory.[9]

All-computer models

In many cases the relevant variables in a decision problem are too numerous or the interrelations too complex to be handled analytically. In this instance, instructions are written for a high-speed computer and the model, therefore, appears as a computer program. In contrast to analytical models, any particular operation of a computer model deals with a specific situation. Each situation to be looked at must be fed into the model and operated separately.

It should be noted that a computer model as described here is not any model run on a computer. Nor is it a computer program in the sense of a programming language. It refers specifically to a set of instructions regarding the interrelation and manipulation of variables which comprise a model—instructions embedded in a computer

Table 8-2. A typology of models.

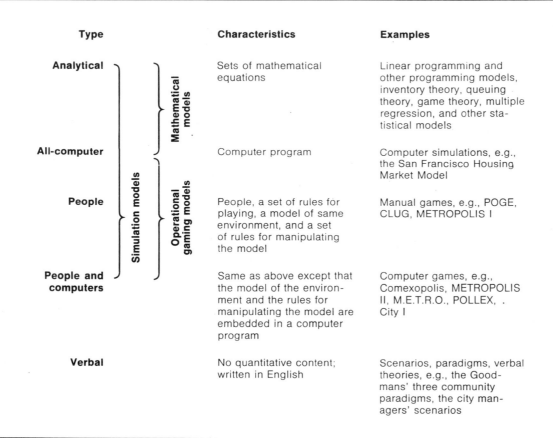

Type			Characteristics	Examples
Analytical		Mathematical models	Sets of mathematical equations	Linear programming and other programming models, inventory theory, queuing theory, game theory, multiple regression, and other statistical models
All-computer	Simulation models		Computer program	Computer simulations, e.g., the San Francisco Housing Market Model
People		Operational gaming models	People, a set of rules for playing, a model of same environment, and a set of rules for manipulating the model	Manual games, e.g., POGE, CLUG, METROPOLIS I
People and computers			Same as above except that the model of the environment and the rules for manipulating the model are embedded in a computer program	Computer games, e.g., Comexopolis, METROPOLIS II, M.E.T.R.O., POLLEX, . City I
Verbal			No quantitative content; written in English	Scenarios, paradigms, verbal theories, e.g., the Goodmans' three community paradigms, the city managers' scenarios

program. Monte Carlo simulation models, the San Francisco CRP model,[10] and the New York Port Authority simulation models of the Midtown Manhattan Bus Terminal and the PATH rapid transit system are examples.[11] As these examples suggest, computer models employ simulation techniques.

People models
While people are involved in all models—as designers, experimenters, users—they are an integral part of the model in this category. The most common type of people models are those used for gaming. The components are people or players, a set of rules which governs the activity of the players, a model of some environment in which the players are operating, and a set of rules for manipulating the environmental model. Thus, business games, war games, and urban community games are people models. So are crisis exercises. POGE (Planning Operational Gaming Experiment),[12] CLUG (Cornell Land Use Game),[13] and Metropolis I[14] are specific examples.

People and computer models
As the name implies, this category involves a mix of people and all-computer models in the overall structure of the situation being modeled. Thus, in the gaming situation just mentioned the model of the environment in which the players are operating and the rules for manipulating that environmental model would be embedded in a computer program. Computerized games such as Metropolis II, Comexopolis, M.E.T.R.O.,[15] and City I[16] are illustrative of this class of models.

Verbal models
Verbal models are those which have no quantitative content. Nevertheless, they involve deciding

what factors in a situation are relevant, determining the relations between and among them, and tracing out their interactions and implications. Everyone uses models of this type in their everyday deciding and acting. In most cases these models are implicit and may be difficult to make explicit. When they are made explicit these models fall into the verbal category. Scenarios, paradigms (see Chapter 7), and verbal theories are examples. The Delphi technique and scenario writing (discussed in Chapter 10) are techniques used in constructing such models. Probably the most familiar examples of verbal models are the urban future scenarios recently developed by several groups of city managers in conjunction with the Brookings Institution.[17]

General models versus specific models
The feasibility of a general model for all problems is, at present, questionable and unlikely. The more suitable approach is to develop a series of submodels and to link them by verbal arguments. Thus, a model of a large system or process will usually comprise many interlinking submodels. For example, Lowry's Model and Metropolis[18] consists of nine submodels relating to land use, employment, and population. The models are operated individually and linked to each other by simulating the effects of decisions in each submodel.

While a general model for all problems is not feasible, models have been developed which can be applied to certain types of problems in widely different contexts. These are the models used in linear programming, inventory theory, information theory, general systems analysis, and game theory. Some of these are discussed in the next chapter.

Table 8-3. Cross-classification scheme relating types of models and techniques of analysis.

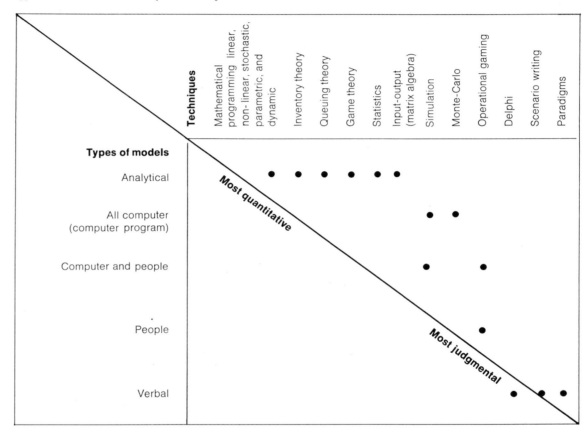

A map of models and techniques

Policy analysis is essentially concerned with developing a framework which permits the judgment of experts in numerous subfields to be utilized. The usual framework for systematizing this judgment is some form of model. It is not necessary that the framework or model be expressed in quantitative terms for the policy analyst to provide sound advice. What is essential is reliance on systematic judgment. Thus, the tools of policy analysis can be viewed as a continuum. At one end, precise computation is emphasized and judgment and intuition, while present, are played down. At the other end, computation is deemphasized and judgment is relied upon heavily. The techniques discussed in the next two chapters represent points along such a continuum. From most quantitative to most judgmental, they are: mathematical and statistical modeling (analytic), computer simulation, operational gaming, Delphi technique, and scenario writing.

Table 8–3 is a cross-classification scheme relating the types of models discussed in this chapter to the various techniques. It is essentially a map of the techniques to be discussed in the next two chapters. Chapter 9 deals with quantitative techniques and Chapter 10 with nonquantitative techniques.

Notes

[1] Richard Stone, *Mathematics in the Social Sciences and Other Essays* (Cambridge, Mass.: The M.I.T. Press, 1966), p. 68.

[2] Robert Specht, "The Nature of Models," in *Systems Analysis and Policy Planning; Applications in Defense,* ed. by E. S. Quade and W. I. Boucher (New York: American Elsevier Publishing Co., 1969), p. 212.

[3] Models built for planning purposes, as defined here, are often referred to as analytical models in most of the literature.

[4] Specht, in Quade and Boucher, *Systems Analysis,* p. 213.

[5] Note: On the average, the value of citizens' time is estimated at $2.00 per hour; on the average, the time loss is eight hours or one working day per large storm; on the average, 50 percent of the citizens suffer time loss in each large storm. Therefore, $C_T = \$2.00/hr. \times 8\ hr. \times 0.50 \times 10,000 = \$80,000$.

[6] Note: Here, 50 percent better will be interpreted to mean that 25 percent of the citizens will suffer time loss in the event of a large snowfall. Then, $C_T = \$2.00/hr. \times 8\ hr. \times 0.25 \times 10,000 = \$40,000$.

[7] Russell L. Ackoff and Patrick Rivett, *A Manager's Guide to Operations Research* (New York: John Wiley & Sons, Inc., 1963), p. 27. Copyright © 1963 by John Wiley & Sons, Inc. Reprinted by permission of John Wiley & Sons, Inc.

[8] This classification is adapted from Specht, in Quade and Boucher, *Systems Analysis,* pp. 222–25.

[9] See, for example: Colin E. Bell and Daniel Allen, "Optimal Planning of an Emergency Ambulance Service," *Journal of Socio-Economic Planning Sciences,* XXX (August 1969), 95–101.

[10] San Francisco Department of City Planning, *Status of the San Francisco Simulation Model* (San Francisco: Department of City Planning, 1968).

[11] J. Browne, "Simulation Scores for PATH," *Modern Railroads* (October 1966); J. H. Dickins and N. H. Jennings, "Computer Simulation of Peak Hour Operations in a Bus Terminal," *Management Science,* V (October 1958), 106–20; Leslie C. Edie, "Vehicle Traffic," in *Operations Research for Public Systems,* ed. by Philip M. Morse and L. W. Bacon (Cambridge, Mass.: The M.I.T. Press, 1967), pp. 83–94.

[12] Francis H. Hendricks, "Planning Operational Gaming Experiment," paper prepared for the Northern California Chapter, American Institute of Planners, November 19, 1960. (Mimeographed.)

[13] Allan G. Feldt, *The Cornell Land Use Game* (Ithaca, N.Y.: Center for Housing and Environmental Studies, Cornell University, 1965).

[14] Richard D. Duke, *Gaming Simulation in Urban Research* (East Lansing, Mich.: Institute for Community Development and Services, University of Michigan, 1964).

[15] Tri-County Regional Planning Commission, *M.E.T.R.O.* (Lansing, Mich.: Tri-County Regional Planning Commission, 1966).

[16] Washington Center for Metropolitan Studies, *City I* (Washington, D.C.: Urban Simulation Laboratory, Washington Center for Metropolitan Studies, 1969).

[17] "Predicting the Future of Cities," *Public Management,* September 1969, entire issue.

[18] Ira S. Lowry, *A Model of Metropolis* (Santa Monica: Rand Corporation, 1964).

Quantitative Techniques

9

There is no sharp distinction between analytic techniques and simulation techniques or the models they employ (analytic models and all-computer models). What difference there is lies primarily in the degree of generality or abstractness of the models employed in the techniques and the way in which the models are manipulated. Analytic techniques employ models that are abstract and deal with aggregated entities expressed by a set of equations which can be solved. The analytic model is formulated primarily for the purpose of finding a best solution to the equations. For example, an analytical model could be used to find an optimal strategy such as an assignment of trips over all possible routes so that time is minimized. The trips could be work, shopping, and pleasure trips on a highway network, or garbage collection trips, or police, ambulance, or fire call response trips on a city's street network.

In simulation, a computer model and a set of rules for determining what happens in the model under various circumstances are used. Simulations are used to investigate specific cases, such as the outcome of assigning a specific trip to a specific route. Each trip and route combination must be individually explored and some criterion applied to determine which is best. Thus, simulation is likely to be used in an experimental fashion, to generate specific case studies or instances from which a best solution can be determined, whereas analytic techniques will be used to directly compute a single best solution.

The analytic techniques discussed here include some standard ones, but the list is not all-inclusive. The techniques in order of discussion are: mathematical programming, inventory theory, queuing theory, and input/output analysis. Simulation and Monte Carlo simulation are discussed next.[1] Operational gaming, a form of simulation, is discussed in the following chapter.

MATHEMATICAL PROGRAMMING

Basically, programming is a method of determining the optimum allocation of available resources for a number of interdependent activities, actions, or jobs. Historically a *program* is a schedule of the quantity, timing, and spatial distribution of the various actions in a plan—actions which involve the use of resources. The problem is to find, from a large number of feasible action/resource combinations, that combination which either minimizes the total cost or maximizes the total return. The costs to be minimized may include such things as physical loss, time, or expenditure. The returns to be maximized may include service, investment, or income. Thus, the central feature of mathematical programming problems will be a concern with *allocation*. There are several standard allocation problems.

The first, *assignment* problems, involve the allocation of one resource to each job, under the following conditions:

1. There is a set of jobs (of any type) to be done.
2. Enough resources [people, equipment, supplies] are available for doing all of them.
3. At least some of the jobs can be done in different ways and hence by using different amounts and combinations of resources.
4. Some of the ways of doing these jobs are better than others [e.g., less costly or more profitable].
5. There are not enough resources available, however, to do each job in the best way.[2]

Therefore, the problem is to allocate the resources to the jobs in such a way that the overall effectiveness is maximized, e.g., so that total cost is minimized or total service maximized. For example, the resources may be classrooms and the jobs may be the housing of students; or the resources may be garbage trucks of different types and sizes and the jobs may be collection routes of varying characteristics; or the resources may be highway networks (existing or planned) and the jobs may be various kinds of trips. The problem becomes more complex if some of the jobs require more than one resource and if the resources can be used for more than one job. This variation is referred to as the *distribution* problem.

The second type of allocation problem arises when there are more jobs to be done than available resources permit. Thus, a selection of jobs must be made as well as a determination of how they are to be done. Most budgeting problems are of this type, but as yet no one has been able to formulate a municipal budgeting problem (not even capital budgeting) in a way that permits the use of mathematical programming. The evaluation of alternative transportation networks in transportation planning is another example: here the effort has been successful.

The third type of allocation problem arises when one has control over the amount of resources and hence can determine what resources should be added where, or what resources should be disposed of. The location of new facilities and budgeting problems are of this type.

Types of mathematical programming
A variety of programming techniques have been developed to try to account for various real world complicating features of programming problems. The most basic technique is *linear programming*. As the term suggests, it can be used when the relationships between or among the elements (variables) in a decision problem can be treated in a linear fashion, that is, when they can be represented by a straight line. *Nonlinear programming* is used for that class of problems in which the relations between or among the elements cannot be treated linearly but must be represented by a more complex function, e.g., a curve or a series of curves. *Integer programming* is a technique to be used where the values describing the elements must be expressed as a whole number. *Stochastic programming* treats situations where the values of the elements are known to be probabilistic in nature rather than assured of taking only one value. *Dynamic programming* is a way of treating decision situations which involve multistage processes and in which the stages are all mathematically similar.

Use of mathematical programming
Mathematical programming has been used in regional land use and transportation planning.[3] For example, the Penn-Jersey transportation study utilized linear programming in its household allocation model. The resources in this case were sites (of various types and locations) and the jobs were households (of various incomes and family size). The assumption was that different households have certain specific amounts that they can budget for the bundle of public and private services associated with a particular type of house. The model was aimed at seeking a market-clearing solution in which households and sites would be matched. The solution was found by a linear program which assigned households to sites so as to maximize the aggregate rent-paying ability of the region's population.[4]

Mathematical programming has also been used in various decision problems of local schools. One such use is in the assignment of students to classrooms given a previously developed master schedule of class meeting times. Another use is in the development of the master schedules themselves.[5] Here the problem is more complex and may be stated as: given a set of students with a set of course requests, a set of teaching staff members, and a certain limited set of physical facilities, find a master schedule of meeting times in which:

1. All students receive their requested course
2. The requirement for staff does not exceed those available and uses them optimally
3. The requirement for facilities does not exceed those available and uses them optimally.

Another use of mathematical programming in the local school situation is that of establishing school attendance areas, i.e., assigning students to various schools within a school district. Because population shifts occur continuously in urban school districts, schools are frequently overcrowded in one area and under-utilized in another. A related problem is that of school rezoning to achieve racial balance. Both situations can be viewed as resource allocation problems. The problem is to achieve an optimum balance between students and school facilities taking into account such things as: travel time and cost, racial mix, school capacity, and the total number of students to be served. Linear programming is one method of determining school attendance area boundaries, whether the aim is desegregation or better utilization of existing resources.[6]

Finally, mathematical programming has been applied to a variety of other problems faced by local governments. Among these are: nonpartisan political redistricting;[7] refuse collection and waste disposal;[8] municipal fiscal policy;[9] and synchronization of traffic signals.[10]

INVENTORY THEORY

Inventory theory is concerned with the problem of idle resources. An inventory consists of useable, but idle, resources. The resources generally of concern to local government policy makers are people, property (land, structures, equipment, material), and money. In simplest terms, an inventory problem arises because there are costs associated with keeping resources in inventory and there are also costs associated with running out of these resources. The costs of idle resources are basically storage costs but may include spoilage and obsolescence costs. The costs of running out of resources are basically those of failing to meet some need, including the cost of time delays. In such instances the objective is to minimize total expected cost. The problem in doing so is to find the quantity and/or frequency of resource acquisition so that the sum of these two costs is minimized.

Use of inventory theory
The most common occurrence of inventory problems is in supply systems.[11] However, education and training problems are another instance. The question here is, "How often should a class be run and how large should each class be?" Cash management also involves an inventory problem, i.e., "How much operating

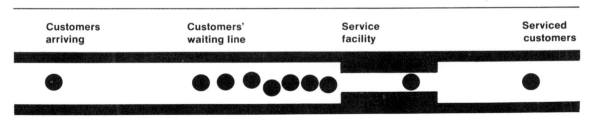

Customers arriving   **Customers' waiting line**   **Service facility**   **Serviced customers**

Figure 9-1. A queuing system.

capital should a municipal government keep available?" If too much capital is kept available, earnings from possible investments of the excess are lost—an inventory carrying cost. If too little is kept available, additional capital will have to be borrowed at premium rates—a shortage cost. There are also costs associated with preparing, processing, and closing out a loan.

While a variety of potential inventory theory applications exist in local government, few have been made outside the supply system area.

QUEUING THEORY

Queuing theory deals with problems of congestion at service facilities—that is, waiting-line problems. The waiting line is called the queue. Queuing problems arise whenever service demands exceed the rate at which the required service can be provided. And these problems are complicated by the fact that people usually arrive at random and at irregular intervals to receive a service. This situation characterizes a number of urban services: dispatching of police cars and ambulances to answer calls for

service; municipal or county vehicle maintenance stations; telephone switchboard operators; and public parking lots.

The nature of queuing problems is best indicated by a diagram, as in Figure 9–1.

The diagram shows the arrival of customers to the end of the queue, the waiting of customers within the queue until they are served, and, finally, the completion of the customer servicing. *Customers* refers to the jobs to be carried out at a service facility rather than to people. A job may be the processing of people at a service counter, equipment at a maintenance center, supplies at a central store, patients in a hospital, or vehicles at a tollgate on a highway, bridge, or tunnel. A *service facility* is the location at which the jobs are carried out.

A queuing problem arises because, on the one hand, there are costs associated with having waiting lines, and, on the other hand, there are costs associated with having idle service facilities. The costs of waiting lines are basically those associated with loss of time, for example, the suffering of a patient waiting for ambulance service. The costs of idle facilities are basically those of personnel or labor to man the facilities, and the facility costs themselves. The objective in such cases is to minimize the total of these two types of costs.

Most often, the decision makers have little control over the arrival of customers, but they can control the number of service facilities. Thus, the problem generally is to determine the number of service facilities needed to meet some level of service in the handling of arriving customers. What queuing theory does is to provide a way of predicting the probable length and delay of a waiting line formed by random arrival of customers at a servicing facility of some given capacity. Thus, the decision makers can choose either to accept the waiting line or to increase the number of service facilities to reduce the waiting line, i.e., to increase the level of service.

Types of queuing problems
It should be noted that there are several different types of queuing problems. They can be categorized broadly as: (1) jam-ups or bottlenecks; (2) idle or below capacity usage; (3) special type service demands. Certain services or facilities are jammed up at particular hours of the day or night and create operational bottlenecks. These are referred to as peak-hour bottlenecks and occur routinely in such places as airport or similar public parking lots and tollgates on highways, bridges, and tunnels.

At other times, services or facilities are relatively idle or are not used to their full capacity. There may also be variation in their usage at times during off-peak hours. Problems of idle times are frequently met with on transportation and communication facilities, in recreation and park facilities, and in schools, where the traffic (demand for service or usage) drops to the lowest ebb during a substantial time period, particularly at night and on certain days of the week.

Another aspect of queuing or waiting-line problems emerges from special activities or occasions in which existing facilities are inadequate and need supplementation — e.g., court proceedings, claim processing, police and fire services during and in the wake of civil disorders. The provision of services under such special demands can be enhanced through hiring additional help on a temporary basis, through personnel or other adjustments within the organization, or through cooperative arrangements with other organizations. However, there are many other temporary or emergent special activities and occasions which require substantial increase in the level of service for short periods. At the same time, the nature of these services is such that it is not readily possible to increase their level or capacity. These situations require a built-in mechanism in the overall system or organization to provide for such special demands. This kind of problem is readily observable in a nationally reputed football match which draws, say, 90,000 to 100,000 people. In such a case, traffic jams, parking problems, lines at ticket booths and other facilities, and all related aspects are congested, extend up to several hours, and put onerous stresses and demands on the overall system.

Use of queuing theory
Queuing theory has been used by the New York Port Authority in improving the management of toll collection operations on its six interstate tunnels and bridges, and for both improving service and reducing the cost of its bus terminal telephone information service.[12] It has also been applied to determining the number of ambulances that would be required to service a small community where the community maintains a single ambulance garage. This particular application, by Bell and Allen,[13] could also be applied to a larger city. In other words, if different ambulance services, or different garages for the same service, could be assigned to different districts or areas of the community with little or no overlap then the models could be used separately for each ambulance service or garage. Finally, queuing theory is being applied to the problem of congestion at airports in the Washington, D.C., area.[14]

INPUT/OUTPUT ANALYSIS

Input/output analysis is a technique for portraying inter-industry relationships, or the economic interdependence of industries, in an urban setting.[15] It provides a means of describing the structure and functioning of the urban economy. The importance of such replication rests on the fact that the destiny of an urban area is largely determined by the extent and character of its productive or income-producing activity and its general vitality. Input/output analysis of the economic basis for this activity provides a key to how the city has developed to where it is and what its future prospects are.

In input/output analysis the total economy is divided into endogenous and exogenous sectors, corresponding to the local economy and the "rest of the world." respectively. The input/output model traces all exchanges of money and goods among producers and consumers in the local area, and between local industries and the rest of the world. The technique postulates that any given sector of the economy bears a measurable relationship to every other sector. That relationship is expressed by a unique set of input/output ratios (coefficients) for each sector in relation to all other sectors. The problem, generally, is to determine what effect a change in demand (i.e., requirements for goods and services) in one sector will have on change in demand on all other sectors. The mathematical solution of this problem is accomplished through the use of matrix algebra.

The structure of input/output tables

The basic structure of an input/output table using dollar transactions for a single urban area is shown in Figure 9–2. The table is divided into the producing sectors, along the left-hand side, and the consuming sectors, along the top row. The producing sectors provide the output of goods and services to the local economy and the consuming sectors account for the total input to the local economy. Read horizontally, the table shows output for each particular sector of the economy measured in terms of receipts from sales to every other sector. For example, producing sector A sells to consuming sectors A, B, and C in the local economy. A also sells to firms outside of the area, the final demand sector, or D. The total output of sector A is then recorded at the far right-hand side of its row.

Read vertically, the table shows input in terms of dollars spent in purchases in a particular sector from all other sectors. Thus, sector A along the top of the table is a consuming sector.

Inputs / Outputs	Consuming sectors (purchases)			Final demand sector	Total output
	A Purchases from	**B** Purchases from	**C** Purchases from	**D** Exported goods and services to rest of the world	
A Sells to	$XXX	$XXX	$XXX	$XXX	$XXXX Total sales or output of A
B Sells to	$XXX	$XXX	$XXX	$XXX	$XXXX Total sales or output of B
C Sells to	$XXX	$XXX	$XXX	$XXX	$XXXX Total sales or output of C
Non-local inputs Imported goods and services from rest of the world	$XXX	$XXX	$XXX	$XXX	
Total inputs	$XXX Total purchases of A	$XXX Total purchases of B	$XXX Total purchases of C		**Gross volume of activity** Inputs = outputs

(left side label: **Producing sectors (sells)**)

Figure 9-2. Basic format of an input/output table (using dollar transactions for a single urban area). Source: Arthur D. Little, Inc., *The Metropolitan Stockton Economy, Analysis and Forecast* (San Francisco: Arthur D. Little, Inc., 1964), p. 21.

It has a certain number of inputs from sectors A, B, and C. Because many goods are not supplied locally, it must import from the rest of the world, sector D. The total volume of inputs necessary for sector A to produce its total output appears at the bottom of its column as a consuming sector. Since an input/output table always requires that the total amount of a sector's input

Figure 9-3. Inter-industry flow of goods and services in Stockton urbanized area. Input/output analysis—in thousands of dollars. Source: Little, *Metropolitan Stockton Economy*, p. 23.

		Consuming sectors—endogenous to the Stockton economy												
Sectors		Manufacturing 1	Food processing 2	Transportation, communications, and public utilities 3	F.I.R.E., business and personal services 4	Wholesale and retail inside CBD 5	Wholesale and retail outside CBD 6	Commercial, industrial construction 7	Residential construction 8	Maintenance and repair construction 9	Household labor (year-round) 10	Household labor (other) 11	Local government services Stockton city 12	Local government construction Stockton city 13
Producing sectors endogenous to the Stockton economy														
Manufacturing	1	1,292	5,968	1,921	369	6,262	2,785	3,280	1,227	196	559	27	612	—
Food processing	2	2	56	—	—	2,917	2,952	—	—	—	1,455	292	—	—
Transportation, communications, and public utilities	3	11,734	6,849	2,970	770	4,634	4,201	421	275	655	33,235	545	76	—
F.I.R.E., business and personal services	4	2,241	497	2,506	4,508	3,548	2,682	1,733	1,416	354	61,047	3,940	372	—
Wholesale and retail inside CBD	5	3,588	1,957	1,819	2,948	15,862	13,549	2,794	1,916	1,402	63,008	7,422	575	—
Wholesale and retail outside CBD	6	10,191	4,138	9,069	1,668	19,674	40,918	4,983	5,399	4,524	117,662	9,833	1,183	—
Commercial, industrial construction	7	1,451	1,998	2,212	163	539	3,359	3,919	535	428	4,454	39	—	2,122
Residential construction	8	64	99	402	345	291	363	378	557	94	5,641	215	—	600
Maintenance and repair construction	9	50	30	70	290	200	70	440	1,180	760	2,840	430	—	10
Household labor (year-round)	10	30,150	10,941	25,255	54,206	20,656	49,763	16,055	2,930	1,785	—	—	6,000	—
Household labor (other)	11	1,828	5,611	808	3,096	1,993	4,802	2,025	370	225	3,730	—	—	—
Local government services	12	352	299	540	313	65	749	33	29	15	4,565	937	190	—
Local government construction	13	92	66	164	115	520	325	19	22	10	1,146	231	31	—
Sectors which are exogenous to the Stockton economy														
Other government services	14	242	115	526	479	142	1,200	94	81	45	22,288	26,720	72	—
Other government construction	15	23	8	68	55	13	169	12	12	6	2,307	598	4	—
Semipublic services	16	144	119	64	166	54	116	27	8	10	5,292	1,325	12	—
Semipublic construction	17	20	16	14	37	12	25	6	2	2	913	255	2	—
Unallocated inputs	18	96,859	85,674	70,893	57,789	98,891	382,167	16,873	—	949	—	9,076	—	155
Total Stockton urbanized area input		160,323	124,441	119,301	127,316	176,273	510,195	53,092	15,959	11,460	330,142	61,885	9,129	2,887

Sectors which are exogenous to the Stockton economy													
Other government services				Other govern-ment services Total	Other government construction				Other govern-ment construc-tion total	Semipublic services	Semipublic construction	Exports	Total Stockton urbanized area output
Special districts	County	State	Federal	**14**	Local special districts	County	State	Federal	**15**	**16**	**17**	**18**	
57	298	1,637	2,726	4,718	—	—	—	—	—	432	—	130,676	160,323
141	148	177	2,141	2,607	—	—	—	—	—	449	—	113,711	124,441
53	41	225	6,898	7,217	—	—	—	—	—	6,055	—	39,664	119,301
1,194	1,253	904	1,653	5,004	—	—	—	—	—	1,515	—	35,953	127,316
1,295	1,536	1,073	820	4,724	—	—	—	—	—	2,577	—	52,132	176,273
3,981	4,388	3,415	1,465	13,249	—	—	—	—	—	3,533	—	264,171	510,195
—	—	—	—	—	1,432	822	2,930	908	6,092	—	2,123	23,658	53,092
—	—	—	—	—	158	390	382	185	1,115	—	143	5,652	15,959
—	—	—	—	—	190	400	250	260	1,100	—	630	3,360	11,460
1,191	5,866	5,613	21,500	34,170	—	—	—	—	—	18,228	—	60,003	330,142
—		37,397		37,397	—	—	—	—	—	—	—	—	61,885
		238		238	—	—	—	—	—	595	—	209	9,129
		52		52	—	—	—	—	—	94	—	—	2,882
		369		369	—	—	—	—	—	190	—	57,503	110,066
		10		10	—	—	—	—	—	6	—	5,016	8,307
		255		255	—	—	—	—	—	49	—	26,093	33,734
		56		56	—	—	—	—	—	11	—	1,525	2,896
—	—	—	—	—	—	—	—	—	—	—	—	—	—
—	—	—	—	110,066	—	—	—	—	8,307	33,734	2,896	—	1,857,406

SECTORS 1–13 are endogenous to the Stockton economy: i.e., sectors whose sales, employment, and income are mutually sensitive to change in each other's level of output.

SECTORS 14–17 are exogenous to the Stockton economy: i.e., outside sectors which effect the Stockton economy but are not affected by local activity.

SECTOR 18. Unallocated inputs consist of: (1) development of local capital, i.e., profits, dividends, etc.; (2) all goods imported into the Stockton economy; (3) any statistical error.

Input/output analysis—in thousands of dollars.

be equal to its total output, gross volume of economic activity for the area (the lower right-hand corner of the table) must be a figure that represents total output equal to total input for all sectors.

Use of input/output models

In all input/output models it is possible to test the effects on the local economy of increases in sales (exports) to the rest of the world, given a forecast of increased demand for goods and services.[16] The increase of local output resulting from forecasted changes in exports can then be translated into equivalent changes in local employment and population, the land requirements to be met as a result of such increases (by sector), and increases of local property tax revenue.

The use of input/output models has been extended further by the work of Arthur D. Little, Inc., on a model of the Metropolitan Stockton Economy.[17] Two innovations were introduced: (1) the inclusion of local government as a sector in the local economy, and (2) the further division of certain local sectors to account for geographic location and seasonal employment.

First, the Stockton model treats local government as a producing and consuming sector (see Figure 9–3) of the local economy (producing services and facilities), whereas previous models have dealt only with the private sectors. Local government is further divided into services and construction sectors. As a result, it is possible to trace the impact of local government expenditures on the other sectors of the economy. For example, the model permits testing out in advance the effect on the local economy of

increases or decreases in a hypothetical municipal operating budget or capital improvements program. The assumption behind this inclusion was that urban government expenditures do, or can, have substantial impact on the local economy.[18]

It is also possible to run the model in reverse and, by so doing, to determine the impact of changes in the nongovernmental sectors on the demand for urban government services and facilities. In this way the model provides a basis for forecasting urban government expenditures. When linked with cost-benefit evaluation, the technique may further be used to determine the economic feasibility of attracting new business and industry, or of increasing government expenditure as a stimulus to the local economy.

The second innovation of the Stockton model was that it divided the wholesale and retail trade sectors of the economy to take account of geographic location, that is, those activities located in the central business district versus all others. Further, it divided the household labor sector into "year round" and "other," to achieve some accounting of seasonal labor. Thus, if local government officials wish to benefit a particular sector of the local economy (for example, the central business district, or household labor with less than year-round employment), any budget or capital program can be tried out and the effect on these two sectors measured directly from the model. The kinds of effects measured are: increases in sales and employment for producing sectors (e.g., the CBD), and increases in wage payments or income for households (e.g., the seasonally employed).

SIMULATION

The analytic techniques discussed in the previous sections involve highly generalized or "standard" models. Thus, the techniques can be applied to various classes of problems in widely different contexts. Queuing theory, for example, can be applied to any of a class of problems in which the objective is to provide a reasonable level of service to a demand whose timing cannot be predicted exactly. This includes a wide range of situations: accommodating aircraft arriving at an airport or vehicles arriving at a tollgate; dispatching police cars and ambulances; operating telephone switchboards; and ordering supplies in a warehouse.

However, often problems cannot be forced into one of the standard types. Or, even after all acceptable simplifications, a problem may be so large or complicated that the equations describing it cannot be solved. Simulation is a technique developed to handle such situations.

Simulation is essentially a technique which involves setting up a model or representation of a real situation and then performing experiments on the model. Simulation could be applied to a civil defense field exercise, a group of subjects in a laboratory where the individuals play various roles, or a computer routine which describes the year-by-year changes in the physical structure, population, political structure, or economy of a community. In all of these cases the real object of interest is difficult or impossible to study directly. A representation of the process or system, one which is similar to the real system in its essential properties, is investigated instead and inferences are made to the real world from the results of manipulating the representation.

For the purposes of this work, discussion is limited to a few cases of simulation. Simulation models which "physically" resemble the process or system of interest are not discussed. Models in which human subjects play the analog role or in which human judgment and decisions influence the course of a simulation exercise are discussed in the following section on operational gaming. This section contains the case in which the representation is an all-computer model.

An example
Simulation consists of the step-by-step imitation of the behavior of a system or process described by a model. When linked to computers this process of imitation can be performed swiftly, and thereby "live through" many weeks of experience in a situation in a few minutes or hours. For example, John P. Crecine has developed an all-computer simulation model of municipal budgeting.[19] This model reproduces the output and procedures of municipal budgeting through a computer program which represents the structural form of: (1) the decision processes (i.e., the sequence of decisions); (2) the functional form of individual decision rules (i.e., equations representing actual decision rules); and (3) the decision parameters (i.e., values of constants or empirically determined variables embedded in the structure and functional relations of the model). The model considers three separate decisions processes:

1. Departmental requests, as formulated by the department heads in city government
2. The mayor's budget for consideration

3. The final appropriations as approved by the city council.

The model for the mayor's budget recommendation is illustrated by the flowchart in Figure 9–4. The mayor's model is written in the form of a computer program. Into it are fed numerical estimates of revenues, departmental budget requests (both current and past), actual previous appropriations and expenditures in various account categories, salaries and wages for employees, estimates of allowable increase over current appropriations, and the like. Further, the model contains procedures for various types of calculations relating to the numerical estimates (preliminary calculation of total budget, check of preliminary total against revenue estimate, etc.). Finally, as indicated in the model flowchart, there is also a series of decision rules describing the behavior of the mayor with regard to departmental budgets (e.g., if the departmental request is less than current appropriations, it is tentatively accepted).

When data representing various numerical estimates are fed into the computer, the program executes the steps indicated in the flowchart, makes calculations, and applies decision rules as indicated at each step, imitating the decision process of the mayor in preparing his budget recommendation. The output is a final budget.

This model can then be experimented with to determine, for example, what happens when expected revenues are high or low, when outside funds (e.g., federal or state) become available in some functional area, or when a different set of rules is applied at various points in the process. In this way it is possible to study the

effects of changes in revenues or changes in policies on the budgeting process.

Uses of simulation
Simulation can be used to study almost any problem, and therefore its uses are many and varied. A few are mentioned here. Simulation has been used by the New York Port Authority in the scheduling of trains in the port-owned rapid transit system[20] and in determining the number of berths in the port's midtown bus terminal in Manhattan.[21]

The San Francisco housing market model described in Chapter 6 is a simulation model designed to determine the impact of various governmental action programs on the supply and demand for housing in that city. The model was developed for use in making action recommendations for that city's Community Renewal Program (CRP). Simulation has also been used by other cities[22] in renewal programming and in several transportation planning projects.[23]

Szekely, Stankard, and Sisson[24] have developed several simulation models to assist in overall planning for an urban school district. The first model, "S.D. One," is a very general model of the financial and operational aspects of a school district, which estimates the cost of operating the district under an overall policy. Overall policy is defined by setting policy factors such as: staff-per-student; space-per-student; materials-per-student. Different policies can be hypothesized and, using the model, the cost of operating the district can be determined for each policy. The model does not, however, try to assess the effect of one policy versus another on improvements of the students' behavior (i.e., on achieve-

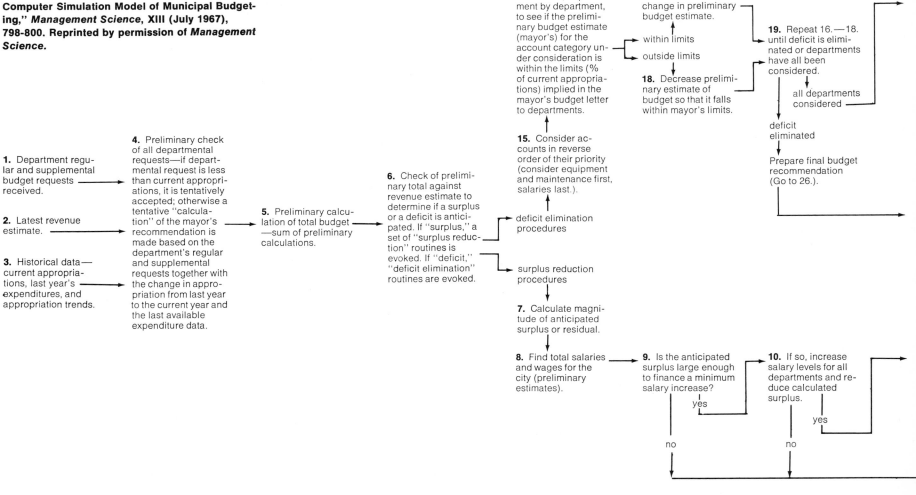

Figure 9-4. Flowchart of model for mayor's budget recommendation. Source: John P. Crecine, "A Computer Simulation Model of Municipal Budgeting," *Management Science*, **XIII (July 1967), 798-800. Reprinted by permission of** *Management Science.*

1. Department regular and supplemental budget requests received.

2. Latest revenue estimate.

3. Historical data—current appropriations, last year's expenditures, and appropriation trends.

4. Preliminary check of all departmental requests—if departmental request is less than current appropriations, it is tentatively accepted; otherwise a tentative "calculation" of the mayor's recommendation is made based on the department's regular and supplemental requests together with the change in appropriation from last year to the current year and the last available expenditure data.

5. Preliminary calculation of total budget —sum of preliminary calculations.

6. Check of preliminary total against revenue estimate to determine if a surplus or a deficit is anticipated. If "surplus," a set of "surplus reduction" routines is evoked. If "deficit," "deficit elimination" routines are evoked.

deficit elimination procedures

surplus reduction procedures

7. Calculate magnitude of anticipated surplus or residual.

8. Find total salaries and wages for the city (preliminary estimates).

9. Is the anticipated surplus large enough to finance a minimum salary increase?

yes

no

10. If so, increase salary levels for all departments and reduce calculated surplus.

yes

no

15. Consider accounts in reverse order of their priority (consider equipment and maintenance first, salaries last.).

16. Check, department by department, to see if the preliminary budget estimate (mayor's) for the account category under consideration is within the limits (% of current appropriations) implied in the mayor's budget letter to departments.

within limits

outside limits

17. If within limits, no change in preliminary budget estimate.

18. Decrease preliminary estimate of budget so that it falls within mayor's limits.

19. Repeat 16.—18. until deficit is eliminated or departments have all been considered.

all departments considered

deficit eliminated

Prepare final budget recommendation (Go to 26.).

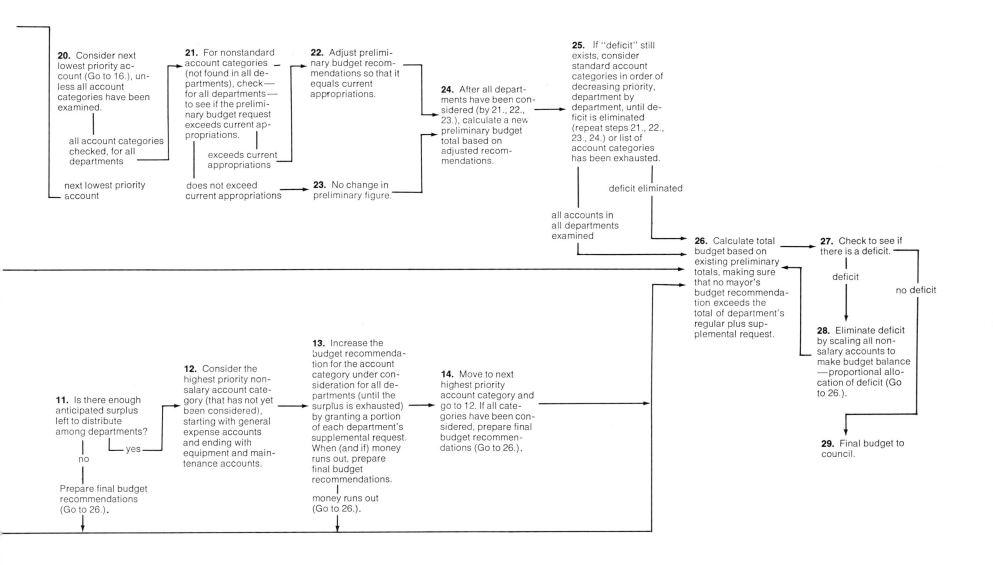

20. Consider next lowest priority account (Go to 16.), unless all account categories have been examined.

all account categories checked, for all departments

next lowest priority account

21. For nonstandard account categories (not found in all departments), check—for all departments—to see if the preliminary budget request exceeds current appropriations.

exceeds current appropriations

does not exceed current appropriations

22. Adjust preliminary budget recommendations so that it equals current appropriations.

23. No change in preliminary figure.

24. After all departments have been considered (by 21., 22., 23.), calculate a new preliminary budget total based on adjusted recommendations.

25. If "deficit" still exists, consider standard account categories in order of decreasing priority, department by department, until deficit is eliminated (repeat steps 21., 22., 23., 24.) or list of account categories has been exhausted.

deficit eliminated

all accounts in all departments examined

26. Calculate total budget based on existing preliminary totals, making sure that no mayor's budget recommendation exceeds the total of department's regular plus supplemental request.

27. Check to see if there is a deficit.

deficit

no deficit

28. Eliminate deficit by scaling all non-salary accounts to make budget balance—proportional allocation of deficit (Go to 26.).

29. Final budget to council.

11. Is there enough anticipated surplus left to distribute among departments?

no

yes

Prepare final budget recommendations (Go to 26.).

12. Consider the highest priority non-salary account category (that has not yet been considered), starting with general expense accounts and ending with equipment and maintenance accounts.

13. Increase the budget recommendation for the account category under consideration for all departments (until the surplus is exhausted) by granting a portion of each department's supplemental request. When (and if) money runs out, prepare final budget recommendations.

money runs out (Go to 26.).

14. Move to next highest priority account category and go to 12. If all categories have been considered, prepare final budget recommendations (Go to 26.).

ment). Such assessment must be made by the school officials (board members, administrators, teachers) by looking at each of the policy factors and making a judgment about their effect on achievement.

"S.D. Two," the second model, is considerably more detailed than the first model and includes

achievement assessments within the model. It permits exploration of the effect of alternative educational programs (or program mixes) on both achievement and the use of resources. The first model is already in use in the school district of Philadelphia, which supported the study. The second model will soon be put into operation.

Finally, simulation has also been used to study: emergency ambulance service[25] and air pollution monitoring and control in New York City;[26] the design of school bus routes;[27] the impact of Community Action Programs on communities and specific subpopulations thereof;[28] problems of design and utilization of hospital facilities;[29] and the Criminal Justice System, in California.[30]

Notes

[1] The discussion of techniques in this chapter is pur- posively brief. For a more extensive, but still introductory, discussion see any of the following: Herbert A. Simon, *The New Science of Management Decision* (New York: Harper & Row, 1960); Russell L. Ackoff and Patrick Rivett, *A Manager's Guide to Operations Research* (New York: John Wiley & Sons, Inc., 1963); Franklin A. Lindsay, *New Techniques for Management Decision- Making* (New York: McGraw-Hill Book Company, 1958); Stafford Beer, *Management Science* (Garden City, N.Y.: Doubleday and Company, 1968); Eric Duckworth, *A Guide to Operational Research* (London: Methuen, Ltd., 1962).

For readings beyond the introductory level, see: Russell L. Ackoff and Maurice W. Sasieni, *Funda- mentals of Operations Research* (New York: John Wiley & Sons, Inc., 1968); or Harvey M. Wagner, *Prin- ciples of Operations Research* (Englewood Cliffs, N.J.: Prentice-Hall, Inc., 1969).

[2] Ackoff and Rivett, *A Manager's Guide*, p. 38. Reprinted by permission of John Wiley & Sons, Inc.

[3] For a general discussion, see: Peter S. Laubal, "The Evaluation of Alternative Transportation Networks," in *Operations Research for Public Systems*, ed. by Philip

M. Morse and L. W. Bacon (Cambridge, Mass.: The M.I.T. Press, 1967), pp. 95–126. (Hereafter cited as Morse and Bacon, *Operations Research*.)

[4] J. D. Herbert and B. H. Stevens, "A Model for the Distribution of Residential Activity in Urban Areas," *Journal of Regional Science*, II (Fall 1960), 21–36.

[5] James F. Blakesley, "Administration-Integrated Records and Procedures," in *Computers and Edu- cation*, ed. by Ralph W. Gerard (New York: McGraw- Hill Book Company, 1969), pp. 183–228; and Dwight W. Allen, "Computer Built Schedules and Educational Innovation," in *The Computer in American Educa- tion*, ed. by Don D. Bushnell and Dwight W. Allen (New York: John Wiley & Sons, Inc., 1967), pp. 51–58.

[6] S. H. Clarke and J. Surkis, "Application of Electronic Computer Techniques to Racial Integration in School Systems," *Journal of Socio-Economic Planning Sciences*, II (July 1968), 259–72; Leila B. Heckman and Howard M. Taylor, "School Rezoning To Achieve Racial Balance: A Linear Programming Approach," *Journal of Socio- Economic Planning Sciences*, III (September 1969), 127–33; Ernest Koenigsberg, "Mathematical Analysis Applied to School Attendance Areas," *Journal of Socio- Economic Planning Sciences*, II (August 1968), 465–75; and T. Ploughman, W. Darnton, and W. Heuser, "An

Assignment Program To Establish School Attendance Boundaries and Forecast Construction Needs, *Journal of Socio-Economic Planning Sciences*, II (July 1968), 243–58.

[7] S. W. Hess, et al., "Nonpartisan Political Redistricting by Computer," *Operations Research*, XIII (November 1965), 998–1006. Heuristic programming was used here to draw nonpartisan constitutional political districts in Delaware and Connecticut.

[8] S. J. Wersan, J. E. Quon, and A. Charnes, "System Analysis of Refuse Collection and Disposal Practices," *1962 Yearbook, American Public Works Association* (Chicago: American Public Works Association, 1962), pp. 195–211. This is really a discussion of how mathe- matical programming (and other techniques) can be applied to refuse collection and disposal problems, rather than an actual application.

[9] Charles B. Woodward, "Optimization of Long-Range Municipal Multiple-Resource Fiscal Policies," *Journal of Socio-Economic Planning Sciences*, II (July 1968), 273–82. Here, a linear programming model was developed to assist the Metropolitan Water District of Southern California in determining the optimum mix of various fiscal policies (e.g., levying taxes, selling water, issuing bonds) so as to minimize the cost of providing water to the citizens of the area served.

[10] J. D. C. Little, "The Synchronization of Traffic Signals by Mixed-Integer Linear Programming," *Operations Research*, XIV (July 1966), 568–94. This article deals with the problem of synchronizing traffic signals so that a car, starting at one end of a main artery and traveling at preassigned speeds, can go to the other end without stopping at a red light. The application is theoretical.

[11] See: R. A. Ward, *Operational Research in Local Government* (London: George Allen and Unwin, Ltd., 1964); Morse and Bacon, *Operations Research*, pp. 17–47. Although several British studies are described in these works, the study referred to here is that of buying policy and inventory control in local government warehouses.

[12] L. C. Edie, "Traffic Delays at Toll Booths, *Operations Research*, II (May 1954), 107–38; "Planning and Control of Service Operations," *Proceedings, Operations Research in Industry Symposium* (Ann Arbor, Mich.: University of Michigan, June 1957); and Morse and Bacon, *Operations Research*, pp. 83–94.

[13] Colin E. Bell and David Allen, "Optimal Planning of an Emergency Ambulance Service," *Journal of Socio-Economic Planning Sciences*, III (September 1969), 95–101.

[14] Paul Feldman, "On the Optimal Use of Airports in Washington, D.C.," *Journal of Socio-Economic Planning Sciences*, I (September 1967), 43–49.

[15] Input/output analysis was first developed and applied to the national economy by Leontief and has since been extended to the regional economy by Isard and others. Wassily Leontief, *The Structure of the American Economy, 1919–1939* (Oxford: Oxford University Press, 1951); and Walter Isard and Robert Kouesh, "Economic Structural Interrelations of Metropolitan Regions," *American Journal of Sociology*, LX (September 1954), 152–62.
It has also been extended to the metropolitan economy: Werner Z. Hirsch, "Interindustry Relations of a

Metropolitan Area," [St. Louis] *Review of Economics and Statistics*, XVI (November 1959), 360–69; Amanda S. Rao and David J. Allee, *An Application of Interindustry Analysis to San Benito County, California* (Berkeley: Giannini Foundation of Agricultural Economics, University of California, 1964); Roland Artle, *The Structure of the Stockholm Economy: Toward a Framework for Projecting Metropolitan Community Development* (Ithaca, N.Y.: Cornell University Press, 1965); B. R. Berman, B. Chinitz, and E. M. Hoover, *Projection of a Metropolis* (Cambridge, Mass.: Harvard University Press, 1960); Bureau of Business and Economic Research, *Economic and Population Base Study of the Lansing Tri-County Area* (East Lansing, Mich.: Bureau of Statistics and Economic Research, Michigan State University, 1960); Harold T. Smith, *The Kalamazoo County Economy* (Kalamazoo, Mich.: The W. E. Upjohn Institute for Employment Research, 1960); Pittsburgh Regional Plan Association, *Region with a Future: Economic Study of the Pittsburgh Region*; Vol. III (Pittsburgh: University of Pittsburgh Press, 1963).

[16] This must be obtained from economic forecasts for the larger region of which the urban area is a part. For example, in California, these can be obtained from the California State Economic Model, which forecasts statewide demand. See: Richard P. Burton and John W. Dykman, *A Quarterly Economic Forecasting Model for the State of California* (Berkeley: Center for Planning and Development Research, University of California, 1965).

[17] Arthur D. Little, Inc., *The Metropolitan Stockton Economy: Analysis and Forecast* (San Francisco: Arthur D. Little, Inc., 1964).

[18] A preliminary test of this assumption in the Stockton area indicates that, for Stockton at least, local government is not a significant sector in the local economy. That is, when a hypothetical increase in local government expenditures was run through the model, its impact was slight. David A. Lyon, *A Public Expenditure*

Model for Local Government: A Case Study (Berkeley: Center for Planning and Development Research, University of California, 1967).

[19] John P. Crecine, "A Computer Simulation Model of Municipal Budgeting," *Management Science*, XIII (July 1967), 786–815; and John P. Crecine, *Governmental Problem Solving: A Computer Simulation of Municipal Budgeting* (Chicago: Rand McNally & Company, 1969).

[20] Edie, "Traffic Delays."

[21] J. H. Dickens and N. H. Jennings, "Computer Simulation of Peak Hour Operations in a Bus Terminal," *Management Science*, IV (October 1958), 106–20.

[22] For example, Pittsburgh and Boston. See: Ira S. Lowry, *A Model of Metropolis* (Santa Monica: Rand Corporation, 1964); and Donald M. Hill, "A Growth Allocation Model for the Boston Region," *Journal of the American Institute of Planners*, XXXI (May 1965), 111–20.

[23] For a comprehensive discussion of the use of simulation and other techniques in transportation planning, see: Ralph E. Schofer and Bernard M. Levin, "The Urban Transportation Planning Process," *Journal of Socio-Economic Planning Sciences*, I (December 1967), 185–97; and Peter S. Laubal, in Morse and Bacon, *Operations Research*, pp. 95–126.

[24] Miguel Szekely, Martin Stankard, and Roger Sisson, "Design of a Planning Model for an Urban School District," *Journal of Socio-Economic Planning Sciences*, II (July 1968), 231–42.

[25] E. S. Savas, "Simulation and Cost-Effectiveness Analysis of New York's Emergency Ambulance Service," *Management Science*, XV (August 1969), 608–27. This study provides an excellent contrast to that done by Bell and Allen ("Emergency Ambulance Service") referenced in the section on use of queuing theory. The

Bell and Allen study dealt with a fairly uncomplicated ambulance service situation and, therefore, the authors were able to develop a mathematical model for the problem. However, in the New York case there were so many real world complicating factors to be handled that mathematical models could not be utilized to solve the problem; therefore, simulation was used.

[26] Emanuel S. Savas, "Computers in Urban Air Pollution Control Systems," *Journal of Socio-Economic Planning Sciences,* I (December 1967), 157–83. This paper outlines a conceptual scheme for a simulation system (i.e., a system of linked computer models) to assist planning by local air pollution control agencies. Several of the models that would be used in the system are de-

scribed; some are already in existence, while others remain to be built.

[27] Rita M. Newton and Warren H. Thomas, "Design of School Bus Routes by Computer," *Journal of Socio-Economic Planning Sciences,* III (June 1969), 75–85. This deals with the problem of school bus scheduling, that is, determination of a route and a time schedule for each bus.

[28] Gilbert Kruschivitz, Alan Colker, and Donald Lamb, "A Community-Action Program Impact Model," *Journal of Socio-Economic Planning Sciences,* III (June 1969), 37–63. This particular application employs a set of fifteen models which are linked to one another to form

an integrated system for evaluating alternative sets of public programs aimed at increasing employment and/or income for specific subpopulations in a community.

[29] R. B. Fetter and J. D. Thompson, "The Simulation of Hospital Systems," *Operations Research,* XIII (September–October 1965), 689–711; and William J. Horvath, "Operations Research in Medical and Hospital Practice," in Morse and Bacon, *Operations Research,* pp. 127–57.

[30] Alfred Blumstein and Richard C. Larson, "A Systems Approach to the Study of Crime and Criminal Justice," in Morse and Bacon, *Operations Research,* pp. 159–80.

Nonquantitative Techniques

In urban policy analysis there are always decision situations where quantitative techniques are inadequate. Some problems simply do not lend themselves to measurement, quantification, and analytic solution, or solution by simulation. Even when decision situations can be handled by technique there are attendant problems of inventing alternatives, developing policies, and setting goals for which quantitative techniques do not exist. Generally, these limitations are minor at the level of operational problems. However, in dealing with programming and developmental problems such limitations are a basic fact of life. Most existing models cannot take account of complex organizational, political, social, and economic factors, or else they do so only under greatly oversimplified and unacceptable assumptions. Reality is that the models needed for many urban policy problems have not been developed—or even conceived.[1]

This chapter discusses some ways of handling those aspects of policy analysis that cannot be quantified. The techniques range from using the judgment and intuition of a single expert, to bringing together the opinions of many experts.

Such experts may be of the same specialty or may represent varied disciplines, professional interests, subject matters, or experimental bases. Basic to all of these nonquantitative techniques is that, for purposes of analysis at least, they are keyed to tapping the judgment of such experts. Thus, these techniques, like the models discussed previously, constitute a framework for systematizing and utilizing judgment. And judgment, as Olaf Helmer says, is an inescapable feature of all policy analysis.

While model-building is an extremely systematic expedient to promote the understanding and control of our environment, reliance on the use of expert judgment; though often unsystematic, is more than an expedient: it is an absolute necessity. Expert opinion must be called on whenever it becomes necessary to choose among several alternative courses of action in the absence of an accepted body of theoretical knowledge that would clearly single out one course as the preferred alternative. [This can happen if there is] a factual uncertainty as to the real consequences of the proposed courses of action, or, even if the consequences are relatively predictable, there [is] a moral uncertainty as to which of the consequent states of the world would be preferable. The latter kind of doubt

often arises even when there is a clear-cut basic ethical code, because the multiple moral implications of a complex change in the environment may not be directly assessable in terms of the basic code.[2]

The techniques discussed in this chapter, in their order of presentation, are operational gaming, the Delphi technique, and scenario writing. Others could be included and probably should. However, the aim here is not to be exhaustive but to describe some of the more promising techniques that can be used in the "art of judgment."[3]

OPERATIONAL GAMING

Operational gaming is a technique similar in form to simulation but different in objective. Formally, gaming is simulation with human intervention. For example, to "game" Crecine's budgeting example discussed in the previous chapter the decision rules in the mayor's model (and in the other submodels comprising Crecine's model of municipal budgeting) would be omitted from the computer program and replaced by the following procedure.

Each time a departmental budget (or all departmental budgets) is to be reviewed by the mayor, the computer would print out the results of comparison of the current budget submitted with past requests, appropriations, expenditures, and total estimated revenues. Then a subject, playing the role of the mayor, would decide on the basis of judgment what that department's share of the total estimated revenues should be. This would be read into the computer and the mayor's review process and would be repeated for each departmental submittal until all had been considered individually. The total budget would then be computed by the computer and a printout prepared indicating the relation between total budget and total estimated revenues, i.e., deficit or excess.

Assuming new sources of revenue will not be sought to increase the total estimated revenue, the subject would then decide where cuts could be made to eliminate a deficit or how any excess might be allocated among the departments. This might require a rereview of departmental budgets. Or a simple rule might be adopted for allocating the excess, such as a 10 percent increase (or decrease, if a deficit exists) for all departments. Such review would continue until a final balanced budget was achieved.

What such a gaming procedure would permit that Crecine's computer model does not is the active introduction of pressures from various individuals or groups (community groups, department heads). Such pressures might include attempts to influence the mayor's handling of a deficit or excess, or they might include attempts to secure an increase in a particular department's budget regardless of the overall budget condition.

As described, such a game would not disclose the optimal policy to be followed. However, if such a gaming model were linked to a model which accurately depicted the consequences of various budget allocations in terms of their impact on the community environment, this hybrid model could be utilized to provide crude tests of the effectiveness of alternative budgetary policies. Richard D. Duke's M.E.T.R.O.[4] does just this.

A definition of gaming
A game is an organizing device to pull things together. It can be used as a training and indoctrination technique and as an analytic tool by which different concepts, strategies, or plans and programs can be investigated in a two-or-more-sided confrontation. Conversely, a game is not:

1. An attempt to convince people to believe the results obtained by gamers.
2. A complete substitute for testing or experimentation. As will be seen later, however, gaming simulations can be used as laboratory experimental models for testing the gross effect of strategic changes in a system.
3. A technique for predicting the future, although it may be linked to other models that are predictive.

Types of games
Games take many different forms. They can be field exercises, such as the civil defense and Red Cross emergency operations exercises which involve real people in mock disaster situations, or they can be manual exercises conducted in a classroom. It is also possible to put certain aspects of games on computers which can carry out some of the formal and routine calculations and prepare maps, charts, tables, and various other materials for the players.[5]

Purposes and uses of gaming
All games have a purpose or objective. These may be any of several:

1. *Training.* The game is carried out with the purpose of using the simulated environment to create a greater awareness of the multitude of factors and actions that are involved in a situation and to develop an appreciation of these factors or actions in any real world counterpart of the environment.
2. *Research and experimentation.* The game is generally in the form of an evaluative or a developmental device, and the purpose is to arrive at specific conclusions with respect to policies, plans, programs, or actions.
3. *A stepping-stone toward a better model.* The game is used as a device for examining the various factors involved in a situation in the expectation that the important aspects can be established and some value assigned to various factors.

Any particular game may be designed to serve all of these purposes. The game M.E.T.R.O., described later, is such an example.

Components of games
In games there are usually two or more "sides." The basic characteristic of these sides is that they have conflicting objectives. Both sides are trying to attain their own objectives and frequently they have different resources which they can use to try to achieve these objectives. All games contain an abstraction of an environment —a model. Finally, games have rules. One set of

rules is for manipulation of the model—a simulation. Another set governs the activity of the sides in relation to the simulation—a game. The competitive activity is governed by the environmental model, which is a facsimile environment (e.g., a community or an organization) whose basic design the sides cannot control. However, the sides do influence the development of the facsimile environment in the game by the implementation of their decision-making strategy.

The phases of gaming
Gaming is more than just "play." It is a three-phased activity including preparation, play, and analysis.

Preparation phase. Preparation must start with definition of the purpose of the game. Unless this is done, it is extremely difficult to control all the possible data required, the events that might be considered, the moves that might be made, and the analyses that might be made. It is then necessary to choose a geographic locale and time period which are adequate to provide answers to the research questions. Although it is possible to use a fictitious locale, increasing emphasis is being placed on using real-world locales and situations rather than imagined ones in order to assure consistency in the data represented in the gaming model. For example, all of Duke's gaming models are based on Lansing, Michigan. The time period selected will depend upon the situation. Organizational games will usually extend two to four years beyond the present, whereas community games may extend ten to twenty years.

The next step is development of the gaming model itself. This involves developing an environmental model or a model of the situation being gamed, together with a set of rules for manipulation of the environmental model and for prescribing the behavior of the players.

Play phase. The play phase involves two or more teams in competition with one another—but a gain for one is not necessarily a loss for another. The teams may or may not operate in a game setting—a scenario—that provides the context in which the game is to be played.

The game is started by a briefing to all teams describing the general situation. The briefing may be oral or it may consist of a vast compendium of historical and other data about the environment and the situation. Each of the teams prepares its plans separately. When a course of action has been chosen, the plans are evaluated and an assessment of the outcome is made. This may be done by a control team, by a game director, or by a computer. Following completion of one cycle, the entire process is repeated for a series of cycles until some predetermined termination point is reached.

Analysis phase. Analysis begins when play ends. One type of analysis focuses on outcomes. In addition, special analyses may focus on the strategies and tactics developed in the game, or on the manner in which the environmental model operates. Finally, follow-on work may be done. This may involve replay of the game using different concepts, strategies, or assumptions about the roles of the players. It may also involve the conduct of field tests to increase the validity of game results and to make them more reliable.

M.E.T.R.O.: a hybrid gaming-simulation
The most sophisticated gaming model developed to depict the urban community to date is

M.E.T.R.O.[6] It is a hybrid of operational gaming and computer simulation models. The game is described by its creators as follows (the original format is changed to make it more readable):

The M.E.T.R.O. Project is designed to quickly and efficiently get across long- and short-run urban social processes to laymen, politicians, urban planners, and social science students. The M.E.T.R.O. instrument is:

1. An interlocking and crosscutting set of games. Each player belongs to two types of teams and is appropriately cross-pressured. There are three prototypical urban area governments (central city, suburb, and urbanizing townships) as one kind of team (each with four functionally differentiated members); and metropolitan-wide professional associations as a second type of team (politicians, planners, land developers and educators, who represent their respective areal teams).
2. An interlocked set of computerized simulation models (voters' pressure groups in the voter response model, exogenous and endogenous firms in a growth model, and a distribution model to tie them together) as well as a data bank and programs for printouts of maps, charts and other display materials to aid the game.

Player decisions are basic to the simulation inputs, and simulation results generated each "year" ($1\frac{1}{2}$ hours real-time) condition player decisions in turn. M.E.T.R.O. uses from twelve to sixteen players and requires an operating staff of half a dozen. The game and simulations are modelled from Lansing, Michigan, economic, demographic, ecological and political data, slightly abstracted and generalized.

The M.E.T.R.O. gaming-simulation joins the approaches of the Cornell Land Use Game and "METROPOLIS," and then adds refinements of its own to increase the sophistication of the instrument. A specific "game" will be played by each team; it is linked into the overall game with realistic interaction between all types of roles. Gamed decisions are injected into the simulation of the metropolitan area, and feedback from the computer relates both to player positions and to the growth pattern that results from the aggregate of gamed decisions. Typical decisions required of each team (different in detail and scope, as appropriate to the particular governmental unit or professional role) will be of three main types: budgets, issues, and policies, both explicit and implicit:

Budgets — Each unit of government is accustomed to making an annual commitment of funds. Many policies and relationships are implicit or revealed in the distribution of funds by a unit of government, and these decisions can represent a more meaningful revelation of actual policy than can more explicit statements drawn from these office holders. The budget function will have to recognize the need for the distribution of formal funds — governmental expenditures — as well as that pressure exerted on or by informal funds (influence on or by private investment capital);

Issues — Each governmental unit will have to be confronted with various issues in the form of a referendum or simply a secret poll on opinions. These will be translated into an index by a conversion program.

Policies — Each governmental unit has a series of policies under which they operate. Some of these are explicit, many more are implicit, based on tradition or custom for that particular unit. In either case these policies are the standards, or decision rules, which control the behavior of that unit of government under certain circumstances. . . .

In each case the results of fresh decisions (annual budget) or of changed policy (e.g., change in ratio of assessed value to real value) must be recorded for each cycle, converted to an appropriate index, and applied, through the use of growth models, to all geographic units having similar characteristics, thus setting the stage for a new machine interaction of the appropriate growth model [see Figure 10-1].

M.E.T.R.O. deals with ideal-types of governments,

roles, issues, programs and budgets, all abstracted from Lansing area data. To each modular unit is attributed the gamed results to all like units in interpreting any given run. Similarly, in the simulation, we have abstracted characteristics of organizations and subpopulations in the Lansing area. For example, there are three dominant industries:

1. A heavy industrial manufacturing plant that is tied to the fluctuations in the national economy and whose urban area employees are predominantly blue collar workers.
2. A fairly large firm with a slow-growing but highly stable employment outlook (an abstraction of the state government, whose role in the area is like that of a national commercial firm's branch offices).
3. A high-growth, technologically-oriented "firm" whose major product is concerned with innovation and the knowledge of research and development industries, whose employees are heavily professional, technical and managerial types who are oriented to world and national markets and who are sophisticated in their demands for urban services and culture (this is an abstraction of Michigan State University, comparable in its urban role to aerospace firms and other research and development firms oriented to the new technologies).

Our rationale is that basic industry *products* are unimportant compared to the kinds of employees the firms hire, the inherent stability of their economic activities, their growth rates, and the ancillary firms they support. We give this example in detail to illustrate the processes of ideal-typing that go on. We have similar rationales for selecting five social classes for the region, which are translated into household types for correlation with consumption patterns, residential mobility, and voter responses on political candidates and issues. For the modelling, regression equations have been used on historical data to establish baseline and response-to-change parameters. The game

starts with 1965 and goes on from there, so it is *future* oriented, and concerned with exploring possibilities of innovations, technological and social, in metropolitan areas.

The major simulation models are:

1. A Monte Carlo type of *voter response model* which generates turnout and support rates on issues and candidates. Its parameters are largely abstractions of historical tendencies in the Lansing area, and its workings are very sensitive to player decisions in the game.
2. A macro-economic and demographic *growth model* which generates growth of population, employment and income for the whole metropolitan region. It is a series of lagged finite difference equations relating basic industries, the regional growth pattern, and the pattern of the national economy. It is sensitive to the aggregate decisions of players with respect to investment in firms, housing, capital plant, public facilities, and urban welfare services.
3. A population and economic firm redistribution model which allocates the above growth to specific areas of the city (consolidated pairs of census tracts) on the basis of transport accessibility to employment and urban services, attractiveness to residential use by social class, density constraints, and the particular locations of facilities, etc., determined by player decisions. It is an elaboration of the T.O.M.M. model developed by J. P. Crecine for a Pittsburgh land-use simulation, and is a complex gravity-type model.

Figure 10-1. M.E.T.R.O. functional interactions. Source: Tri-County Regional Planning Commission, M.E.T.R.O. (Lansing, Mich.: 1966).

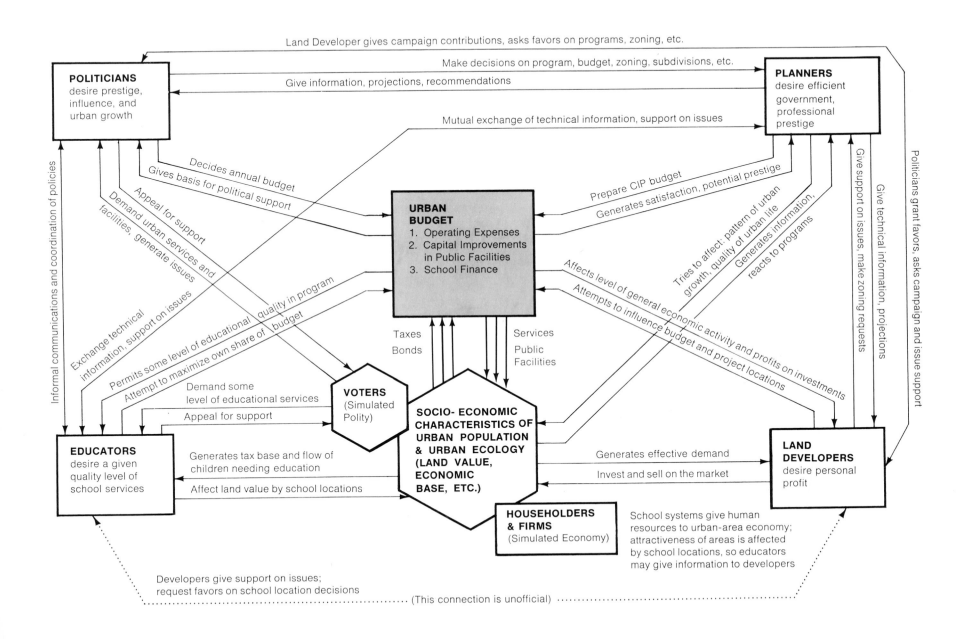

In addition to the simulation models, we use computer printout mapping to represent growth of various kinds, or any other variables that are spatially distributed and are held in the data bank. The technique, called "SYMAP," was developed by Howard Fisher of Harvard University. The establishment of a miniature prototype of a computerized data bank in the game means that players can query the system on a variety of issues, population projections, the areas of blight or unemployment, or of recent growth, etc. Players must *buy* information, however, so that this becomes a problem of rational adaptation like everything else.

We see the typical M.E.T.R.O. run as involving seven cycles of play in one day, each cycle representing one year. If players are already familiar with the game, all seven cycles may be active play, and sets of seven may be indefinitely strung together over several days to make for many years of hypothetical urban development. But for naive players, the first two cycles will involve learning the nature of the game, its tasks, operations, and strategies. The third cycle will start actual play and this will run five "years" at the end of which the computer will calculate the projected growth of the city on the basis of trends established by the players. Projections will be printed out for the next year, five years, ten years and twenty years hence. These will be part of the critique session that follows the run of the game.

Cycles are carefully elaborated into a tight sequence of activities and interactions among players, and between the player and the computer. The structuring of interaction is facilitated by the layout of the room in which the gaming takes place. There is an inner ring of tables for the first half of the cycle when areal teams meet to make key decisions and outer ring of tables for the second half of the cycle when players change hats and meet as metropolis-wide teams to discuss area-wide problems. Since the computation time, even given the speeding-up by computerization, cannot be less than half an hour, the meeting of metropolitan functional teams keeps the players on the track during this period, as well as ensuring a useful perspective on the metropolitan area. The intertwining of the operation of the computer (for simulation and game-supporting output) and the gaming allows a maximum of learning activity with a minimum of wasted time.

This phasing directly affects player interaction patterns. Their content within areal teams is given in "M.E.T.R.O. Functional Interactions" and the sequences of who interacts with whom is given in "General Paradigm for Interaction and Decision Patterns within a Gaming Cycle." Few unilateral decisions are possible; most player plans and enterprises are highly interdependent, leading to extensive bargaining and coalition formation. Players mutually define their own and others' roles in response to gamed constraints, interaction contingencies, and simulated outcomes. Much of a player's personal standing (likelihood of winning the next election, or personal profit position, etc.) depends on his accurate estimation of how the world will move next year, and his ability to modify, or to take advantage of, the course of events. Though his predictions are aided by data bank outputs and the opinions of his colleagues, his is not a mere optimizing task so much as development of a strategy, bargaining and balancing of power equations in a complex social system. Interaction focuses on the urban budget, upon short-term feedbacks of particular rewards and punishments, and upon the prospects for enhancing most players' chances by growing the area to make a larger base from which to get rewards.[7]

Finally, it should be noted that while most operational gaming tends to be nonanalytical, the M.E.T.R.O. hybrid gaming-simulation appears to have sufficient predictive ability to be regarded as at least a quasi-analytical tool for decision making. That is, it can actually be used as an instrument for testing alternative development policies in the context of the Lansing environment.

Other urban gaming models
The Cornell Land Use Game (CLUG)[8] is a manual community game which focuses on the factors influencing land use decisions in a city.

The game is based on data from the Syracuse Metropolitan Area. The game attempts to reduce the broad range of "factors" affecting urban land use decisions to a small number of basic characteristics of cities and surrounding territories. The factors are those which appear to make up the more universal and important components of urban areas and which affect the development of particular locations. The players take the role of competitive investors in the urban community, although their behavior in this role is not prescribed. CLUG is presently being prepared for play on a computer (which will perform the mass of calculations and provide printouts summarizing the results of play and other information). At present, this game is largely a communication and teaching device.

POGE (Planning Operational Gaming Experiment)[9] is a manual game dealing with the interactions and competing strategies of planners and real estate speculators in attempts to change zoning regulations in a previously zoned city. It is probably the first urban game developed. Metropolis I (manual) and Metropolis II (computerized), also developed by Duke, are first generation versions of M.E.T.R.O. Comexopolis is an adaptation of Metropolis II to include a role for an air pollution control officer and includes some decisions specifically relating to problems of pollution. These were simply grafted onto the existing model.[10] POLLEX (Pollution Exercise) is an adaptation of M.E.T.R.O. to an air pollution environment, and, in this case, the model is changed substantially to account for the roles and environmental situation of air pollution control.

City I, developed by the Washington Center for Metropolitan Studies,[11] is a general simulation of a hypothetical metropolitan area. The game is essentially oriented toward physical development decision making in the context of an economic model of the community and political forces (introduced by the players through structured roles).[12]

It should be noted that none of the games developed thus far begins to model the social system of a community in any important way. They are all physical-development-oriented and try to introduce social and political considerations largely through role specifications for the players.[13]

THE DELPHI TECHNIQUE

Most short-term planning by individuals or by governments is based on extrapolation from the recent past, some knowledge of alternative possibilities, and some planning against unforeseen hazards. For the more distant future—ten, twenty, and fifty years ahead—it is often necessary to rely on more intuitive judgments. The Delphi technique is essentially an effort to obtain such intuitive judgments as systematically as possible from persons who are regarded as experts in the area to be predicted. Basically, the technique involves exposing the views of experts to one another by a program of sequential individual interrogations, interspersed with feedback of prior and preliminary consensus. It is probably best used for situations in which the experts are all of one specialty rather than for situations in which the experts represent different disciplinary, professional, or other interests.

The method
The Delphi technique attempts to improve the panel or committee approach in arriving at a

forecast or estimate. The traditional panel approach involves achieving consensus through open discussion. The Delphi technique eliminates this kind of committee activity altogether. It reduces

the influence of certain psychological factors, such as specious persuasion, the unwillingness to abandon publicly expressed opinions, and the bandwagon effect of majority opinion. This technique replaces direct debate by a carefully designed program of sequential individual interrogations (best conducted by questionnaires) interspersed with information and opinion feedback derived by computed consensus from the earlier parts of the program. Some of the questions directed to the respondents may, for instance, inquire into the "reasons" for previously expressed opinions, and a collection of such reasons may then be presented to each respondent in the group, together with an invitation to reconsider and possibly revise his earlier estimates. Both the inquiry *[and the estimates] adduced by others may serve to stimulate the experts into taking into due account considerations they might through inadvertence have neglected, and to give due weight to factors they were inclined to dismiss as unimportant on first thought.[14]

An example
As an illustration of the Delphi technique, consider the problem of a policy group trying to determine what physical measures might be used to deter property crime in the city. Here the Delphi technique could be used to generate ideas and to use the respondents to trace out the interrelationships among these ideas and the consequences of their adoption. The kind of survey involved would not be a statistical survey of the Gallup type, and, therefore, it would be immaterial whether the respondents formed a representative sample of initially known points of view. What matters is that the viewpoints of persons with all major relevant backgrounds

have a chance of being voiced. The study would involve a range of experts who might be divided into several units[15] so that the task of running the experiment could be managed. Each unit might consist of a central committee of three plus a panel of six to twelve respondents. The committee chairman would be responsible for organizing his unit's activity, maintaining liaison with the study director, and transmitting the responses of his unit as well as receiving responses from other units.

The inquiry would be broken into several rounds, each based on a suitably formulated questionnaire. Round one would involve all participants.

The first questionnaire could contain, in addition to the questions themselves, a brief background statement explaining the purpose of the study. It could include a statement that the responses would be handled anonymously, except that approval for the use of names eventually may be asked in case certain suggestions are deemed worthy of further action. Only the members of the steering committee would initially be aware of the authorship of ideas. The respondents would be urged to include all suggestions they think should be examined, even though they might be dubious about advocating them. Figure 10–2 incorporates some of these suggestions. However, before actual use, considerable reworking would be required.

When the responses from the first questionnaire have been received, the steering committee would sort, collate, and tabulate them, clarifying their meaning with the respondents where necessary, eliminating proposals obviously not operational, doing some minor editing, and generating additions to the list. The results would then be

This questionnaire is being submitted to you to elicit ideas on what physical measures might be developed for the prevention of crime in the city. Crime deterrence and prevention today rely almost exclusively upon legislative penalties (prison or jail sentences, fines, probation), or the morality of citizens in society. There is considerable evidence that while vital, neither of these two forms of criminal deterrence are sufficient to prevent all criminal acts. A third method—deterrence through physical means (including policies, instruments, careful planning of physical layout)—is being increasingly considered as potentially useful, desirable, feasible, and important. This method has received little attention except for a few selected crimes such as embezzlement. While it is doubtful if crimes of passion and personal violence can be reduced by such methods, such crimes constitute only a small portion of

total crime. Most crime is property crime, and this type is susceptible to influence by physical means.

This effort is being conducted in the spirit of a brainstorming session, except that it sets out to collect ideas in written form rather than through open debate. At this stage, it is entirely appropriate for you to submit ideas even if you consider them far out, or if you merely consider them worthy of further exploration without wishing to endorse them. This survey is in no way intended as a substitute for research; rather, its chief value might be to highlight areas needing detailed study to stimulate further research.

Therefore, would you compose a list of specific physical means that, in your opinion, could effectively be used in combating property crime?

Figure 10-2. Questionnaire I (hypothetical).

submitted to the respondents directly, or to the unit committees as an intermediate step. The result of this review might be the elimination of several proposals. The remainder would then be annotated by the steering committee with brief arguments pro and con; they might also be ranked in some way.

Since the specific wording of every questionnaire depends on the outcome of preceding rounds, the likely form of the remaining questionnaires can only be suggested. For round two, it might look like Figure 10–3. This questionnaire would

be accompanied by written arguments, pro and con, for each proposal listed. If the results of this appraisal indicated that an item ranked no higher than Doubtful in any category, it would be eliminated from further consideration. For the remaining items, some of which would be controversial, more exacting standards of acceptability would be set.

The third questionnaire would explore the reasons for any divergence of opinion and might take the form shown in Figure 10–4. If the replies to this questionnaire continue to move towards

a consensus on some of the proposals, or if irreconcilable differences of opinion are inadequately documented, one or more additional questionnaires might be worthwhile. Such questionnaires would resemble that shown in Figure 10–4 in form.

The result of this study would be a series of proposals, ranked in some way and probably divided into those which are immediately operational and those which require research and testing. The technique is, of course, applicable to many other areas than that illustrated, for example, developing proposals for recreation programs and facilities, fire prevention, or educational innovation. It can also be applied to questions of long-range planning and development.

Uses of the Delphi technique
Delphi has been applied in several situations relevant to local urban governments. It has been used to study educational innovation,[16] the factors comprising the concept "quality of life,"[17] alternative urban and regional futures, and technological forecasting at the national level.[18] One of its greatest potential uses is in setting organizational and community goals, whether for parts of the organization or community, or for the whole.

SCENARIOS

At some time or other, policy makers need and would like a broad-based view of the future, or of conditions and events that might lead to some envisaged future. That is, they require descriptions, predictions, imaginings, or fictions of the circumstances in which their organizations and

The tabulation given below contains a list of proposals to prevent crime through physical means. We would like you to give us your judgment of each in terms of its desirability, utility, feasibility, and potential importance. For each item, check one box under columns A, B, C, and D. In making this evaluation, consider the *intrinsic* rather than the *relative* merits of the proposal.

Comparison Factors	A Desirability				B Utility				C Feasibility					D Importance				
Prevention Proposals	Desirable	Mildly Desirable	Doubtful	Mildly Undesirable	Undesirable	Useful	Slightly Useful	Doubtful	Not Very Useful	Definitely Feasible	Possibly Feasible	Doubtful	Possibly Infeasible	Definitely Infeasible	Very Important	Important	Doubtful	Slightly Important	Unimportant
1 Street Lighting Improvement																			
2 Television Surveillance																			
3 Helicopter Patrol																			
4 Communication Equipment																			
5 Auto Ignition Devices																			
6 Telephone Monitoring System																			
7 Layout of Streets, Alleys																			
8 Design of Parking Areas																			
(etc.)																			

Figure 10-3. Questionnaire II (hypothetical).

communities might operate in the future. They require projections of existing trends and predictions of future events, and also imaginings of what could be and might be. The policy makers may be interested in: the overall outlook for and character of cities in the seventies and eighties; the problems that government officials will face at some future period; the manner in which technology (the SST, mass-produced housing, computers, etc.) will change the responsibilities of local governments; or the conditions under which collective violence in the city might be increased or decreased. Scenario construction is a way of systematically thinking about and developing descriptions of such conditions and events.

Definition of a scenario

A scenario is a description of the conditions and events under which some system being studied is assumed to be operating. Most scenarios are future-oriented, although they may be reconstructions of the past or synoptic descriptions of the present. Further, scenarios may describe conditions and events at a single point or period in time, or over a period of time. Scenarios that involve the tracing of events over time are referred to as "transition" scenarios. Those describing conditions and events at a single period are "state" scenarios. Thus, a scenario may be a detailed description of a hypothetical sequence of events that could lead to some envisaged future state, e.g., events that could lead to an increase or decrease in government strikes, civil disorders, or flight to the suburbs. The scenario also may be a very broad and impressionistic description of the future character of the city as a whole, of local governments, or of some population group or class, e.g., alternative city futures or profiles.

Scenarios are particularly suited to dealing with conditions and events taken together, to integrating several aspects of a situation more or less simultaneously. They provide a way of exploring chains of events and the branching points in those chains dependent upon critical

The following items out of the list previously submitted to you have been eliminated for the reasons checked.

Item No.	Description	**Reason for Elimination**			
		Undesirable	Not Useful	Infeasible	Unimportant
3				X	
7		X	X		X
8					
—					X
—					

The remaining items are controversial in one or more ways. In those cases where a check mark is circled, your previously expressed opinion differed from the opinions of several other of the respondents. For each, please indicate why you hold this particular opinion. Alternately, if on reconsideration you do not feel strongly enough about your previously expressed opinion to defend it, please indicate this by stating a revised rating.

Item No.	Description	**Controversial as to**				Reason For Previous Rating or Revised Rating
		Desirability	Utility	Feasibility	Importance	
1						
2						
5						
—						
—						

Figure 10-4. Questionnaire III (hypothetical).

choices of decision makers. They are also a way of exploring, as a whole, alternative sets of conditions that might characterize a system.

The system for which the scenario is constructed could be anything: the city, municipal government, a school district, an operational exercise, a gaming situation, a transportation system, or a transportation vehicle. The possible scenarios relating to such systems could include the following, among others:[19]

1. A caricature of the system and its environment at some future time, e.g., an urban future
2. An outline of a sequence of hypothetical events, e.g., various technological breakthroughs; crises relating to air, water, or noise pollution, or to race relations
3. A record of the actions and counteractions taken by parties to a conflict, e.g., public employee unions and local government officials in a labor dispute, or interest groups in a public confrontation over some policy issue
4. A plan of actions to be taken during a projected exercise, e.g., a civil defense–civil disaster exercise or a riot control exercise
5. The estimate of a situation made by a decision maker (or provided to him), e.g., as in a gaming exercise.

Utility of scenarios

Kahn and Wiener cite the following advantages of scenarios as an aid to thinking:

1. They serve to call attention, sometimes dramatically and persuasively, to the larger range of possibilities that must be considered in the analysis of the future. They are one of the most effective tools in lessening the "carry-over" thinking that is likely even when it is

clear to all that 2000 cannot be the same as 1965 or even 1985. Scenarios are one way to force oneself and others to plunge into the unfamiliar and rapidly changing world of the present and the future: They dramatize and illustrate the possibilities they focus on in a very useful way. (They may do little or nothing for the possibilities they do not focus on.)

2. They force the analyst to deal with details and dynamics that he might easily avoid treating if he restricted himself to abstract considerations. Typically no particular set of the possible sets of details and dynamics seems specially worth treating, so none are treated, even though a detailed investigation of even a few arbitrarily chosen cases can be most helpful.

3. They help to illuminate the interaction of psychological, social, economic, cultural, political, and military factors, including the influence of individual political personalities upon what otherwise might be abstract considerations, and they do so in a form that permits the comprehension of many such interacting elements at once.

4. They can illustrate forcefully, sometimes in oversimplified fashion certain principles, issues, or questions that might be ignored or lost if one insisted on taking examples only from the complex and controversial real world.

5. They may also be used to consider alternative possible outcomes of certain real past and present events such as [urban disorders, campus strife, or rejection of bond issues at the polls].

6. They can be used as artificial "case histories" and "historical anecdotes" to make up to some degree for the paucity of actual examples.[20]

The relation of scenarios to other analyses

Usually, scenarios are related to other analytic tools, either as imputs to formal models or as supplemental analyses to model outputs that are essentially quantitative in nature. For example, scenarios may provide data for quantitative models, serve as the setting for an urban gaming situation, or constitute a way of handling nonquantitative organizational, social, and political aspects of a problem where other aspects are handled analytically. However, scenarios may also constitute analyses in their own right, serving to stimulate and stretch the imagination or show the complex relation of social and other factors in a decision situation.

Scenarios and problems

The form and content of a scenario is related to the type of decision problem being studied and to the scenario's function in relation to other analyses that may be conducted as part of a total policy analysis study. While scenarios may be used in dealing with operating and programming problems, their greatest need and utility is at the level of planning or developmental problems (determining major policy alternatives).

For example, scenarios could be used in developing and analyzing transportation policies or transportation systems. Starting with various philosophical assumptions and introducing technological, social, political, economic, and physical factors and events, alternative urban futures could be developed which would depict the various environments in which transportation policies and systems would operate. These environments might depict the preferred or optimal urban future, the worst possible future, or both, and numerous other futures in between. Various policies and systems could then be tested in terms of their effectiveness in achieving the optimal future, or in terms of their ability to operate at some level of effectiveness under the worst conditions. Those policies and systems which meet this test could then be compared in terms of more quantitative and traditional criteria, such as the costs, convenience, safety, comfort, flexibility, and environmental impacts.[21]

There is an additional important feature of scenarios in relation to decision problems. As the problems move along the scale from operational to developmental, the philosophical, political, and social content and context surrounding decision problems assume more importance. Further, at the lower end of the continuum the scenario content may be dictated by the decision makers, who wish to have some aspects explored which are relevant to *them*. At the other end, the scenario is more likely to serve, and is more valuable, as a device that alters what the decision makers perceive as important, the models and the criteria they use to evaluate alternatives, and even the alternatives perceived. In this last case the scenario serves as a crystal ball. It may be used to alert the decision makers to state-of-the-world changes and specific situations which may require new systems and new responses that are not now planned for, or which may alter prevailing expectations of what planned-for systems can accomplish. Thus the scenario serves as a way of questioning old assumptions and fashioning new ideas.

The form and content of scenarios

As indicated above, the form and content of a scenario is related to the problem and the specific function it is to serve in the analysis. Thus, the scenario may be presented in computer language or it may resemble a historical essay (i.e., a "future history"), rich in detail, with the purpose of conveying not only the tangible features of a situation but also its tone and mood. For example, if the scenario is to be used in a community gaming situation, it might look as follows: written on pieces of 8½-by-11-inch paper, mostly in English words, and combining the attributes of a "policies plan" drawn up by government officials and the *New York Times'* "News of the Week in Review." If the scenario is to be used for developing and testing transportation policies and systems, as in the previous example, it might look like the three community models described in Chapter 7.

Use of scenarios
Recently a series of ICMA–Brookings Institution seminars[22] was directed towards consolidating the thinking of thirty-two city managers about the nature of the environment and the management problems that will be presented by different size American cities in two time frames: 1969–75 and 1975–85, with some reference to the time period 1985–2000. Major emphasis was placed on projection of present trends in cities and the manner in which these trends will extend and intersect in the immediate and longer-term future. Some consideration was given to prediction of future events. The aim was not simply to develop a list of predicted individual conditions or events but also to view these as an interrelated set and to explore the way in which the various individual predictions might affect the total set.

Using various readings and their own experience as backgrounds, the managers prepared descriptions or scenarios of what they thought would be the management environment and the problems of cities in 1975, and ten years later in 1985. Four scenarios were developed by the various teams. In addition to the detailed predictions

themselves, what is really interesting about this particular set is the unanimous pessimism implicit and explicit in the urban futures developed. In every case the managers predict a sizable increase in the number, kind, and complexity of problems to be faced, but no corresponding increase in the ability of local governments to act on these problems. Each predicts increasing reliance on the federal government to solve the problems of cities. While important changes are predicted for 1975 and 1985, the more interesting changes are those predicted for the year 2000. Some of these are shown in Table 10–1.

PARADIGMS

Scenarios and paradigms are closely related but differ somewhat in purpose and use. A scenario is used as an aid to stimulate thinking about future conditions and events and to develop alternative futures. Paradigms are used to compare or to show side by side a set of ideas such as those which might be developed in a scenario. They are used to analyze the set of ideas. Thus, a paradigm is a structured set of assumptions, concepts, propositions, and questions about a subject. It brings these together in a compact form, thereby permitting simultaneous inspection and evaluation of the set, or of several sets. The paradigm does not represent a set of ideas constructed *de novo*. Rather, it is a codification of concepts, ideas, or problems found in existing theory, research, or experience related to a particular subject. The purpose of constructing the paradigm is to expose the underlying logic of the ideas as a basis for correction, improvement, or choice among them.

Table 10-1. Some projections of the operating environment of cities for the year 2000. Source: International City Management Association, "Predicting the Future of Cities," *Public Management,* LI (September 1969), p. 15.

Functions of paradigms
First used in sociological analysis, paradigms are equally valid and applicable for the analysis of public policy problems. Robert K. Merton points out five closely related functions of paradigms:

First, paradigms have a notational function. They provide a compact parsimonious arrangement of the central concepts and their interrelations as these are utilized for description and analysis. Having one's concepts set out in sufficiently brief compass to permit their *simultaneous* inspection is an important aid to self-correction of one's successive interpretations, a result difficult to achieve when one's concepts are scattered and hidden in page after page of discursive exposition. . . .

Second, the explicit statement of analytical paradigms lessens the likelihood of inadvertently importing hidden assumptions and concepts, since each new assumption and each new concept must either be logically *derivable* from the previous terms of the paradigm or explicitly *incorporated* in it. The paradigm thus supplies a pragmatic and logical guide for the avoidance of *ad hoc* (i.e., logically irresponsible) hypotheses.

Third, paradigms advance the cumulation of theoretical interpretation. In this connection, we can regard the paradigm as the foundation upon which the house of interpretations is built. If a new story cannot be built directly upon the paradigmatic foundations, if it cannot be derived from the foundations, then it must be

Political developments

Centralization of certain services at the federal level, probably in health, safety, and welfare activities.

Nationalization of police activities, probably related to technology such as computer identification of persons or police activities which lend themselves to this type of analysis or use.

Regional land use controls with localities having minimal or no control over land within their own boundaries.

Disappearance of nonpartisan politics at the local level, with major parties becoming increasingly responsible for the condition of cities. This will, of course, result in increased interest among national parties in local government.

Economic developments

A 30-hour work week with continuing increases in leisure time.

Reduction in the economic differential between populations developed by such devices as a guaranteed income or a minimum base income.

Regional economic homogeneity with reductions in extreme differentials among income levels in various sections of the country.

Social developments

Birth control by government action with governmental rewards and penalties for birth, depending upon governmental policies.

Life control, with the legal and moral right of an individual to destroy himself.

The reduction of interracial conflict and social differences.

Higher family incomes for young persons with nonwork becoming socially acceptable.

The disappearance of currency as we know it, with a credit balance system supplanting the exchange of money as it occurs today.

Psychological developments

Governmentally arranged national health programs with a national policy of psychological control. This might include psychological assistance or psychiatric care for a much broader group of the population than is presently available.

National control of the educational process with limitation of subject matter and reduction in the breadth of subject matter available. This will involve a reorientation of advanced training from present disciplines, with greater emphasis on the productivity of training. The individual will be tested and productive; selection and placement will be made prior to the beginning of his schooling, possibly as early as age one year.

Institutionalization of individuals, starting as early as age one year, with some form of family substitution occurring where necessary.

Education and business conducted in the home due to the availability of advanced communications systems. Activities will be more home- than office-oriented as they have been in the past.

Technological developments

Home disposal of solid and liquid waste with development of internal home energy systems. The home will become a self-contained unit with regenerative power and waste disposal sources.

Development of new and more systematized transportation devices with government regulation of use.

Nationalization of public and private information systems, with possible cooperation between government and private investment sources for the establishment of these systems.

Control ecology through weather control and food synthesization.

Increasing use of video forms of communication with reduction of face-to-face contact between individuals. This will also involve a significant improvement in video systems to create a greater sense of reality in their transmission.

Reorientation of professions and occupations resulting in part from their psychological obsolescence or their inability to adapt to new disciplines and social requirements.

A reduction in the labor force devoted to manufacturing. The population required for manufacturing functions may be no more than 5 percent of the total U.S. population.

Industrialization of housing production, with greater emphasis on mobility and flexibility in the type of living available through new housing developments.

Structural developments

Increasing development of regional governments and councils of governments with small units within each performing limited functions to satisfy resistance to a mass society. This will also involve imposition of regional standards over existing small units of government.

Value changes

Increased racial mixing with racial barriers becoming less apparent.

Continuing institutionalization of people, with more emphasis upon their formal position in the social structure.

A reduction in competitive activity or a change in orientation away from the survival concept of competition.

Cultural developments

Increased education resulting from leisure time, but with the educational process made easier and more pleasurable for the assimilation of knowledge.

considered a new wing of the total structure, and the foundations (of concepts and assumptions) must be extended to support the new wing. Moreover each new story which can be built upon the original foundations strengthens our confidence in their substantial quality just as every new extension, precisely because it requires additional foundations, leads us to suspect the soundness of the original substructure. . . .

Fourth, paradigms, by their very arrangement, suggest the *systematic* cross-tabulation of presumably significant concepts and may thus sensitize the analyst to types of empirical and theoretic problems which might otherwise be overlooked. They promote *analysis* rather than concrete description. . . .

Fifth, and . . . finally, paradigms make for the codification of methods of *qualitative* analysis in a manner approximating the logical, if not the empirical, rigor of *quantitative* analysis. . . . [Quantitative] procedures are expressly codified as a matter of course: they are open to inspection by all, and the assumptions and procedures can be critically scrutinized by all who care to read. In frequent contrast to this public character of codified quantitative analysis, the . . . analysis of qualitative data is assumed to reside in a private world inhabited exclusively by penetrating but unfathomable insights and by ineffable understandings. Indeed, discursive expositions not based upon an explicit paradigm often involve perceptive interpretations; as the cant phrase has it, they are rich in "illuminating insights." But it is not always clear just which operations with analytic concepts were involved in these insights. There consequently results an aggregate of discrete insights rather than a codified body of knowledge, subject to reproducible research. . . .[23]

Use of paradigms

Paradigms are probably used most frequently in urban planning as a means of developing planning proposals and communicating them to government officials and citizens. The Washington metropolitan area plan, prepared in 1961 by the National Capital Planning Commission, is an example.[24] In the plan, the population of the Washington metropolitan area was projected to grow from a level of 2,000,000 to an estimated 5,000,000 by the year 2000. Since federal employment bulks large in the metropolitan total, a separate projection was made for it. In the past this employment has been concentrated largely in the center of the metropolitan area. The plan assumed that it would become federal policy to create subcenters of federal employment on the fringes of the metropolitan area, as had been done in recent years by several major agencies. This decentralization of federal employment would presumably be accompanied by a comparable and contiguous growth of other employment on a decentralized basis. The plan further assumed that any scattered pattern of development was uneconomic and socially and aesthetically bad. Finally, it assumed that the reservation of large amounts of open space in the form of green belts was a desirable goal and could be achieved through a combination of planned transportation systems and public controls.

On these assumptions, the plan briefly examined the following alternatives:

First, the restriction of metropolitan growth by a combination of federal policy, which would move future federal employment centers to other cities, and local policy, which would restrict areas available for urban growth. The effect of these policies would be to increase the density of the remaining areas and deter the movement of people and enterprises to metropolitan Washington. This alternative is rejected as neither feasible nor desirable.

Second, a pattern which would accommodate present growth in new independent cities. This alternative was described as attractive but difficult to attain, particularly in view of its dependence upon the co-operation of the areas affected and the difficulties of channeling growth into such cities.

Third, a pattern called "planned sprawl." This alternative assumes that the present pattern of residential expansion will proceed, but that sub-centers for community services, commercial services, and federal employment will emerge, linked by highways; and that these will form a sprawling but partially nucleated suburban pattern. This alternative is rejected on the grounds that it would be undesirable, would increase journeys to work, would reserve no open space, and would limit housing and employment choices to those now available in the suburban areas.

Fourth, the emergence of a number of dispersed cities. This alternative differs from the second only in that several more proposed cities of smaller size are suggested.

Fifth, a ring of cities. This pattern would have certain communication and transportation advantages over the dispersed city pattern, but, like it, would tend to generate pressures for development in the green belt and would tend to deemphasize the importance of the metropolitan center.

Sixth, peripheral communities. This alternative is not essentially different from the preceding two, but it poses another possible pattern of growth with narrower open spaces and slightly more concentrated radial transportation routes. Again it assumes less control over the pattern of development than would be the case in preceding alternatives.

Finally, the radial corridor plan, based upon the establishment of major radial transit and expressway systems. This plan assumes that such transit axes can be built, usually in advance of population growth, that employment and community service centers will be generated along them and lead to the development of a fairly high-density core along each corridor and surrounding the stops in the transit system. It is claimed that this pattern would provide a wider choice of housing types, including single family detached homes, garden apartments, and elevator apartments along each corridor. This pattern would supposedly facilitate employment choices by providing employment centers along each linear axis and in the center. The report argued that this plan would lead to the growth and renewal of the metropolitan center as a major business and employment district. Growth could thus be restricted in the interstitial green spaces, preserving access to the countryside at convenient distances from most of the population. A radial transit system and a radial and ring highway system are conceived as the most important development forces to effect the plan.[25]

Needless to say, the radial corridor plan was the development plan recommended for adoption. While the plan suffered from a number of analytic defects,[26] it was one of the first attempts to try to present alternatives for public choice and to

indicate clearly and simply some of the public issues requiring attention.

Although paradigms have not been used much in other policy areas of local government, they can be used to depict alternative plans in any functional or programmatic area or to depict alternative schemes for organizing or reorganizing some existing government, department, or activity. Organization charts are paradigms of a sort. To be really useful for analysis, however, the traditional job-task pyramids must be supplemented with a series of overlays such as those suggested by Pfiffner and Sherwood.[27] These writers argue that traditional organizational charts say very little about the real character of

organizations and suggest that at least the following overlays are required to adequately represent the structures and functions which occur in organizations:

1. The sociometric network
2. The system of functional contracts
3. The gird of decision-making centers
4. The pattern of power
5. Channels of communication
6. [Information flows].[28]

While Pfiffner and Sherwood illustrate these overlaps graphically, they could also be depicted verbally, or as networks in a computer program.

Notes

[1] This is the case not only in local government but in higher levels of government as well. See: Yehezkel Dror, *Public Policy-Making Reexamined* (San Francisco: Chandler Publishing Company, 1968).

[2] Olaf Helmer, *Social Technology* (New York: Basic Books, Inc., 1966), p. 11.

[3] Geoffrey Vickers, *The Art of Judgment* (London: Chapman and Hall, 1965).

[4] Richard D. Duke, "The M.E.T.R.O. Urban Game-Simulation: An Experiment in In-Service Training," *Fourth Annual Conference on Urban Planning Information Systems and Programs* (Berkeley: Center for Planning and Development Research, University of California, 1966), pp. 142–53.

[5] Metropolis I, a gaming simulation which focuses on the capital budgeting process in municipal government, is an example. Metropolis II is a computerized version of the same game.

[6] Tri-County Regional Planning Commission, *M.E.T.R.O.* (Lansing, Mich.: Tri-County Regional Planning Commission, 1966).

[7] Duke, "The M.E.T.R.O. Urban Game-Simulation," pp. 144–49.

[8] Allen G. Feldt, *The Cornell Land Use Game* (Ithaca, N.Y.: Center for Housing and Environmental Studies, Cornell University, 1965).

[9] Francis H. Hendricks, "Planning Operational Gaming Experiment," paper prepared for the Northern California Chapter, American Institute of Planners, November 19, 1960. (Mimeographed.)

[10] Air Pollution Control Institute, *COMEXOPOLIS* (Los Angeles: Air Pollution Control Institute, University of Southern California, 1967).

[11] Washington Center for Metropolitan Studies, *City I* (Washington, D.C.: Washington Center for Metropolitan Studies, 1968).

[12] City II, a revised version of the City I game, attempts to introduce social awareness and considerations into the game, but does not model the social system; it is still physical-development-oriented. Enviromentrics, Inc., *Environmental Modeling: The Method for Total Solutions* (Washington, D.C.: Enviromentrics, Inc., 1970).

[13] Nathan Grundstein has outlined a proposed game which would explicitly model the social system. See: Nathan Grundstein, "Computer Simulation of a Community for Gaming," paper presented at the annual meeting of the American Association for the Advance-

ment of Science, Denver, Colo., Dec. 29, 1961. (Mimeographed.)

[14] Norman Dalkey and Olaf Helmer, "An Experimental Application of the Delphi Method to the Use of Experts," *Management Science*, IX (April 1963), 458–67.

[15] The units would probably be oriented around a discipline or profession or a grouping of related ones. A second experiment might deliberately mix the units to provide a check on the results of the first.

[16] Marvin Adelson, ed., "Planning Education for the Future," *American Behavioral Scientist*, X (March 1967), 1–31; and Olaf Helmer, *The Use of the Delphi Technique in Problems of Educational Innovations* (Santa Monica: Rand Corporation, 1966).

[17] Norman C. Dalkey, *Quality of Life* (Santa Monica: Rand Corporation, 1968).

[18] T. J. Gordon and Olaf Helmer, *Report on a Long-Range Forecasting Study* (Santa Monica: Rand Corporation, 1964). See also: *Daedalus*, XCVI (Summer 1967), entire issue.

[19] Seyom Brown, "Scenarios in Systems Analysis," in *Systems Analysis and Policy Planning: Applications in Defense*, ed. by E. S. Quade and W. I. Boucher (New York: American Elsevier Publishing Co., 1969), p. 300.

[20] Herman Kahn and Anthony J. Wiener, *The Year 2000* (New York: Macmillan Co., 1967), p. 263. Copyright © 1967 by Macmillan Co. Reprinted by permission of Macmillan Co.

[21] For example, see: F. S. Pardee, et al., *Measurement and Evaluation of Transportation System Effectiveness* (Santa Monica: Rand Corporation, 1969).

[22] A report on these seminars is contained in: "Predicting the Future of Cities," *Public Management*, September 1969, entire issue.

[23] Robert K. Merton, *Social Theory and Social Structure* (Glencoe, Ill.: The Free Press, 1949), pp. 14–15. Copyright © 1949 by The Free Press. Reprinted by permission of Macmillan Co.

[24] U.S., National Capital Planning Commission, *A Policies Plan for the Year 2000: The Nation's Capital* (Washington, D.C.: Government Printing Office, 1961).

[25] William L. C. Wheaton, "Operations Research for Metropolitan Planning," *Journal of the American Institute of Planners*, XXIX (November 1963), 251. Reprinted by permission of the *Journal of the American Institute of Planners*, XXIX, 6 (November 1963).

[26] The plan showed a static future state for the year 2000. There was no indication of the intervening states and little discussion of the processes necessary for their achievement. There was no analysis of the economic, social, or other implications of the choices offered, nor was there any calculation of the costs or benefits of any alternative.

[27] John M. Pfiffner and Frank P. Sherwood, *Administrative Organization* (Englewood Cliffs, N.J.: Prentice-Hall, Inc., 1960), pp. 16–32.

[28] Ibid., p. 119.

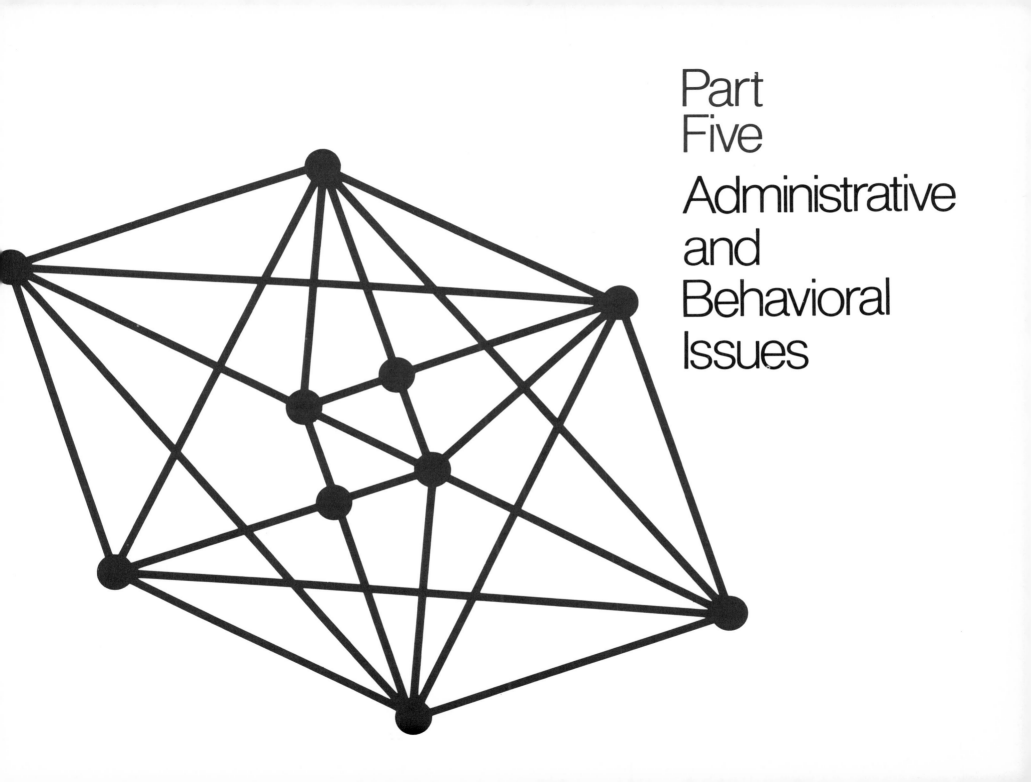

Part
Five

Administrative
and
Behavioral
Issues

**Administrative Issues:
The Infrastructure for Analysis**

Analysis essentially begins with a decision to use it. Once that decision is made — and in its making — several administrative issues must be considered. How shall a group be created and organized for carrying out analysis? Where shall the group be located in the governmental structure? How shall it be comprised? How financed? How shall people, both analysts and decision makers, be trained? On which problems does one start?

All of these questions but the last relate to the foundation or infrastructure for analysis. The last refers to a strategy for initiating policy analysis. This chapter, therefore, considers the following issues in the use of analysis: organizational arrangements; the analysis group; financing; training; and equipment and facilities. In addition to considering the above, this chapter discusses alternative strategies for choosing the problems on which to work.

ORGANIZATIONAL ARRANGEMENTS

Assuming that a decision has been made by a particular government to use policy analysis, a basic question is how to start. In order to begin, an analysis group is needed. Three ways in which such a group can be obtained are: (1) externally, by hiring consultants or outside organizations; (2) internally, by recruiting experienced personnel or training people already in government; or (3) by some combination of these.

Initially, outside consultants will probably be used by most governments. Consultants will prove useful over the longer run also in working on specialized problems and as members of a team on very large and complex problems. However, in general the ultimate place of the policy analysis group should be within government. The reason that the analysis group should be within government will become clear as each of the alternative arrangements is discussed below. Basically, it is because policy analysis is a continuous process oriented not simply to one-time solutions, but to increasing an organization's capacity for defining problems, designing alternatives, and developing solutions over time — as the problems, the organization, and the potential solutions change.

Alternative arrangements for performing analysis

The use of outside groups. If a government has an urgent problem and needs a solution quickly, it may be useful to engage an experienced outside organization to perform the analysis.

Presently, organizations such as universities, management and planning consultants, research and development firms, and the aerospace companies contain the bulk of people skilled in policy analysis. Few trained analysts are available in local government.

The usual type of consultant arrangement involves a contract for a specific end product, to be prepared essentially by the staff of the outside organization. As a result, there are several disadvantages to this approach. First, it generally does not leave government with any greater internal capacity for doing analysis. Second, it does not provide government with a capability for adapting the particular solution derived as conditions change. Third, while many consultant organizations have the skilled personnel, few have had experience in dealing with the problems of urban areas and those of their governments.

When consultants are used, at least one technically competent person in government should work with them along with several operations or management personnel. However, the problem in government generally is that the technical people are not available. If a technically competent person is unavailable in-house (or cannot be recruited), the government unit may require the consultant to engage in a training program for one or more government personnel as part of the analysis effort.[1] In this way, the results are more likely to be understood and utilized subsequently, and modified as conditions change. The people in government best suited for such training are those already serving in staff and analytic positions, for example, management and budget analysts, planners, engineers, staff aides, and assistants to political leaders, chief executives, and department heads.

Finally, before engaging an outside organization to perform a policy study, at least three things should be done in the selection process:[2]

1. Discuss the problem with a number of consultants as a basis for comparison
2. Obtain a list of previous clients and projects, and discuss the performance of the consultants with government agencies or others who have used them
3. Determine how willing the consultants are to have internal government personnel work with them on problems.[3]

Several cities have used outside organizations for specific policy analysis studies (San Fran-

cisco, Los Angeles, Pittsburgh, Stockton, Fresno, New York). In addition, a significant variation on the use of outside organizations has been initiated recently. New York City has engaged the Rand Corporation for a large-scale consulting effort (about $2 million a year), extending over a period of years and focusing on the application of policy analysis to the problems of eight major units within the city.[4] Two things are significant about this effort. First, it differs from the usual consulting arrangement in that it represents a long-term, continuous enterprise, at least as presently planned. Second, the Rand staff is committed to training in-house government personnel while also working on actual problems. Thus, the New York–Rand arrangement is probably closer to the third approach of using mixed groups.

The use of internal groups. Ultimately, the best approach is to develop a policy analysis group within government. However, sudden initiation of policy analysis studies by a full compliment of trained analysts is impracticable because of recruitment difficulties, existing personnel classification and salary structures, and budget limitations. An evolutionary approach often is required. At least one qualified policy analyst is needed to start an in-house group. This person should be supplemented by several other analytical personnel in government and by periodic consultant help.

If internal recruitment is used to form an analysis group, sufficient time and resources should be provided to permit adequate training. One year would probably be required in which the individuals would immerse themselves in the pertinent literature, take formal classes, and

visit established policy analysis groups and organizations. Part of this training may be done by temporary groups and organizations. Another part may be accomplished through temporary assignment of individuals to government units that have a strong analytic capability.

The following guidelines, suggested by Ackoff and Rivett, and others,[5] are offered for internal selection:

1. At least two people should be chosen to start the group. In this way there will be a greater likelihood of the group expanding and developing, and each person can provide counter viewpoints and arguments for the other's ideas.
2. One of the two people (assuming this is the initial number) should have a comprehensive grasp of the government and the city, as well as a working relationship with the people involved in each department or unit, so that the group will have access to key people.
3. The two people selected should have command of mathematical thinking. At minimum, they should understand the basic concepts of research design and of probability theory, statistics, marginal analysis, and decision analysis. An understanding of more specialized techniques such as those discussed in this book is desirable. It is unnecessary for both people to be proficient in the application of the full range of techniques, but at least one technically proficient person is required. Persons from such fields as policy science, mathematics and statistics, science, engineering, operations research, management science, and computer science are likely to have the needed skills. If the people selected lack the

minimum skills, they should acquire them during the first year.

4. The two people chosen should like to work on real problems.
5. They should be interested in coping with problems as they exist rather than in trying to simplify them out of existence.
6. They should appreciate the primacy of problems over techniques. The task of analysis is to develop techniques for existing problems, not to search for problems to fit existing techniques.
7. The two people should be articulate and be able to use the language of politicians, managers, and operating personnel alike. At the same time they should be prepared to be misunderstood and to cope with it. Further, they should want others to be aware of what they are doing and to participate in the analysis efforts—not merely accept them.
8. They should supplement one another in background and temperament. It would be very useful, for example, if one person's main interest was in the analysis of problems and the other's in data collection and manipulation.
9. The two people should exhibit mature judgment and imagination. They should be able to see their work in perspective, including the limitations of analysis and the behavioral realities of their task. At the same time, they should be eager to innovate, to seek out new objectives and alternatives, and to induce others to exercise imagination.

If internal groups are utilized, the policy makers should be committed to trying out policy analysis for a time period that allows results to be seen. This means a commitment for at least one year,

and probably two. Commitment can also be made in stages. If trained people can be brought together, a temporary group can be established with a limited life (say six months or a year). At the end of this period the results can be reviewed and a decision made about future commitment, including the direction, size, and scope of continued efforts.

The Port of New York Authority is an example of a local government agency that has developed internal analysis groups.[6] Its use of policy analysis (largely for operations-type problems) dates back to 1952. Presently, it has three groups. The first performs analysis across all operations of the Port Authority and is located within the Operations Services Department. The second group focuses on analysis to improve the operation and design of tunnels and bridges and is located within the Tunnels and Bridges Department. The third group is located within the Engineering Department and is concerned with applying analysis to long-range problems of importance to the Port Authority as a whole or to a group of its facilities. Thus, while all three groups are located at the departmental level, two of them cut across the entire organization and its problems.

Fort Worth,[7] another example, has a single group of analysts, directly under the city manager but serving the departments as well. Generally, their work has focused on operational problems (e.g., waste collection routing, street maintenance operations, and delinquent traffic ticket procedures), although attention has been given to some management problems (e.g., capital improvements programming and community renewal programming).

Finally, a significant variation of the in-house approach has been initiated in Los Angeles. The city recently formed a nonprofit research corporation (LATSCO—Los Angeles Technical Services Corporation) which is loosely tied to City Hall (under the mayor) and provides technical assistance to all units of government. LATSCO has employed people from the aerospace industry and receives federal, city, and foundation support for its work. Three of LATSCO's first assignments have been: (1) preparation of Los Angeles's Model Cities application; (2) management of the Community Renewal Program (elsewhere called CRP); and (3) solution of a highly controversial freeway location conflict. LATSCO is a significant experiment in that it suggests a way of using skilled people from outside government to create an ongoing analytic capability which is tied to government but retains some autonomy. The long-range impact and success of this arrangement presently is unclear. On the one hand it provides expert advice and fresh perspectives from people free from daily operations. On the other hand, its semiautonomous position may render it ineffective in influencing policy decisions and may tend to diminish the development of analytic capabilities within the departments. None of these limitations is insurmountable, however.

The use of mixed groups. Probably the most effective way of starting a policy analysis operation involves using an outside group in combination with a newly formed group within government. The joint group can work on a common problem, supplement one another's knowledge and skills, and engage in training in the course of doing the analysis. Approximately one year of such joint effort would be required to prepare internal personnel for competent work.

However, even after internal personnel are trained use of outside consultants probably should continue. Objectivity and a fresh perspective are important. It is too easy for internal personnel to acquire the preconceptions and misconceptions of managerial and other government personnel and thus to try to prove or disprove their perspectives. Further, it is often easier for outsiders to gain access to the appropriate decision makers. They will be listened to more, and they tend to have both broader and different perspectives to bring to the organization.

Location of the analysis group in government
Several approaches to location of the analysis group are possible, since there is little evidence that a best approach exists. To some degree the appropriate location is a matter of common sense. The analysts should report to someone who is sympathetic to what they are trying to do. They should be located to provide sufficient security so that if their superior moves on elsewhere the analysts will not be out on a limb. They should have access to top management and to information on the various departments.

The following approaches are possible:

1. Place the group under the chief executive (mayor, city manager, chief administrative officer).
2. Locate the group under one of the staff departments, e.g., management analysis, planning, or budget.
3. Place the group under an operating department, e.g., police, fire, public works, finance.

In either (2) or (3) there is a danger that the group will work only on the problems of the particular department: in (2) the group may work only on long-range problems; in (3), only on short-term problems.
4. Create a management services group consisting of staff planners, budgeteers, organization and methods people, work study groups, cost analysts, etc. Here, there is a danger that the policy analyst will become like the others or that they will become like him.
5. Place the group under the elected governing body. Here the danger is that the group will become isolated from the mainstream of government administration.

The location of the analysis group also depends on the size of the government agency, the number of groups to be established, and the type of problems government officials deem urgent and important. For example, most small and medium-sized cities will probably have only one analysis group. It is best located directly under the chief executive and related to, but distinct from, existing staff activities such as budgeting, planning, and traditional management analysis.

In large cities, several groups will probably be required, one at the level of top management, others within the operating departments, and possibly another serving the elected officials. Regardless of how many groups are created, the first should probably be located directly under the chief executive. It is here that the best perspective on government activities can be obtained, the necessary support can be marshaled, and the danger of getting bogged down in day-to-day operational analysis is minimized.

Further, it is at this level that the greatest opportunity exists for working directly with the elected government officials on the problems they deem important.

Size and makeup of the analysis group
Most individual problems in government require no more than six persons to work on them;[8] many require only two or three persons. In general the analysis group should comprise three equally represented disciplines: behavioral science and economics; mathematics and statistics; physical science and engineering. Thus, a group of six persons might comprise the following:

1. A management scientist, operations researcher, or systems analyst
2. A mathematician or statistician
3. An engineer or physical scientist
4. A political scientist, public administrator, or planner
5. An economist or cost analyst
6. A behavioral scientist.

Increasingly, the graduates of schools of administration and planning are being trained in analytic methods and, therefore, constitute the ideal type of person for smaller analysis groups. Because their education is broad, they often make good team leaders for larger groups.

FINANCIAL ARRANGEMENTS

Generally speaking, large-scale analysis is expensive. Therefore, most small and medium-sized cities will tend to work on small problems and use techniques already developed. Cities also can extend their resources by obtaining outside financial support and by joining with others.

Time and cost requirements

The time and cost of a particular analysis depends upon the type of problem. Most operational problems can be completed in six to twelve months by two or three persons. Management and development problems may require several years and a very large team supplemented by consultants.[9] For example, Aerospace Industries Association officials[10] roughly estimate that for every dollar spent in system analysis, $10 are spent in system engineering, and $100 in system development and implementation. The total time span may be seven to ten years and more. The context of these estimates is that of large-scale military hardware system development (e.g., a new aircraft and its support facilities), but transportation, housing, and school systems are equivalents in the urban setting. Table 11–1 indicates the time and the costs of some recent projects for various types of problems.

Approximately two-thirds to three-fourths of the time spent on a policy study may be devoted to gathering and processing data. Therefore, the availability and quality of data is probably the most important factor affecting the length and cost of a study. The use of government personnel in collecting data has two advantages. First, they are far more likely to know where to find the data than is an outside group. Second, they can usually collect and process data more cheaply than an outside group by doing so in conjunction with daily activities. Often a significant by-product of policy analysis efforts is a greatly improved information handling capability that reduces the time required for future policy studies and that has supplementary advantages for many other data users.

Financing policy studies

If urban governments are to engage in analysis they will have to be prepared to finance the efforts. A figure of 1 percent of the agency's total budget seems reasonable. In addition to their own finances, local governments can expect aid from the federal government and, probably, the state. Policy studies are presently funded under several federal programs.[11] In addition, private research foundations are also beginning to provide limited support for policy analysis in local government.[12]

Another approach is for local governments to pool their resources in a joint effort. This has been done by eleven cities in the San Gabriel Valley of Los Angeles, although in the context of computerization rather than policy analysis. These cities, under a joint powers agreement and in conjunction with an outside consultant, have been developing a central computer facility and certain common computer applications. The project was scheduled for thirty months (from June 1968), at a cost of $550,000, and was funded by the cities ($340,000) and the Carnegie Foundation ($210,000). A cost sharing formula among the cities was based on estimation of data processing loads.[13]

Finally, it is possible for cities to cooperatively fund analysis on a regional or national basis. At the regional level, a group of California school districts has cooperatively supported a research and development project (School Construction Systems Development—SCSD) to test a method of building better schools more rapidly and economically. The project staff, as technical advisers to the thirteen school districts grouped together as the First California Commission on

School Construction Systems, analyzed the building needs posed by new secondary school programs. They then asked manufacturers to develop new products to meet new types of specifications—ones emphasizing the need for compatibility of the various building components. The manufacturers then bid competitively to the commission for multimillion dollar contracts to supply and install their products. The individual school districts employed their own architects to design their schools. These architects utilized the new SCSD components in much the same manner as they use standard building components. Local general contractors bid on each school, with the component manufacturers becoming their subcontractors to deliver and install the SCSD components.[14] The actual cost of the components developed was about a 20 percent reduction of what the school districts had been paying to buy available products. At the same time, the total performance characteristics of the building system were substantially higher.[15]

The American Public Works Association (APWA)[16] has operated a national cooperative research program since 1966, with the cost of a specific project prorated among the participating governments in accordance with a cost-benefit formula. The costs have ranged from a minimum of $200 to a maximum of $10,000 for any single participant, and participation has been largely voluntary. In 1967, APWA spent $1.3 million examining such problems as snow removal, solid waste disposal, storm and sanitary sewers, and detection of flyash in the atmosphere.

The International City Management Association recently began a similar cooperative program for urban policy studies under Technology Appli-

Table 11-1. Recent civil sector system-related contracts.

Contractor	Type of [1] Organization	Description	Client	Completion date and/or duration	Contract amount
Arthur D. Little, Inc.	ND	San Francisco CRP	City and County of San Francisco	24 months 1965	$ 800,000
AEROJET-General (Von Karman Center)	D	California Waste Management	California Department of Health	6 months August 1965	100,000
AEROJET-General	D	Solid Waste Management Study for Fresno Area	California Department of Public Health	24 months	175,000
AEROJET-General (Space General)	D	Prevention and Control of Crime and Delinquency	California Youth and Adult Corrections Agency	July 1965	100,000
AEROJET-General (Space General)	D	Welfare Report	California Department of Social Welfare	March 1967	225,000
Booz, Allen and Hamilton	ND	Performance Budgeting	Bureau of Public Roads	18 months 1968	N/A [2]
Building System Development Corp.	ND	College Facility Design	State of California	N/A	N/A
Center for Urban Studies, University of Chicago	ND	Selection and Use of Social-Economic Data in Urban Planning	Department of Housing and Urban Development	N/A	62,598
Consad Research Corporation	ND	Pittsburgh CRP Land Use Model	City of Pittsburgh	N/A	N/A
City of New York	ND	Design of Program Planning and Budgeting System for the City of New York	Department of Housing and Urban Development	1967	N/A
City University of New York	ND	Urban Documentation Storage and Retrieval (URBANDOC)	Department of Housing and Urban Development	N/A	186,442
Columbia University	ND	Mental Health Programming in Urban Areas	Public Health Association	N/A	42,600

[1] Type of Organization: D—Defense-related; ND—Nondefense.
[2] N/A means information is not currently available.

Contractor	Type of [1] Organization	Description	Client	Completion date and/or duration	Contract amount
Cornell Aeronautics Laboratory, Inc.	D	Feasibility Study and Report on the Application of a Dual-Mode Small-Transportation System (URMOBILE) in one selected city	Department of Housing and Urban Development	N/A	$ 99,912
Institute for Defense Analyses		Air Traffic Control (North Atlantic Area)	Federal Aviation	6/30/65	137,000
Institute for Defense Analyses	D	Law Enforcement and Criminal Justice	President's Commission on Law Enforcement and Administration	4/30/67	498,000 [3]
Issacs-Dobbs, Inc.	ND	San Gabriel Valley Cities Time-Sharing System	? Cities in SGU of Los Angeles	N/A	N/A
International City Management Association	ND	Use of Systems Analysis in Urban Planning	Department of Housing and Urban Development	N/A	80,000
Lockheed Missiles and Space Co.	D	Design of a Statewide Information System	California Department of Finance	6 months 7/30/65	100,000
Midwest Research Institute	ND	Special Transportation Requirements in Small Cities and Towns	Department of Housing and Urban Development	N/A	29,750
Midwest Research Institute	ND	Study of Packaging, Materials, and Waste Disposal	Public Health	1/18/68	53,884
National League of Cities	ND	Guide to Capital Improvement Programming for Officials and Citizen Leaders in Smaller Cities and Counties	Department of Housing and Urban Development	24 months 1967	N/A
New York City	ND	Development, Design, and Testing of the Design of a PPB System	Department of Housing and Urban Development	N/A	50,000
North American Aviation	D	Design of a Study to Develop an Integrated Transportation System for California	California Division of Highways	6 months 9/15/65	100,000

[3] Additional funding of $38,000 requested.

Table 11-1. (continued).

Contractor	Type of [1] Organization	Description	Client	Completion date and/or duration	Contract amount
North American Aviation (Subcontractor to Burns and Roe)	D	Develop Personnel Training System	California Department of Water Resources	mid-1968	$1,900,000
Philco-Ford	D	Computer Model of Poverty	Colorado State Department of Education	N/A	N/A
Philco-Ford	D	Automated Education System	Philadelphia School System	N/A	1,300,000
Polytechnic Institute of Brooklyn	ND	Computer Simulation Model of Urban Police System	U.S. Department of Justice	Two years; completion 8/31/68	43,000
Regional Planning Council (Baltimore)	ND	Development of New Techniques for Planning Sewage and Water Disposal Systems for Metropolitan Areas	Department of Housing and Urban Development	1967	26,650
Research Foundation of State University of New York	ND	Community Health Services Research and Development Program	Department of Health, Education and Welfare—PHS	35 months August 1967	424,250
School Construction Systems Development	ND	School Construction System Development Project	Educational Facilities Laboratory (Ford Foundation)	1961–1967	750,000
School of Architecture, University of Minnesota		Experimental City	Department of Housing and Urban Development	N/A	80,000
Southeastern Wisconsin Regional Planning Commission	ND	Use of Computer Technology to Forecast Urban Growth Patterns Resulting from Public Improvements and Changes in Land Use	Department of Housing and Urban Development	1967	N/A
Sperry Rand Corporation	D	Traffic Control System	New York City	N/A	5,400,000
Standard Research Institute; Westinghouse Air Brake; Day and Zimmerman, Inc.; Defense Research Corporation	D	New Systems of Urban Transportation	Department of Housing and Urban Development	N/A	1,500,000

Contractor	Type of [1] Organization	Description	Client	Completion date and/or duration	Contract amount
System Development Corporation	D	Technical Monitoring and Evaluation of Four Aerospace Systems Contracts	California	6 months 1965	$ 30,000
System Development Corporation	D	Criminal Justice Identification and Intelligence System	New York State	48 months	1,027,000
System Development Corporation	D	Police Information System Design Study	City of Los Angeles	6 months 1966	50,000
System Development Corporation	D	Evaluation of Automated Comprehensive Planning and Programming Systems	Department of Housing and Urban Development	8 months	48,000
University of North Carolina	ND	Adapting the "benefit-cost analysis" approach to comprehensive metropolitan planning	Department of Housing and Urban Development	N/A	28,000
University of North Carolina	ND	Environmental Engineering Policies	Department of Health, Education and Welfare: PHS	36 months August 1968	240,187
University of Oklahoma Research Institute	ND	Health Services System Simulation	Department of Health, Education and Welfare	12 months January 1968	N/A
University of Southern California	ND	Prototype Design of Integrated Municipal Information Systems	Office of Civil Defense and City of Burbank	24 months 1968	200,000
University of Washington	ND	Regional Forecasting Models: Analysis and Training	U.S. Department of Commerce: EDA	1968	N/A
Westinghouse	ND	Design and Demonstration of a Transit Expressway System	Department of Housing and Urban Development	N/A	5,000,000

cation Program — now Public Technology, Inc. (PTI). This project has been supported by membership contributions from local governments, federal and state financing, and the Ford Foundation.

Analysis in small government units

The time and cost involved in policy analysis often seem to preclude its use by small government units. However, there are several alternatives in addition to the cooperative efforts mentioned above. These alternatives include:

1. Retaining one person who can be used in policy analysis and in other research activities as well. When conducting a policy study, supplemental personnel can be borrowed for the specific problem, or people can be recruited or hired from outside.
2. Supporting one or more graduate students who are willing to do a thesis on a government policy problem. This would require from about $2,000 to $4,000 a year per student.
3. Forming an areawide policy analysis group of several governments in an area, to work on common problems.

TRAINING FOR POLICY ANALYSIS

The long-range effectiveness of analysis will depend heavily on capabilities within the governmental jurisdiction. Periodic use of qualified analytical personnel from outside government is helpful but is not sufficient to assure a continuing capability in policy analyses and its effective use. To provide the capability for and use of policy analysis, two types of training programs should be considered. The first is internal orientation for administrative staff, functional agency personnel, and political leaders, to give them the necessary understanding of the purposes and uses of analysis and to ensure the support required for its successful application. The effectiveness of analytical efforts will be increased if carried out in an environment of acceptance and cooperation.

A second type of training program on the fundamentals of policy analysis is important because fully trained and experienced personnel are scarce in local governments. It is probable that, as more governments undertake policy analysis, colleges and universities will respond with degree programs and course offerings that will increase the supply of such people. Meanwhile, cities must devote their efforts to developing the needed skills. Programs like those mentioned above can have recruitment value also, because training in a new field with wide employment possibilities is often a strong inducement for people to enter public employment. With experience in government, these people may develop a commitment to public service and to solving the complex problems present in urban areas.

Types of training programs

The following is a list of the types of training programs possible — some of which have been used by various governmental agencies.[17]

On-the-job training. City personnel can receive training while working on policy studies under the guidance of senior analysts, consultants, or specialists who work on projects for the city or who assist temporarily. Few in-depth courses on policy analysis are now available, so this type of training may be key for inexperienced persons who will be used in connection with policy analysis in the near future. However, on-the-job training should be supplemented by more intensive study under available special courses, seminars, symposia, and university programs.

Specially designed in-service orientation. The content, duration, and frequency of such orientation depends on the strengths, background, and duties of the staff assembled. For example, academically-oriented economists may need orientation in "government"; public administrators and mathematicians may need illumination in economic theory and analysis. Both groups may need introduction to the specialized techniques of policy analysis.

Specialized policy analysis course offerings. In recent years specialized courses and programs in policy analysis have been developed by universities and colleges, research organizations, government agencies and private organizations. Though limited in number, such programs appear to be on the increase, at least among the large universities. The federal government currently sponsors mid-career training programs in systematic analysis for its personnel at several cooperating universities. State and local government people may also attend some of these programs under special arrangements.

Formal course work in the disciplines contributing to policy analysis. Since policy analysis draws from many disciplines, training can be obtained through the study of such subjects as economics, mathematics, statistics, social science research, and operations research.

Course work in these subjects is likely to be provided at nearby educational institutions.

Financial aid for support of staff training
Local governments traditionally spend money for the education and training of their personnel, and policy analysis appears to warrant such expenditures. If additional financial support is required, the following are potential sources of such support:[18]

Foundation grants. Ford, Carnegie, National Science, and similar foundations contribute to personnel training in the state and local field, particularly when governments seek to initiate innovative programs and exhibit a continuing commitment to those programs.

Special federal aids. Programs developed under Title I of the Higher Education Act include provision for training of state and local employees. Programs of specific federal agencies sometimes provide funds for improving planning and evaluation skills in certain areas. For example, the National Defense Education Act authorizes funds for improvement of statistical services and strengthening state departments of education; the Comprehensive Health Planning Acts authorize project grants for training to improve planning skills to meet health needs; schools of public health and other institutions training for the health professions may also receive federal project grants for improved training in public health administration. Similar possibilities exist in other federal grant programs.

Training costs as an administrative cost in federally aided programs. In many federal grant programs, staff development and training may be included as an administrative cost in computing the federal grant.

EQUIPMENT AND FACILITIES

Supporting equipment and facilities for the analysis group will depend upon the type of problems studied and the number and size of such groups. Obviously, office and conference space is needed. In addition, one fully automatic desk calculator is required for every five persons, as is a large blackboard space so that it is easy for several persons to be involved in working out a problem. A reference library of basic works and professional journals is also needed.

Access to electronic computers is extremely helpful, as large amounts of data must be processed and analyzed in any policy study. Where simulation techniques are used, access to a computer may be essential. However, the policy analysis group should be independent of the computer organization.

THE PROBLEMS ON WHICH TO START

The first problem which the analysis group tackles is extremely important, as it will shape viewpoints of all concerned. When the group starts work many people in the organization will know that they are beginning, but most will be unclear about what the group is trying to do, why they are trying to do it, how they are going to do it, what is likely to be achieved if they are successful, or what the impact on the people in the organization will be as a result of the work. This last is probably the most critical, for if some people feel threatened during the course of the work, even the best results may not be utilized, or may be considerably delayed in use.

While the initial work may have to be on small problems and related largely to operational problems, the real benefit of policy analysis will come primarily when it is applied to bigger problems which, if solved, may prevent crises in the future. There is a close parallel between starting policy analysis efforts and data processing systems.

Urban governments initially focused on transforming housekeeping applications to computers — because it was relatively easy, produced rapid results, and promised savings. Many government officials have concluded recently that applications so developed fall short of an information system capability, fail to provide information needed for the management of operations, and effect little improvement in government administration generally. As a result, recent data processing efforts have been oriented to tying together many applications in a single function or department, and some have sought to create a unified data processing system for all governmental functions. It is now recognized that this is the only way to achieve real payoffs from electronic data processing systems.

However, it is also clear that, because of financial limitations, departmental resistance, shifts in power relations brought about by information systems, and other factors, integrated information systems for urban governments may be achieved only downstream — except, perhaps, in a few experimental projects.[19]

The point is that initial policy analysis studies will probably focus largely on operational problems and subproblems; and the improvements in administration will be less than those which would result from solving large-scale problems. However, urban governments will be building up a capability for handling the larger problems and will probably support cooperative efforts of this sort. Further, by applying the mixed analysis strategy discussed in Chapter 3, the smaller studies can constitute component analyses for larger ones. Finally, it is also possible that the growing alliance of governmental and private agencies focused on urban problems may result in massive efforts which will substantially change the presently foreseeable evolution of policy analysis in local government.

SUMMARY

In the end, the overall approach, concepts, and principles, and the tools and techniques of policy analysis depend upon a foundation or infrastructure which paves the way for analysis, permits it to be accomplished, increases the likelihood that it will be utilized, and provides feedback on the results achieved. The best ultimate arrangement for conduct of policy analysis is through groups within government rather than through the use of outside consultants. Initially,

consultants will be required because of the present lack of trained people. Consultants can serve in both a problem solving and a training capacity and can be used effectively after an analytic capability is created in government.

Analysis groups may be located at several levels in government, but, wherever located, they should have access to the people and information necessary for conducting studies on the problems chosen for analysis. Generally, they should be related to—but independent of—traditional staff and analytic activities of government. The team of analysts will also vary in size but should represent a mix of disciplines. Some analysts may be recruited from other government organizations, from private industry, or from universities. Most will probably have to be recruited from inside government, and here people with analytic backgrounds should be selected. Training of these people will be required, and a variety of alternatives exist for getting appropriate training.

Few policy studies can be completed in less than a year. Usually, two or three persons will

be required even on a small project. Financial support for analysis will have to come from local government, but, increasingly, outside funds are being made available—often for a substantial part of the effort, including training costs. Cooperative research programs among government units in an urban area can be undertaken for the purpose of sharing the cost burden, particularly for large studies beyond the financial capability of any one unit.

The first studies conducted by an analysis group are often critical for gaining continued support. On the one hand, there is merit and need for choosing small problems which are easily handled and produce quick results. On the other hand, the biggest payoffs of policy analysis generally lie elsewhere—in the large, complex problems that may never be totally solved and in which the results may be seen only over a considerable time period. This dilemma can be managed by using a mixed analysis strategy in which the smaller problems which have been chosen for analysis are part of larger problems and contribute to longer-term solutions.

Notes

[1] This was done in the San Francisco Community Renewal Program. In addition, upon completion of the study one staff member of the consulting organization (Arthur D. Little, Inc.) joined the planning staff of the city and county of San Francisco.

[2] There have been instances in which the government agency has felt unable to evaluate the consultants. If this is the case, there is some question as to whether the study should be undertaken. However, the importance of a problem may demand action regardless of this limitation. Here, another consultant can be used to help in selection, to monitor the study, or to evaluate the results. For example, in the case of the California

aerospace studies, the System Development Corporation (in addition to various state agencies) was contracted to perform the latter two functions.

[3] This is a critical issue in view of the need for the consultant to train government personnel while working on a problem jointly with them. Ida Hoos has criticized the California aerospace studies contractors for being

intolerant of the people they worked with. Ida R. Hoos, *A Critique on the Application of Systems Analysis to Social Problems* (Berkeley: Space Sciences Laboratory, University of California, 1967).

[4] Prior to contracting with Rand in 1967, New York City had created an internal policy analysis group in June 1966. This group, located directly under the mayor, was charged with *planning* for the introduction of new management techniques to the city government and for increased use of computers as a management tool. See: Nachman Bench, "New Management Techniques," paper presented at the Third Annual Conference on ADP Systems in Local Government, Barbizon-Plaza Hotel, New York, June 21, 1967.

[5] Russell L. Ackoff and Patrick Rivett, *A Manager's Guide to Operations Research* (New York: John Wiley & Sons, Inc., 1963); and State-Local Finances Project, *Staffing and Training for a PPB System in State and Local Governments* (Washington, D.C.: The George Washington University, 1967).

[6] The Port Authority has two basic responsibilities: development and operation of transportation and terminal facilities within its district boundaries (an area within a twenty-five-mile radius of the Statue of Liberty), and the promotion and protection of the commerce of the port. In carrying out its responsibilities, the Port Authority has developed and operates twenty-three facilities, including: six interstate tunnels and bridges; a regional system of four airports and two heliports; six marine terminals; a bus terminal; two motor truck terminals; a truck terminal for railroad freight; and a rapid transit system.

[7] Jerry L. Brownlee and Errol H. Colley, "A City Manager Looks at the Management Sciences," in *Using Advanced Management Techniques*, ed. by Arthur D. Little, Inc., Arthur D. Little, Inc., Series on Critical Issues in Urban Management (Washington, D.C.: Communication Service Corporation, 1968), pp. 1–15.

[8] However, as in the case of New York with forty persons from Rand, the size of the analysis group can be large.

[9] Consultants in private industry may charge out at $250 per day; academicians may cost less, but may take longer to do the work because of other demands on their time.

[10] U.S., Congress, Senate, Committee on Labor and Public Welfare, *Scientific Manpower Utilization, Hearings,* before a Special Subcommittee on the Utilization of Scientific Manpower, 90th Cong., 1st sess., 1967 (Washington, D.C.: Government Printing Office, 1967), pp. 34–62.

[11] See particularly: U.S., Office of Economic Opportunity, *Catalogue of Federal Assistance Programs* (Washington, D.C.: Government Printing Office, 1967). HUD's Urban Observatories program and the National Science Foundation's Interdisciplinary Research program also provide assistance for research jointly carried out by local governments and universities. See also: National League of Cities, *Urban Research and Metropolitan Community Services Group System* (Washington, D.C.: National League of Cities, 1969); and U.S., National Science Foundation, *Summary of Awards, Fiscal Year 1972, Division of Social Systems and Human Resources, Research Applied to National Needs* (Washington, D.C.: National Science Foundation, 1972).

[12] For example the Ford Foundation is providing assistance to LATSCO and the American Public Works Association (APWA). See: William C. Pendleton, *Technology and Cities: A Foundation Viewpoint* (New York: Ford Foundation, 1968).

[13] The formula weighted cities by the number of water bills per month, size of budget, population size, and current expenditure on data processing. Herbert H. Isaacs, *The Feasibility of a Central Computer System for San Gabriel Valley Cities* (Los Angeles: Isaacs-Dobbs Systems, Inc., 1967), p. 122.

[14] Educational Facilities Laboratories, *SCSD: The Project and the Schools* (New York: Educational Facilities Laboratories, 1967).

[15] For example, the lighting levels were doubled, structural spans were doubled (permitting greater flexibility in changing classroom sizes to meet changing needs), the schools were air-conditioned summer and winter to plus or minus two degrees for any space the size of half a classroom or larger and were given a maintenance contract guaranteeing performance for twenty years.

[16] American Public Works Association, *Prospectus for Cooperative Research* (Chicago: American Public Works Association, 1967).

[17] State-Local Finances Project, *Staffing and Training for a PPB System,* pp. 14–15.

[18] Ibid., p. 16.

[19] Anthony Downs, "A Realistic Look at the Final Payoffs from Urban Data Systems," *Public Administration Review,* XXVII (September 1967), 204–10; and Edward F. R. Hearle, "Urban Management Information Systems," paper presented at the Symposium on Application of Computers to Problems of Urban Society, sponsored by the Association for Computing Machinery, New York, November 10, 1967. (Mimeographed.)

Behavioral Issues and Organizational Preconditions

There are a number of behavioral and organizational issues in the use of policy analysis which local government policy makers must face if their efforts are to achieve the desired improvements. One set of issues relates to pitfalls in the conduct of analysis, the proper uses of it, and its limitations as an approach to decision problems. A second set relates to the policy makers' understanding of their role in the whole process of analysis, the organizational impacts of using it, and special features of the urban setting which influence the character of the analysis process. A final set of issues relates to organizational preconditions for policy analysis. Included are: integrating it into other governmental decision processes; improving organizational structure; developing personnel; increasing knowledge about policy analysis; changing the organizational milieu so that policy analysis will be accepted and used.

BEHAVIORAL ISSUES

Pitfalls in policy analysis

Policy analysis is still more art than science. There is no set of principles which will guarantee successful results. The techniques of analysis frequently leave out many more important factors than they include. Further, what may be most helpful to policy makers and analysts alike is neither quantification nor technique, but is discussion and debate of issues—discussion in which each group tries to understand the other's viewpoint.

The case discussions in Part Three illustrate a number of errors that policy makers and analysts may make in using policy analysis. This section reiterates some common pitfalls as a guide to what to avoid in carrying out policy analysis and what to look for in evaluating policy studies. It also discusses the appropriate use of policy analysis and some of the limitations of policy analysis. Much of the material discussed here is drawn from the three sources listed below[1] as well as from the case studies and other experiences.

Insufficient attention, inflexibility, and attention bias in problem formulation. A major pitfall in policy analysis is the failure to allocate sufficient project time to deciding what the problem is. This may be a result of time pressures, demand for quick results, desire to get started, or preconceived notions of policy makers and analysts regarding the issues, the methods of analyzing them, or the solutions to them.

Of all these factors, preconceived notions are potentially the most harmful. Generally, the policy makers and analysts will have ideas about an issue, its solution, and methods of approaching the issue to test various solutions. This is both necessary and desirable, for if these people really know nothing about an issue there is some question as to whether they should be working on it. The danger is in choosing a particular problem conception, method, or solution without first considering other possible ways of approaching it.

The greatest difficulty in most policy analyses is deciding on what the problem is, the multiple perspectives from which it can be approached, and how it should be approached. The only reasonable way of handling this potential pitfall is: (1) to allocate sufficient time to problem exploration; (2) to bring numerous perspectives to bear in formulating alternative problem statements; and (3) to subject the alternative problem statements themselves to analysis by working through, in preliminary fashion, the subsequent phases of analysis.

Even then, it is useful to regard the problem statement as though it were tentative. In this way policy makers and analysts may be open to reconsideration of the problem formulation as more detailed explorations continue. Thus, it is not a mistake to hold preconceived notions or to form early ideas about a problem and its solution. A set of tentative ideas helps to guide the analysts and policy makers. It tells them what they are looking for while they are looking. It also offers others a concrete statement that they can probe to test the adequacy of what is being attempted and how it is being pursued.

A related pitfall lies in relations between policy makers and analysts in problem formulation. Analysts frequently accept the policy makers' original statement of what is wanted and set about providing information without sufficient thought as to whether that statement is correct or whether the information to be gathered will contribute to the decisions it is meant to assist. Sometimes policy makers have preconceived notions which they try to get the analysts to accept and to prove or demonstrate through analysis. They may have already decided what to do and may want the analyst to support the decision or to make a particular alternative look better than others. In other instances, this bias is more indirect—as when policy makers disapprove considering certain assumptions or alternatives although not specifying which alternatives they prefer. At its most extreme, this type

of influence causes the analyst to lose his independence of view.

On the other hand, policy analysts are seldom capable of defining problems alone. They may choose simplifications which are useful in bringing a real life problem within the bounds of analytic feasibility, but which would make the resulting analysis irrelevant to the problem of real concern. The implication of all this is that analysts and decision makers should have close contact in the formulation stage.

Limited perspective. Another pitfall in policy analysis is parochialism in the perspective of analysts or policy makers. Frequently, the advocates of particular alternatives or solutions

1. Consider only those alternatives which fall within the individual or unit's area of concern and fail to consider: (*a*) alternatives that overlap unit responsibilities and require cooperation with other units, and (*b*) alternatives that fall entirely within the purview of another unit
2. Compare proposed alternatives with "straw men" (e.g., comparing a new communication system in the police department with a semiobsolete system in the fire department rather than with the new system which the fire department hopes to introduce)
3. Fail to discover the faults of a proposed alternative, or overlook those limitations that have been discovered
4. Discount alternatives developed by parties outside the particular unit in question (i.e., the "not invented here" syndrome).

Perhaps the greatest counterforce in such cases is to foster "devil's advocate" proceedings in

which some people deliberately try to raise counterarguments to proposals and suggest additional alternatives. Multiple analysis groups and multidisciplinary teams also tend to foster wider perspectives and more critical questioning of assumptions and alternatives.

Neglect of subjective elements. One of the most common pitfalls in policy analysis is neglect of the subjective elements of decision. Those issues that cannot be represented quantitatively or cannot be fitted into the perceived decision structure in any satisfactory way often are overlooked or deemphasized in comparison with those that can be explicitly structured and quantitatively represented. A great number of policy problems involve an intermixing of measurable, calculable elements and unmeasurable elements. It is not enough for policy analysts simply to organize and calculate the calculable. They must go beyond and attempt to deal with the subjective elements, using whatever extrarational, qualitative, and creative processes they can bring to bear. Further, when subjective elements are dealt with in a study the analysts must make their subjective judgments known to the policy makers. This is essential, because the policy makers are unable to repeat the study, seldom have time to review it carefully, and will be heavily influenced by their information as to how the analyst reached his conclusions.

In other words, it is not only the product of analysis which is of importance to the policy makers, but also the processes by which the analysis was conducted and the conclusions derived. The policy makers are concerned not only with the analysts' technical and scientific competence but also their judgment. Therefore, they need to have the subjective elements in the study, whether they represent the analysts' judgments or those of the policy makers which the analysts included (or rejected) in conducting the study.

A related problem is that unless the product and process are fully disclosed the analysis may be used by a policy maker who is unaware of, or unwilling to accept, its limitations. Quade points out that:

When a study is presented confidently, but little attention is called to its deficiencies, the recipients are prone to read too much into it. A weak or careless or busy policy-maker may ease his job by transferring a portion of his responsibilities to the analyst or a model, and thus fail to give the study the critical scrutiny it requires.[2]

Misplaced emphasis in model-building. Whatever the type of model used in policy analysis, there is always a danger that the analysts will become more interested in the model itself than in the problem. For example, Quade says:

Technical people with specific training, knowledge, and capability like to use their talents to the utmost. It is easy for the analysts to focus attention on the mechanics of computation or on the technical relationships in the model rather than on the important questions raised in the study. They may find out a great deal about the inferences that can be drawn from the model, but very little about the question they set out to answer.[3]

This pitfall occurs when there is overemphasis on the particular system or process without sufficient focus on what it is that the policy makers and analysts are trying to find out. Frequently, the analysts build a model that treats every aspect of a complex problem simultaneously, that attempts to imitate the real world as realistically as possible. However, unless there is some basis for selecting what things should be included or excluded from the model it will become bigger and more complicated but may never be an aid to decision. The only realistic basis for selecting what to accept or reject in the model is the question being asked, the goals sought. For this reason it is advisable to design the model around the question to be answered, rather than make it a mere imitation of the real world.

A related problem is that sometimes model-building (or the entire analysis effort) is performed with such thoroughness that the analyst finds the decision has been taken before he can complete or report his results. While there are dangers in oversimplifying models, generally they should be simple. The most convincing analysis is one which the nontechnician can understand.

Finally, it is erroneous to accept as useful information results from a model that are incidental to the questions the model was designed to answer. For example, in a comparison of alternative governmental strategies for improving the quality and quantity of housing for various population groups in San Francisco it is possible that subsidizing low-income households could show up as a best strategy. However, if the model has failed to include many considerations important to how households would actually allocate such a subsidy (e.g., how much is spent for housing versus other consumer purchases), these modifying circumstances would have to be considered before the model results could be offered for policy guidance.

Handling of uncertainty. The most critical pitfall in dealing with uncertainty is to simply acknowledge that it exists and to warn that some things have been left out of the analysis because of a lack of information. The policy maker needs to come to grips with the uncertainties in a decision situation. To do this he needs to know what the uncertainties are, their probable effects, when they will occur, and what can be done about them.

A related problem is concentrating on statistical uncertainty while avoiding real or unforeseeable uncertainties. Sometimes the probability of future occurrences is more or less objective or calculable and can be handled readily. The danger here is that the uncalculable uncertainties may be ignored. One way to avoid this problem is to focus on the subjective or real uncertainties first. If these are not so great as to make the statistical uncertainties trivial, then these latter calculations may be performed.[4]

Reappraisal of the work. Another pitfall common to policy makers and analysts is failure to reappraise a study as it progresses. Concern for deadlines, wasted work, and money already spent tend to prevent critical review and redirection of a study. However, such review is essential, because one's understanding of a problem inevitably increases as the work progresses. Stocktaking that results in discarding or redirecting a major portion of the work is itself a demonstration that such reappraisal was necessary.[5]

Misplaced faith in policy analysis. Perhaps the greatest pitfall is to believe that, if the work is done correctly, policy analysis provides unlimited assistance to policy makers. Policy analysis has many limitations. Therefore, policy makers need to be aware of what analysis can do and what must be left to their own judgment. Generally, this is the task of the analysts to point out in particular studies. However, it is also the responsibility of policy makers to be critical in managing and evaluating policy studies conducted for them.

Uses of policy analysis

Whitehead points out that policy analysis can be used in two ways: ". . . in reaching a better conceptual understanding of decision problems and deciding what *should* be done, and in bargaining with other participants in the organizational process of deciding what *will* be done."[6]

Analysis is used in decision reaching to provide the policy makers with an information base that will improve their decisions. Thus, a major use of policy analysis is the development of information about the relationships among the decision makers' objectives and available alternatives. Specifically, analysis can be used in decision reaching to: (1) suggest new or improved statements of objectives; (2) help clarify the policy makers' understanding of the nature of the problem, including the relationships between their objectives and the actions they can take; (3) suggest new or improved action alternatives; and (4) provide information comparing alternatives in the light of the objectives as a basis for choice. Thus, policy makers can use analysis as a sounding board, and through a continuing cycle of analysis and review they can improve

their understanding of the problem, sharpen their judgment, clarify and improve their objectives, and obtain high quality alternatives to choose from.[7]

The uses of policy analysis in the organizational process of deciding what will be done are also important. The participants in the policy-making process almost always have differing perceptions of the environment and of the problem in relation to it. They also have differing concepts of convincing argument and differing organizational responsibilities and loyalties. Policy analysis rarely changes the way people think and interact with one another in the policy-making process. It is only one more consideration for the principal participants in that process. Therefore, the organizational process of bargaining will remain the context within which decisions are made, although that process may be changed by the introduction of policy analysis.

One such change is the use of policy analysis to educate the various participants to each others perceptions. Another is the use of information developed in policy analysis as a base from which all participants develop their arguments and counterarguments. The feasibility of so doing obviously depends upon development of an information base which gives full consideration to the differing points of view.

If key organizational factors (power, leadership, etc.) and relations among the participants are considered in carrying out the policy study, both the process and the results will tend to decrease the tension and strife likely to be felt during the explicit confrontation of different points of view. Also, the likelihood that the

participants can agree to the proposed solutions, or that they can find areas of agreement from which consensus can be built, will be increased by attention to organization and interpersonal factors.

The use of policy analysis in actually taking decisions is clearly the least understood aspect of the whole process. This is also an area susceptible to misuse by those who best understand how to use policy analysis. Nevertheless, assuming that most participants are sincere, responsible men, policy analysis can be a substantial help in deciding what will be done as well as in deciding what should be done.

Limitations of policy analysis

Throughout this book reference has been made to important limitations of policy analysis. A few are singled out here for special comment. First, any inquiry is always limited by time, money, and other costs. Second, even if these limits do not exist analysis can never treat all of the considerations that may be relevant. Some are too intangible. Others may be beyond our present knowledge and understanding. Still other considerations may be arrived at only by political discussion and debate. The policy analysts can apply their judgment to many of the factors in a situation, but the policy makers will and must insist on applying their own judgment in the end.

Third, the choice of alternatives must be governed by broad community objectives, not solely by organizational or subunit standards of success. However, community objectives are multiple, ill-defined, and conflicting. Even when objectives have been defined and ordered in some fashion, measures of their attainment are often only approximations. Often, too, multiple measures must be used, and there is no analytical way of combining these into a single measure of effectiveness.

In a sense, these conditions are an advantage, because they tend to preclude placing over-emphasis on the results of analysis. They also force decision makers and analysts to be clear about what can be shown analytically and what must be determined by collective judgment. In so doing, greater emphasis is placed on qualitative matters and on ways of improving qualitative judgments.

Fourth, policy analysis falls short of being an exact science despite efforts to maintain high standards of inquiry. One of the greatest limitations here is that the models used in analysis seldom can be verified. Further, as Quade points out, the whole process of analysis is shot through with judgment and intuition.

Human judgment is used in designing the analysis; in deciding what alternative to consider, what factors are relevant, what interrelations between these factors to model, and what numerical values to choose; and in analyzing and interpreting the results of the analysis. The terminology may be inherently vague, and the reasoning may be informal. In short, since judgment and intuition are fallible, caution and reservation on the part of both the analyst and the decision-maker are necessary to avoid errors or misconceptions that could bias or even negate the implications of the analysis.[8]

Finally, policy analysis is risky. There is always the possibility that the hypotheses the policy makers set out to test will turn out to be unsupported by the analysis. Few people ever approach problems without some preconceived notions as to their solution. However, most analyses result in changed understandings of the problem and/or its solution. This is not to say that policy makers should be devoid of ideas about the nature of the problem or its solution, but that they may have to change their stand as a result of analysis.

This poses several difficult problems. First, both political and administrative policy makers must frequently take positions on a problem or issue publicly—and before analysis is started. They may be doing so to get elected (or reelected), to obtain support for an idea, or to fund the policy study. In public pronouncements they may overstate their position or the results expected from policy analysis. Thus, when the analysis fails to support their publicly announced position, their credibility, support base, or image may be jeopardized. Second, it is extremely difficult to substantially change one's thinking about a problem, or one's way of thinking about problems in general. It is not that policy makers are more perverse than other people: this is a problem for everyone. In fact, frequently policy makers are willing to change their position on an issue but find that in so doing they alienate their initial supporters.

One simple shift in political posture suggested by Campbell to reduce these problems is the shift from the advocacy of a specific solution to the advocacy of an experimental approach to the problem. The political stance would become: "This is a serious problem. We propose to initiate an experimental approach towards its solution. We will begin investigations into, or actions towards, policy A. If after analysis, or after x time acting under the new policy, there has been no significant improvement, we will shift to policy B." By making it explicit that a given solution is only one of several that the policy makers could seriously advocate, and by having a plausible alternative, the policy makers may be able to afford rigorous evaluation of outcomes. Negative results from analysis, or failure of the first program, would not jeopardize the policy maker's position, for his commitment would be to keep after the problem until something was found that worked.[9]

ORGANIZATIONAL AND BEHAVIORAL PROBLEMS IN APPLYING POLICY ANALYSIS

In addition to the foregoing pitfalls, there are several organizational and behavioral issues that must be considered. Chief among these issues are (1) the role of policy makers in the process; (2) the organizational impacts of using analysis; and (3) the social features of the urban system that complicate the process of analysis.

Policy makers and policy analysis

One of the most important issues in applying policy analysis in local government is the role and involvement of the policy makers in the process. Policy makers have a basic responsibility to come to an understanding of policy analysis—what it is, how it can be used, what its limitations are. In addition, they may be required to perform certain specific roles.

One such role is helping to define the task of analysis, i.e., the problems to be solved or the opportunities to be utilized. In this capacity, policy makers may be acting as initiators and sponsors of a study and/or as direct participants in a study initiated by themselves or by others.

Definition of the analysis task (problem formulation) is essentially a statement of the objectives and is critical to the outcome of any policy study. If this is left entirely to the analysts or to other professionals in the organization, then the policy makers should not be surprised if someone else's problem rather than their own is solved.

Since many policy studies are performed by organizations outside government, two additional roles may be involved. One is as evaluators of policy study proposals made by outside organizations. More than one city has contracted for studies involving large sums of money only to discover: (1) that they were the training ground for some consultant organization's staff; (2) that the problem to be studied was of little consequence—although the initial study proposal may have spelled impending disaster; or (3) that the basic approach and study design omitted consideration of the social, political, and economic realities of government decision and action.

Another role is that of monitor and controller of policy studies conducted by outside organizations. It is insufficient to turn an organization loose on a problem and wait for the results. Policy makers must be intensively involved if the study is to be useful to them. A key reason for this is that public problems are social in nature and are vastly different from the physical problems with which many outside or nongovernmental organizations have worked. Another reason is that the actions recommended in such studies have impacts on organizations and on people—impacts which the outside organization can ignore but which the policy makers cannot.

These impacts must be spelled out and accounted for in policy studies. Unless the policy makers are sufficiently involved in a study to indicate which impacts must be considered and which can be ignored, chances are that the wrong factors will be considered—if any such impacts are considered at all.

Whether analysis is performed in-house or by contract, policy makers will also need to be facilitators of the studies they sanction. Access to people and information, and social support, are critical to most policy studies (assuming reasonable financing). Policy makers also have a role to play in implementation. Assuming a study has been done well and the implementation actions have been spelled out, the necessary organizational arrangements must still be created to facilitate concerted action. This may be as simple as lending support to existing organizational units or as complex as creating new units or a new organization of units to carry out implementation actions.

Finally, policy makers have an important role to play in evaluation of policy studies—during the conduct of the study, upon completion, and during and after implementation. This last is most often overlooked. It is not sufficient for policy makers to perform the other roles well and to fail to evaluate the real world consequences of the actions taken as a result of a policy study. Such evaluation failures have contributed to the tendency of local governments to repeat their own mistakes and those of others. They have also contributed to the tendency to jump from one pat solution to another in the hopes of finding *the* answer without ever facing up to the basic questions involved in successive failures

or dubious achievements. In instances where the policy makers' other roles were performed inadequately, such evaluations are even more critical.

But how to bear the burden of such evaluations? In referring to the lack of critical evaluation of systems analysis studies, Ida Hoos describes the problem as follows:

> Only . . . the protective shroud of politics and pride has discouraged, if not prevented, critical analysis from being conducted so far.
> Public agencies are, understandably, sensitive about their image. Criticism of the expensive study might make it appear that hundreds of thousands of dollars out of strained budgets have been squandered. The completed study, quite irrespective of its worth, is unassailable, and, coincidentally, useful to all parties to the contract. The astute administrator can use it for leverage in obtaining more grant money for follow-on purposes; the contractor parades it as evidence of capability, for he is secure in the knowledge that his claim will go unchallenged.[10]

The basic assumption stated in the introduction to this book was that most local government policy makers seek improvement in the human condition of their communities. If we accept the view that most participants in public policy making are sincere, responsible individuals, then a major use of such evaluations would be the education of these other participants as well as of the responsible policy makers and analysts themselves. Such a view may be difficult to maintain in the wake of political defeat by men who have acted in such fashion in recent years. However, this may be more of an indication of our amateurism in handling such evaluations than of the weakness of the position.

There is increasing evidence, in the federal government at least, that some politicians and administrators are unwilling to continue to promote or to fund programs that fail in critical self-evaluation. Few local government officials have been this demanding of themselves or their organizations as yet. However, as citizens' awareness of and dissatisfaction with their urban environments increases, as it surely will, local government officials will find they can no longer hide behind policy studies that produce no policy and action programs that produce no action. They will find that if they wish to remain in office their most critical function will be to educate themselves and the public about what government should and can do, what it hopes to achieve, and what it actually does achieve — what is learned from its successes and from its failures.

Thus, policy makers may have any or all of several roles in the conduct of policy studies: initiator and sponsor, proposal evaluator, participant, facilitator, monitor, and evaluator. Obviously, few of these roles can be fulfilled directly or continuously by the highest level policy makers. How many of these roles and which of them are handled directly depends upon the type of decision problem and the arrangements made for the conduct of analysis. At minimum, the responsibility of the policy makers will be to define the necessary roles in specific decision contexts and to secure their effectuation. For many decision problems this is done by delegation of continued responsibility to an analysis group or unit in the organization. However, on extremely consequential issues most policy makers may want to consider these questions in the light of the specific situation.

Two additional issues are involved in the use of policy analysis. It is important that policy makers realize that analysis does not relieve them of the task of decision making — of applying their judgment to the process and product of analysis. In fact, policy analysis may well increase the responsibility of and pressure on policy makers for decision and action. It may also result in a shift in the kinds of decisions they must face. In the past, urban public policy makers have focused their attention largely on routine, operational problems. As a result of increasing emphasis on analysis, these routine decisions (and other decisions which will be reduced to routine decisions) will be susceptible to handling at lower levels of the government organization. Therefore, policy makers will be asked to attend to the more complex, long-term, and as yet unsolved issues and questions. Policy analysis will be an aid to increasing understanding of these issues, but it is doubtful whether it will be able to point to optimal solutions. Thus, policy analysis may constitute a threat to some policy makers — particularly to those who are unable to evaluate or use the results of policy studies.

Finally, analysis is becoming increasingly popular for a variety of reasons. In the process, it is often oversold — and so are the results (not only by those performing the work, but also by those for whom it is performed). The really critical problems of urban areas will persist until governments find the will to provide basic economic, social, and political solutions. Policy studies will be useful in defining problems and developing alternatives for government action, but in themselves they will not solve anything. The danger is that decision makers may cloak their unwillingness to do anything about social

problems in the mystique of policy analysis, vigorously pursue study after study, and avoid making the hard political choices which the studies present. Ultimately, those who choose to use policy analysis in this way will be caught short, but in the meantime much harm can be done both by action and inaction.

Organizational impacts

Policy analysis inevitably results in changes in an organization, either directly through the implementation of recommendations for change developed as a result of analysis, or indirectly through its effect on the behavior of the individuals and groups who use it or who are affected by its use by others. Since the indirect impacts have not been discussed previously, and since policy makers must deal with them, several points are in order.

1. Policy analysis is a new way of structuring decision processes. As such, it represents a threat to the power and influence of those not well versed in its language and techniques. Generally, well-organized and technically sophisticated individuals and groups gain power at the expense of those less well organized and less sophisticated because the former are better equipped to engage in, use, and react to the output of policy studies. Further, if the latter groups concede that policy analysis is a useful way of addressing public policy making, they are in fact conceding an advantage to those who are better versed in it.[11]

2. Explicit analysis of policy alternatives represents a communication and decision-justifying process that is alien to many participants in the policy-making process. That is, one can

distinguish between the use of analysis in reaching a choice as opposed to setting out the explicit rationale for that choice. The former involves a synthesis of goals and alternatives and the finding of insights into the relationships between the two. The latter is more a demonstration (to others) of the connections between the chosen (or recommended) alternative and the boundary conditions of the decision. Both activities are involved in policy analysis.[12] Difficulties arise when a conflict occurs between the way people actually reach a decision and the way in which they must justify it. As long as people need not be too explicit about their justification, this conflict can be ignored. However, because policy analysis places such great emphasis on decision-justification, it is difficult to ignore. As a result, many people may be made quite uncomfortable by having to justify their positions on ground rules different from those they used to reach the decision in the first place.

3. By its emphasis on explicitness, policy analysis forces people to face issues they were able to gloss over previously without even being aware that they were doing so. Since policy analysis forces decision participants to be explicit and objective about assumptions and measures, there is a possibility that the analysis will produce results contrary to some of the predispositions of the participants. Some people will view this as a useful result, because it provides a basis for improving and sharpening their judgment. But others will interpret it as a challenge to their judgment and hence to their competence and status.[13]

4. By calling explicit attention to the uncertainties involved in a decision situation, policy analysis emphasizes the limited basis for decision. Many people find this situation uncomfortable, especially when they have a sincere desire to reach the best decision possible. It is dissatisfying to many people to speak of trade-offs among objectives since that implies compromise with what is really needed. Further, by stressing the uncertainties, policy analysis may weaken the decision makers' confidence in the rightness of their decision.[14]

5. Policy analysis helps clarify objectives and ends–means relationships, but doing so may create increased disagreement within an organization. So long as ends and means are vague, basic conflicts between individuals and groups in an organization remain submerged. Further, by couching their thinking and their defense of decisions in technical, problem-solving terms rather than in terms of fundamental trade-offs among objectives, the participants in the decision process avoid a sense of personal responsibility and vulnerability. They are then vulnerable to criticism only by those few people in a position to question technical competence *and* value choices.[15]

6. In policy analysis judgments are regarded as part of the decision problem. Emphasis is placed on clarifying specific judgments that must be made and on using analysis to relate such judgments to one another. The more common approach to decision analysis is to present the facts of the problem and let the decision makers make a lumped judgment. The net result of this difference is that with policy analysis it is much more difficult for the decision makers to foresee the tangible implications of their judgments, because they are made sequentially over a number of subareas in the policy study. Under the "lumped-judgment" approach, the policy makers seemingly have full control over the outcome of the analysis. This control may be used to ensure that a favored alternative comes out ahead, but it probably is more commonly used as insurance against unreasonable results from the analysis. People simply are able to assess the implications and acceptability of concrete alternatives better than they can assess the outcome of judgments separated from analysis. Since a major function of the decision makers is to integrate diverse considerations rather than to delve into the details of each, this shift of the locus of judgment may make it difficult for them to justify a valid but vaguely formulated overview in the face of an analysis that factors the decision problem into a number of subareas.[16]

7. By cutting across established organizational boundaries, policy analysis increases the uncertainty about how a particular individual, unit, or organization will fare in the final decision. This uncertainty tends to increase the ambivalence which most people feel about using policy analysis and may generate opposition.[17]

The most general implication of these points is that when policy analysis is introduced into an organization it will result in gains for some people and losses for others. Therefore, it will generate opposition as well as support. This organizational strife may be a salutary thing. Disagreement can be a help in avoiding the trap of specious analyses and can provide the impetus for development of better alternatives.

The real problem with policy analysis lies in structuring the discussion and debate so that constructive rather than destructive results ensue.

An appeal to the reasonableness of the ideas and methods of policy analysis is probably the worst approach to promoting its use. A more effective approach is to demonstrate that policy analysis results in better decisions. However, since the definition of a better decision depends on one's objectives, and since individuals and groups differ on objectives, this, too, may be an ineffective approach. Perhaps the most constructive way of promoting policy analysis is to make widely available the data and the results of any particular study so that all parties to a decision may operate from a common information environment in arguing the pros and cons of any particular alternative. Since most people structure their thinking to fit the information available, making information available that suggests connections between objectives and alternatives is bound to influence the approaches taken to analysis. In addition, organizational incentives (promotion, status, recognition) to encourage good analysis may be desirable if these are not so great as to produce resentment rather than the desired results. Finally, training, whether provided early in one's career or in mid-career, is an effective way of encouraging the use of policy analysis.

The nature of local government and its problems

A final set of behavioral issues in using policy analysis relates to difficulties presented by the local government environment. Chief among these are: (1) complexity of the social system context; (2) lack of correspondence between problem and jurisdictional boundaries; (3) the necessity for involvement of the constituency; and (4) the difficulty of defining community goals.

The social system context. The city is first and foremost a social system. Cities are physical systems, too, but the physical artifacts are the result of social values and social interaction broadly defined. Ida Hoos illustrates this point well when she says:

One of the most important, and never publicized, results of the now legendary California aerospace studies was the discovery that, in the final analysis most of mankind's problems, even those which superficially appear to fall into the engineering category today, turn out to be *social.* Transportation is not mere networks of roads; it is people's reasons for living and working and playing where they do. It is why the hard core unemployed have given up the job hunt; it is why the sick babies of migrant workers do not receive treatment at free clinics. Air pollution is the one-man, one-car life style of Americans; it is our national reverence for big business which can with impunity load the limited pure air at our disposal with poisonous emissions; it is an international determination to build and test instruments of destruction at all costs.[18]

The most obvious implication of this fact is that physical solutions to the problems of cities may do little to solve problems that are basically social in nature. A second implication is that even when physical solutions are appropriate they almost always have social consequences. Unless these social effects are considered in choosing among alternative proposals, the unanticipated social consequences may negate any physical achievements derived.

Further, because of the social character of cities there are limits to what can be achieved through analysis, particularly through the technology transfer tradition (see Chapter 2) in policy analysis. The city context is vastly different from the context of military and space hardware systems, where many methods and techniques of analysis have been developed and applied successfully. In physical systems the elements are readily identifiable, tangible, and measurable. Control of the decision elements is immediate and direct and predictions about the uncontrollable elements fairly reliable. As a result, the whole process of analysis can be simplified by quantification and mathematical manipulation. In the social sphere the crucial elements often defy identification and measurement. Control is indirect, slow, and subject to interference by a vast number of forces. Predictions about the uncontrollable elements (i.e., essentially social behavior) are uncertain at best. Further, the test of the effectiveness of a system is largely a reflection of human values and may not be amenable to quantitative measurement. Thus, the process of analysis often is complex, uncertain, and subject to negation by failure to consider socially relevant factors (political feasibility, public acceptance, organizational impacts, human consequences).

The basically social character of cities, therefore, presents difficulties not previously encountered or recognized by many people engaged in the technology transfer efforts. Because of this difficulty, not everyone is sanguine about the possibility of using analysis (in whatever form) to solve social problems. For example, William Pendleton cautions against exaggerated claims about the potential contribution of technology (i.e., decision analysis, information systems, hardware systems) to solving the problems of cities:

The really critical and immediately pressing problems —poverty, unemployment, crime, bad housing, poor health, and inadequate education—will persist until the nation finds the will to provide very basic economic, social, and political solutions. The technological approaches . . . appear to offer promise toward solving what may be called the hardware-related problems— pollution, congestion, waste disposal and the like. They may be useful in achieving better understanding of the systems out of which the really critical problems develop, but actually solving those problems will depend upon progress in redistributing population, in tapping greater sources of financing for urban services, in restructuring our antiquated political institutions, and ultimately in a revolution in basic attitudes of both the white and Negro populations. . . .

The potential role of the systems approach to urban problems, at least as the approach has developed in the aerospace industry, is currently being oversold to a rather substantial degree. The findings from the California experiments referred to earlier revealed no spectacular successes. A recent meeting in Washington of the Operations Research Society of America heard systems analysts time and again wring their hands over the complexities, the data problems, and the political obstructions they faced as they tried to tackle some of the most pressing problems of today's cities. . . .

Furthermore, it is not at all obvious that the heritage of Department of Defense and National Aeronautics and Space Administration contracts prepares the aerospace companies to operate in the context of municipal problems. With those agencies, systems people worked for a single identifiable client—one who was extraordinarily well-heeled and in a position to conceal from the prying eyes of the political sector many failures and false starts. Not one of these conditions is likely to be present when and if a bigger push

is made for research and development in the municipal field.[19]

Similarly, C. West Churchman concludes that if scientists are used by government it should be with the realization that the real objective of their employment is to educate scientists about the meaning of people and politics. Churchman feels scientists must "do science" on public policy questions rather than simply doing scientific advising. However, he also has reservations about sole reliance on politics and politicians.

Everyone knows that politics itself is immature, because everyone can see how utterly ridiculous it is. . . . but few people realize how immature science is and how utterly ridiculous in many regards it is. In fact, a large amount of science's activity is simply playroom activity, the making of toys. When science gets serious about people, it is ridiculous and also downright dangerous. . . .

Now, I am not averse to a bit of game-playing in public policy-making. I think that it would be all to the good, and in this regard I think that even current science can be of some real assistance to the policy-maker. It can play some of his games by means of the toy it calls computer simulation, and the game-playing will be delightful. But what I am concerned about, however, is asking this immature child to take on the role of public policy-making. Of course, I am also, like every other citizen of the United States today, very worried about asking another group of children, the politicians, to play the same game.[20]

Boundary problems. An additional area of difficulty in applying policy analysis to the problems of cities lies in defining the boundary of the system in which a problem occurs. The difficulty arises in trying to determine which things must be included in thinking about a problem and which can be excluded, which

things can be controlled by the policy makers and which must be accepted as givens. Many problems are so interrelated they seem to defy all attempts to bound them, however the boundaries are defined. For example, assuming a programmatic definition, problems of poverty intersect with those of education, employment, and welfare; under a functional definition, police problems overlap with those of welfare, education, planning and building, and recreation; in a race definition, the problems of the black relate to those of the Chicano and Puerto Rican. Thus, the choice of an appropriate way to bound policy problems may be exceedingly difficult.

In the choice of levels and boundaries of the intervention (decision) system, a similar difficulty occurs. Is the particular problem something that can be dealt with at the local level or does it require state or federal decision and action? More importantly, what is the purview of local government? Within any particular government there is a further problem of choosing among alternative specifications of the appropriate intervention system. For example, in dealing with problems of poverty the relevant systems may be the public programs for employment, welfare, education, or housing—or all of these.

Finally, many problems overlap legal-jurisdictional boundaries at the local level. Many aspects of police, fire, building, planning, recreation and other governmental problems are resolvable largely within the territorial limits of a single jurisdiction. However, other aspects of these and certain other problems (air and water pollution, transportation, refuse disposal) can be handled only on a multijurisdictional basis. Yet rarely do governmental entities exist that are able to decide and act on these types of problems. There are some cooperative mechanisms, (councils of governments, regional agencies, etc.), but few of them possess the power to secure concerted action from their members. Thus, a compounding feature of many public policy problems in local government is that the boundary of the system (for example, the metropolitan or urban area) in which the problem occurs does not correspond to the system that seeks to deal with the problem (the municipality).

The constituency or client of policy analysis. In the city there are many possible choices of clients (including citizens, public administrators, and politicians)—each choice bringing a different problem definition. In policy analysis, who are considered to be the decision makers, and therefore how the decision problem is stated, determines in large part what will be done, how, and with what results. But "the decision makers" includes more than the political leaders and government professionals. It includes all those affected by particular decisions and actions in some important way. While the actual conduct of policy analysis may involve a much smaller number than this vast set of decision makers, it must be done with full consideration of the points of view of these others.

The increasing demand by citizens for participation and involvement in these decisions which have important effects on their lives complicates the whole process of analysis in the local government context. The critical problem often revolves around the way in which participation and involvement are structured rather than the way in which the technical

analysis is structured. In fact, in many instances professionals, analysts, or politicians may feel they know what should be done. The problem then is to communicate this perception so as to elicit a useful response from other relevant parties. That is, the problem is to create a forum in which issues are debated, alternative goal statements tested, and possible solutions tried out with those who will be affected by choice among the issues, goals, and solutions.

This situation is exacerbated when issues cross jurisdictional, class, race, or other lines. But it cannot be ignored, for the best technical analysis is useless if the preferred solution fails to consider the appropriate mix of interests involved. Indeed, it would be extremely useful if policy analysis studies were viewed as incomplete and inadequate where these considerations are not integral to the whole process of analysis and/or not covered in the resultant recommendations.

Goals and objectives. Determining goals and objectives is closely related to determining the client, that is, "Whose objectives are to be served?" Once the client is defined, an additional task is to determine the *real* objectives of the client. This is difficult because the city is a complex social organization with a wide mixture of goals. Further, as expressed by the inhabitants and the political leaders, these goals are often inconsistent, contradictory, or downright unrealistic. Finally, these people may be unable to express their goals clearly, if at all.

Although there may be no single set of goals and objectives that will be agreed upon by all

the interested parties or the formal client, it is important in the conduct of analysis that at least a satisfactory set be identified. As Ida Hoos says:

What the analyst conceives as the system's objectives molds his ideas, weighs his conceptions, and has impact on so seemingly quantitative an operation as cost/benefit comparisons. Whose cost becomes whose benefit is not a matter of undisputable accounting but rather an issue for interpretation within a given framework.[21]

In a sense all of this has been said before. *What cannot be emphasized clearly enough is that the analysts and policy makers cannot escape from the task of determining goals, whatever the process utilized.* The statement of objectives is the key to subsequent phases in analysis. It is in essence the process of formulating the questions that the analysis is to answer. *It is insufficient to conduct an analysis in the hope that, or on the assumption that, the model developed will be suitable for evaluating whatever goals the policy makers and others may eventually agree upon.*

ORGANIZATIONAL PRECONDITIONS

The introduction to this work sketched the environment of local government policy makers and described a number of organizational problems they face in seeking improvements in decision and action. At various points throughout the book it has been suggested that sometimes substantive issue analysis may be of less importance than organizational analysis and organizational development. The preceding chapter focused on some organizational requirements for the actual conduct of policy studies.

Finally, earlier sections of this chapter identified a number of behavioral issues associated with the use and misuse of policy analysis.

The point, then, of all this is: in addition to analysis of substantive issues, there are organizational preconditions to actual improvement in government (or private) decision and action. That is, the final payoffs of policy analysis are *actual improvements in government or private action* as distinguished from improvements in the information on which such action is based. Policy analysis is simultaneously directed towards achieving both types of improvements through the production of information about substantive issues and about needed organizational changes to achieve the recommendations resulting from issue analysis. But actual change is ultimately brought about by organizational arrangements — by the systems developed to secure concerted action from people towards chosen objectives. Thus, there are organizational preconditions. Some of these preconditions relate exclusively to the governmental organization. Others relate to the environment (the community, region, etc.) and to the relations between the government and its environment. The focus here is on government-related preconditions.

The utility of policy analysis rests in its potential contribution to improving the decision and action processes in local governments. To achieve that potential, policy analysis must be viewed first as a part of governmental decision-action processes and second as a process of producing information for decision. However, improvement of information and decision processes requires

simultaneous improvement in several related dimensions of the governmental system. Chief among these are organization structure, people, knowledge about policy analysis, and the social milieu of government. The key reason for these concomitant requirements is that, given the nature of systems, improvements must reach a critical mass in order to influence the aggregative working of the system. Improvements which do not reach the relevant impact thresholds will be neutralized by countervailing adjustments of other components, or may actually reduce the quality of the system. Thus, a systems approach to public policy improvement in local government requires simultaneous improvements aimed at: (1) integrating policy analysis and other decision processes; (2) realigning organization structure; (3) developing personnel; (4) expanding the stock of knowledge about policy analysis; and (5) altering the social milieu in which policy analysis occurs.

Integration of policy analysis with other decision processes

The policy-making function in local government operates through a wide dispersion of activities, with responsibility for analyzing, deciding, and acting also widely dispersed. Virtually every individual and unit in the system potentially shares in the analyzing, deciding, and acting triad (including some units which specialize in one or more of the triad functions).

The key feature of policy analysis in this context is that it is an information-producing activity. As such, policy analysis largely serves a co-ordinative function in the whole system. It does this through "feedforward" and feedback of

information. On the one hand, policy analysis provides feedforward which is intended to inform decisions and actions over a range of time periods, system locations, and perspectives. Feedforward includes such things as: projections and forecasts about environmental and internal conditions; goals and targets to be achieved by the system; outcomes and impacts of alternative ways of achieving goals. On the other hand, policy analysis provides feedback — soundings, scannings, and evaluations of changing conditions resulting from previous decisions and actions or from conditions and events outside local control.

The task of integrating policy analysis and other decision processes, therefore, is twofold: (1) tying together the feedforward and feedback functions of policy analysis; (2) tying these two into decision and action at all levels of the governmental system. The former is largely a matter of organizing for the conduct of policy studies and of improving policy analysis as a method for dealing with complex issues. The latter is a matter of establishing a capability for using policy analysis throughout the governmental system and of creating a system to handle the multiple flows of information which facilitate its use.

Realignment of organization structure

Related to improvement of information production and using processes are organizational structures. Examination of the information-decision flows in a number of governments indicates that information-decision structures and organization structures are interrelated. Either of the structures may be viewed as the independent variable. In many cases the most desirable way to organize may be determined only after information needs and points of decision have been determined. This is a critical consideration, because, in the social milieu of organizations, almost the only means of modifying behavior is by the transfer of information. The points of information generation, aggregation, and dissemination become key decision centers and the focus of organizational capacity to influence action. Thus, the reworking of old structures becomes an integral part of policy-making improvement. So does the creation of new structures. Among these are units and arrangements for the development of policy recommendations, for the management of programs designed to effectuate chosen policies, for monitoring and evaluating the impacts of programmatic actions, and for the continuous evolution of the governmental system itself.

Development of personnel
Improvement of the human decision makers in the governmental system is also necessary. Nearly everyone in the system is a decision maker and potentially contributes to or utilizes information. Therefore, development of information-related knowledge and skills is required at all levels of the governmental organization. A variety of educational and training programs exist for technical and professional personnel, but most of these fail to be concerned with

matters beyond the mechanics of decision technology. Educational programs for managers and politicians are almost nonexistent.

Indoctrination, technical training, use of the new decision technology, creative invention, the human and organizational impacts of policy studies, and change strategies are basic requisites of personnel development. So is sophistication in the use of information developed from analysis. Recent experiments have indicated that decision makers, when free to call for information from a ready-access source, are extremely wasteful of such a resource. In addition, given the complex problems of urban governments, policy makers are tempted to grasp at measurable dimensions in order to represent an underlying reality. In the process of political discourse and debate the statistical abstraction is often confused with a particular reality. Statistical, mathematical, and logical abstractions are important. Such explanations should make possible a constant reminder that statistics which show, for example, a decrease in the number of poor families can exist side by side with increased militancy of certain poor elements in the population.

Expansion of the stock of knowledge
Improvement is also needed in the basic stock of knowledge about policy analysis. As pointed

out by Whitehead, Dror,[22] and others, few policy studies are documented sufficiently to transmit the considerations involved in a particular analysis. Failures, whether technical or behavioral, are never reported in the literature. Research, frank experimentation, and documentation are needed if the knowledge and experience with policy analysis is to be transmitted and if there is to be a basis for theory building and improvement of practice. Since policy analysis is an activity largely carried on in operational settings, those responsible for its use cannot leave this function solely to academicians. Policy studies can be designed as experiments conducted in a scientific manner and reported on for replication and testing in other contexts.

Alteration of the social milieu
A final area of needed improvement is the culture of government. Policy studies are themselves agents of change. They are intended to bring about changes in the organization and its environment. Further, they cannot be accomplished without changes in attitudes and in existing ways of doing things. More fundamentally, they cannot be accomplished without changes in the way policy analysis is viewed. As long as policy analysis is regarded as something apart from, rather than integral to, the normal processes of government, its full potential will remain unrealized.

Notes

[1] H. Kahn and I. Mann, *Ten Common Pitfalls* (Santa Monica: Rand Corporation, 1957); E. S. Quade, "Pitfalls and Limitations," in *Systems Analysis and Policy Planning*, ed. by E. S. Quade and W. I. Boucher (New York: American Elsevier Publishing Co., 1969), pp. 345–63; and Clay Thomas Whitehead, *Uses and Limitations of Systems Analysis* (Santa Monica: Rand Corporation, 1967).

[2] Quade, in Quade and Boucher, *Systems Analysis*, p. 360; see also: Donald T. Campbell, "Reforms as Experiments," *American Psychologist*, XXIV (April 1969), 409–29.

[3] Quade, in Quade and Boucher, *Systems Analysis*, p. 353.

[4] Ibid., p. 356.

[5] Campbell, in *American Psychologist*, 409–29.

[6] Whitehead, *Uses and Limitations*, p. 108.

[7] Ibid., pp. 108–10.

[8] Quade, in Quade and Boucher, *Systems Analysis*, p. 363.

[9] Campbell, in *American Psychologist*, 410.

[10] Ida R. Hoos, *A Critique on the Application of Systems Analysis to Social Problems* (Berkeley: Space Sciences Laboratory, University of California, 1967), p. 14.

[11] See: Anthony Downs, "A Realistic Look at the Final Payoffs from Urban Data Systems," *Public Administration Review*, XXVII (September 1967), 208. Although the context of Downs' article is urban data systems, his comments relate to the impact of increased and improved information — a product of policy analysis as well as data systems. See also Whitehead, *Uses and Limitations*, pp. 103–4.

[12] Whitehead, *Uses and Limitations*, pp. 93, 105.

[13] Ibid., pp. 104–5.

[14] Ibid., p. 106.

[15] Ibid.

[16] Ibid., pp. 107–8.

[17] Downs, in *Public Administration Review*, 209.

[18] Ida R. Hoos, *Systems Analysis and the Technical Writer's Growing Responsibility* (Berkeley: Space Sciences Laboratory, University of California, 1968), p. 5.

[19] William C. Pendleton, *Technology and Cities: A Foundation Viewpoint* (New York: Ford Foundation, 1968), pp. 10–11.

[20] C. West Churchman, "The Use of Science in Public Affairs," in *Governing Urban Society: New Scientific Approaches*, ed. by American Academy of Political and Social Science (Philadelphia: American Academy of Political and Social Science, 1967), pp. 47–48.

[21] Ida R. Hoos, *Systems Analysis in Government Administration: A Critical Analysis* (Berkeley: Space Sciences Laboratory, University of California, 1967), p. 5.

[22] Whitehead, *Uses and Limitations*; Yehezkel Dror, *Public Policy-Making Reexamined* (San Francisco: Chandler Publishing Company, 1968).

Selected Bibliography

Ackoff, Russell L., and Rivett, Patrick. *A Manager's Guide to Operations Research.* New York: John Wiley & Sons, Inc., 1963.

Banovetz, James M., ed. *Managing the Modern City.* Washington, D.C.: International City Management Association, 1971. See especially Chapters 9, 10, and 11.

Brewer, Garry D. *Politicians, Bureaucrats, and the Consultant: A Critique of Urban Problem Solving.* New York: Basic Books, Inc., 1973.

Churchman, C. West. *The Systems Approach.* New York: Dell Publishing Co. [paperback ed., Delta Books], 1968.

Fisher, Gene H. *Cost Considerations in Systems Analysis.* New York: American Elsevier Publishing Co., 1971.

Goodman, Percival, and Goodman, Paul. *Communitas: Means of Livelihood and Ways of Life.* New York: Vintage Books, 1960 [paperback]. First published in hardback, New York: Random House, 1947.

Goodman, William I., and Freund, Eric C., eds. *Principles and Practice of Urban Planning.* Washington, D.C.: International City Managers' Association, 1968.

Hoos, Ida R. *Systems Analysis in Public Policy.* Berkeley: University of California Press, 1972.

International City Management Association, and U.S. Department of Housing and Urban Development. *Applying Systems Analysis in Urban Government: Three Case Studies.* Washington, D.C.: International City Management Association, 1972.

Kahn, Alfred J. *Theory and Practice of Social Planning.* New York: Russell Sage Foundation, 1969.

Kraemer, Kenneth L.; Mitchel, William H.; Weiner, Myron E.; and Dial, O. E. *Integrated Municipal Information Systems.* New York: Praeger Publishers, 1973.

Lasswell, Harold D. *A Pre-View of Policy Sciences.* New York: American Elsevier Publishing Co., 1971.

Lichfield, Nathaniel. *Cost-Benefit Analysis in Urban Redevelopment.* Berkeley: Real Estate Research Program, Institute of Business and Economic Research, University of California, 1962.

Lindblom, Charles E. *The Policy-Making Process.* Englewood Cliffs, N.J.: Prentice-Hall, Inc., 1968.

Morse, Philip M., and Bacon, L. W., eds. *Operations Research for Public Systems.* Cambridge, Mass.: The M.I.T. Press, 1967.

Quade, E. S., and Boucher, W. I., eds. *Systems Analysis and Policy Planning: Applications in Defense.* New York: American Elsevier Publishing Co., 1969.

Rivlin, Alice M. *Systematic Thinking for Social Action.* Washington, D.C.: Brookings Institution, 1971.

Suchman, Edward A. *Evaluative Research.* New York: Russell Sage Foundation, 1967.

Whitehead, Clay Thomas. *Uses and Limitations of Systems Analysis.* Santa Monica: Rand Corporation, 1967.

Wholey, Joseph S.; Scanlon, John W.; Duffy, Hugh G.; Fukumoto, James S.; and Vogt, Leona M. *Federal Evaluation Policy.* Washington, D.C.: Urban Institute, 1970.

Williams, Walter. *Social Policy Research and Analysis.* New York: American Elsevier Publishing Co., 1971.

Municipal Management Series
Policy Analysis in Local Government

Text type:
Helvetica Light

Composition, printing, and binding:
Kingsport Press, Kingsport, Tennessee

Composition for figures and tables:
Artisan Type Inc., Washington, D.C.

Paper:
Champion Matte

Production:
David S. Arnold, Betty L. Lawton,
and Emily Evershed

Design:
Herbert Slobin